Looking at Early Years Education and Care

Edited by

Rose Drury, Linda Miller and Robin Campbell

David Fulton Publishers
London

David Fulton Publishers Ltd
Ormond House 26–27 Boswell Street, London WC1N 3JD
www.fultonbooks.co.uk

First published in Great Britain by David Fulton Publishers 2000

British Library Cataloguing in Publication Data

A catalogue record for this book is available from the British Library

ISBN 1–85346–659–X

Typeset by Textype Typesetters, Cambridge
Printed in Great Britain by The Cromwell Press Ltd, Trowbridge, Wilts.

Contents

Foreword

This book is being published at a time of great change in the early years field. Recent developments are opening up a wide range of possibilities which have been dreamed of and fought for over many years. Early years and childcare development partnerships have now been established in every local authority, to take a lead in strategic planning for the expansion of provision. These partnerships are across existing boundaries bewtween the maintained, voluntary and private sectors. Like Sure Start, they are designed to bring together a range of services with the aim of meeting the needs of children, families and communities increasingly effectively and responsively. Rightly, the common thread is quality.

The authors come from different disciplines, and speak as experts in their respective fields. The editors have woven together the contributions of their colleagues from the University of Hertfordshire to provide insights into many of the important issues affecting practitioners. They have set book in the context of current developments, and underline key principles. These are exemplified in the chapters which consider aspects of working with others, including parents. Areas of learning are explored in ways which link theory to practice, and there are many thought-provoking commentaries on observations of children together with quotations from them. The importance of play, representation and communication is explained, with particular mention of children with special educational needs and those in the early stages of learning English.

The editors acknowledge that the introduction of a Foundation Stage and the need to interpret the Early Learning Goals will make considerable demands on staff working with young children in schools and nursery settings. However, it introduces invaluable opportunities to counter unsuitable top-down pressures. The authors point out that high levels of training will be required, and ensure that the book provides a good starting point for practitioners who want to refine their understanding of quality care and education in the early years. As a former member of staff at the Watford Campus, and external examiner of initial teacher training there, I have a personal as well as a professional regard for the committed and thoughtful individuals who have contributed to this book. They live up to their belief that children need thoughtful adults, and show by example how learning can be life-long. As Loris Malaguzzi has said, ". . . leave room for learning, observe carefully what young children do, and then, if you have understood well, perhaps teaching will be different from before." This book will help us all to collaborate more effectively in educating and caring for future generations.

Wendy Scott
Chief Executive
The British Association for Early Childhood Education
February 2000

Notes on the contributors

Rosemary Allen is Senior Lecturer in Art Education at the University of Hertfordshire. She has worked extensively in art and design education in a range of settings. Her research interests include art in the early years, assessment in the arts and the importance of creativity and imagination in teaching and learning.

Peter Bloomfield is Senior Lecturer in Geographical and Environmental Education at the University of Hertfordshire. He regularly contributes to the journal *Primary Geography* and his current research is in the area of environmental studies.

Robin Campbell is Emeritus Professor at the University of Hertfordshire. He was previously a primary school teacher and head teacher. His research interest is early literacy development and his most recent books, including *Literacy from Home to School: Reading with Alice* and *Literacy in Nursery Education*, reflect that interest.

Max de Boo is Senior Lecturer in Education (Primary Science) at the University of Hertfordshire. She has considerable experience of teaching in primary schools and in early years contexts. She specialises in science and early years education and has written extensively therein.

Rose Drury is Senior Lecturer in Early Years Education at the University of Hertfordshire. She has extensive experience of teaching bilingual children in the early years. Her research and publications relate to this field.

Joy Jarvis is Senior Lecturer at the University of Hertfordshire who is currently responsible for training teachers of the deaf. She has worked with children with a range of communication difficulties in different contexts, including homes and schools and has published in this field.

Lyn Karstadt is Professional Leader for children's nursing in the University of Hertfordshire. She has been involved in Nurse Education for 17 years and is presently involved in research into the health effects of bullying in primary school children.

Sue Lamb is a speech and language therapist specialising in working with pre-school children with special needs. She is currently employed by North Herts NHS Trust to work in playgroups, opportunity groups and home settings.

Tricia Lilley is Principal Lecturer in Education at the University of Hertfordshire. Formerly head teacher of a primary school, her research interests include school provision for four year olds, children's mathematical experiences outside school, and the implementation of local education authority nursery policy. Publications include co-authorship of *Early Childhood Education and Care* (Trentham).

Jo Medd is Senior Lecturer in the Department of Midwifery and Child Care at the University of Hertfordshire where she has worked for three years. She has been a children's nurse and health visitor in London, Newcastle and Manchester. Her particular interests are chronic illness in childhood and child health in the community.

Linda Miller is Principal Lecturer in Early Years Education at the University of Hertfordshire and has worked both with and for children throughout her professional life. Her research and publications are in the areas of early literacy development, working with parents, play and the early years curriculum.

Pauline Minnis is Senior Lecturer in Education at the University of Hertfordshire. She has taught in reception and nursery classes and worked as an advisory teacher for English. Her current interest is in how literacy initiatives are mediated in the classroom.

Patti Owens spent 17 years in early years education as a nursery teacher and educational visitor. Previously a Senior Lecturer at the University of Hertfordshire, she now combines her psychotherapy practice with work for the Open University. Her publications include *Early Childhood Education and Care* (Trentham 1997). Her current research interest is in developmental theory and Gestalt psychotherapy.

Alice Paige-Smith was formerly a Senior Lecturer at the University of Hertfordshire. She has been involved with and published in the area of inclusive schooling.

Tim Parke is Principal Lecturer in Linguistics at the University of Hertfordshire and has taught in primary and secondary schools, and in language schools. His current research is into the acquisition of languages by bilingual children.

Bernice Rawlings is Senior Lecturer in Education and Geography at the University of Hertfordshire. She has taught all age groups in Hertfordshire and North London, from nursery to secondary, and she continues to maintain close links with a local nursery school, working with them on 'exploring our world'.

Mary Read is Head of Initial Teacher Training at the University of Hertfordshire. Her involvement in Early Years dates from working as Head of Infants in a Hertfordshire primary school. Her current interests are in management, particularly the relationship between managing self and managing others.

Mary Rees is Principal Lecturer in Education at the University of Hertfordshire where she co-ordinates the Specialist Teacher Assistant scheme. She has experience of working in teams in primary schools and in special schools and is particularly interested in the role of Learning Support Assistants.

Gill Smith is Senior Lecturer in Music Education at the University of Hertfordshire. She has worked with young children in a range of early years settings and provides training for adults in the provision of early years music.

Rosie Turner-Bisset is Senior Lecturer in Education at the University of Hertfordshire. She has worked in first and middle schools, as well as in secondary schools. She has worked on numerous research projects, including the Leverhulme Primary Project. Her publications and interests range over history teaching, teachers' knowledge bases and teachers' expertise.

Val Warren is Principal Lecturer in Education at the University of Hertfordshire. She has taught in primary schools and has been an advisory teacher for primary mathematics. Her research interests include maths education, early years maths and ITT for primary mathematics. She has published in the area of early years and primary mathematics.

Susan Westmoreland is Senior Lecturer in primary mathematics at the University of Hertfordshire. She has a wide experience of classroom teaching ranging from early years through the primary age range to Key Stage 3 in three different London LEAs. Her research interests relate to teaching mathematics and to teaching and learning in higher education.

Cindy Willey is Head teacher of Wall Hall Nursery School which is at the Watford Campus of the University of Hertfordshire. The nursery was established in 1971 to meet the needs of the local community and to act as a 'demonstration' nursery school for staff and students.

Acknowledgements

The editors wish to acknowledge the guidance and help they have been given by young children learning at home and in early years settings. Although the children may not have been aware of their essential contributions nevertheless their actions and comments feature throughout this book. The text is about children but it is for those adults who work with, or intend working with, children in early childhood settings. Many of those practitioners and students have added valuable insights which we were pleased to receive.

The collaborative task of completing an edited book is never easy. Nevertheless, the support we received from the chapter authors made the task more manageable than we imagined possible at the start of writing this text. Deadlines were met despite the other demands upon the writers. Amanda Evans collated all of the chapters and brought them together in an efficient and helpful way. We hope that they, and you the reader, will be as pleased with the book as we are. Other colleagues at the University of Hertfordshire Department of Education have added their assistance for which we are grateful.

Chapter 1

Looking at early years education and care: towards firmer foundations

Rose Drury, Linda Miller and Robin Campbell

This is an exciting time to be involved in the field of early years care and education. The needs of children under five and their families are now firmly on the political agenda. Professionals and experts in the field differ in their views regarding the rate and significance of the progress made, but in a sampling of the views of a number of notable 'pioneers' in the early years field O'Grady (1998 p. 2) concluded that the early years community had 'gained hugely in confidence and muscle' and that early years practitioners have 'found their voice'. One example of this progress is that children under six are to be included in the new foundation stage for children in all early years settings (QCA 1999a). This development brings to fruition the recommendations of the *Start Right Report* (Ball 1994) which recognised the need for a new phase of education for three to five year olds. Implementing curriculum guidance in a way which considers both the process and outcomes of learning will continue to be an important issue for early years practitioners and one which is addressed in subsequent chapters (QCA 1999a). As Ball (1994, p. 68) states 'The introduction of a new phase of education cannot be achieved overnight without careful preparation and training of staff'. It is the needs of those staff which this book seeks to address.

The current government has taken heed of a number of reports written over the last decade (DES 1990, Ball 1994) which have argued for a rapid expansion of provision for young children and support and training those who care for and educate them, whether in the home or in early years settings. A range of policy initiatives aim to build upon and enhance the current diverse provision for young children and their families and cut across the traditional care and education divide. These include the establishment of a network of 25 Early Excellence Centres, offering 'wrap around' education and care. Also, Early Years Development Partnerships and Plans which are intended to take into account the local needs of both children and parents and which will bring together providers from the maintained, private and voluntary sector (DfEE 1997). Linked to these developments are proposals for more uniform regulation and inspection of providers (DfEE 1998). The notion of 'joined-upness' across government departments and providers, has been a key theme of the present government. This principle is embodied in The Sure Start project which aims to work with parents to promote the health, development and education of their young children. It requires statutory providers in health and in local education authorities to work together with local communities to identify need and to provide intensive support for children under four and their families. This initiative is intended to identify a gap in provision and initial projects will be situated in areas of high deprivation. However, Peter Moss, of the Thomas Coram Research Unit, argues that we are still a long way from achieving an integrated and coherent service for children aged 0–6 (O'Grady 1998).

The new framework for nationally accredited qualifications in early years education, childcare and playwork should enable opportunities for training and career progression for early years practitioners and support them in developing the skills and knowledge which will be required to work with the developments outlined above (QCA 1999b). However, there will need to be commensurate recognition that additional training should be appropriately acknowledged through increased status, pay and working conditions.

Recent developments in the field of early years education and care provide the grounds for cautious optimism and will hopefully lead to firmer foundations for young children and their families. This book debates many of those developments and the foundations. The text is divided into four distinct sections each with a number of chapters. In the first section key issues are explored. Linda Miller opens that section and reminds us all of the importance of play as a foundation of learning. This is a major issue for everyone concerned with early years education and care because of the pressures from initiatives such as the National Curriculum and the new Early Learning Goals which seem to encourage direct teaching at ever earlier ages. Positive examples are provided in this chapter of children learning literacy through play as they explore, for instance, flight. The children's imaginative play with their 'aeroplane' demonstrates the possibilities for learning. Then in chapter 3 she looks at some aspects of practice in early years settings and in doing so raises wider questions. How does a knowledge of child development support our provision? What are developmentally appropriate practices? Both of those questions can be considered in the context of our society, but they are considered in a wider socio-cultural context. There is also the issue of quality in the early years setting. Questions are raised about who is to define or judge that quality.

A trio of education and health staff look at the variety of professional roles in early childhood in chapter 4. The need for knowledgeable adults who understand something of how children learn is emphasised here and is apparent in the other chapters of the book. Those adults need to be able to respond to external questions and pressures. They do so by being secure as to why practices, such as play, are utilised. A mature student, Tracey, helps us to note how that happens as she reflects on her degree course.

'Working together' is the title of the second section. It contains contributions from staff with differing backgrounds who explore support for young children from various perspectives. First, in chapter 5 Lyn Karstadt and Jo Medd consider children in the family and society. They remind all early years practitioners that a child should not be considered in isolation from the home. The family has a considerable influence on the child's development and it is incumbent upon those in early years settings to create partnerships with parents and carers. The link between home and early years setting is often facilitated by using a key worker to provide security for the child and real dialogue between the adults.

Mary Rees and Mary Read explore working in teams in early years settings in chapter 6. It is inevitable that adults have to work together in a early years setting. However, here it is argued that teamwork has to be seen in a management context which leads to a planned professional activity. Using documents from a large nursery setting the key features which support working together are debated. It is evident that adults in early years settings have to work collaboratively in order to maximise the environment for the children.

Supporting children with communication difficulties is presented by Joy Jarvis and Sue Lamb. In chapter 7 they first describe how those working in the early years can identify and assess communication difficulties. Then they suggest strategies which can be used to support those children. That theory is made specific as we note the observations and subsequent support for Tom and Kia. The two children have different difficulties leading to a variety of suggested strategies. And with adult guidance they are able to make progress.

Alice Paige-Smith explores inclusive education in the early years in chapter 8. Using the example from a Canadian kindergarten class she shows how providing inclusive education from the early years can create positive learning for all the children. The tasks for parents and staff to ensure that inclusive education becomes successful are exemplified as we learn of Karen's pre-school experiences.

Lyn Karstadt and Jo Medd return to debate child health in chapter 9. Their theoretical insights are clarified as we learn of the life styles of three year olds Gemma and Lucy. Issues of diet and exercise are important features for both children. However, to address those there is a need to think of the child, the immediate environment, as well as wider social and economic factors. The implication is that partnerships between the home, early years settings and wider links are required to best serve the needs of the children.

In chapter 10 Rose Drury follows two children in early years settings and provides an analysis of bilingual children in the pre-school years. Nina and Nazma encounter the rules and expectations of their new social world in a nursery. For Nazma the learning of procedural rules and other aspects of nursery life are dependent upon her learning of English as an additional language. But her learning of English depends, for instance, on being able to interact with peers. She is supported by her interactions with bilingual staff who are able to relate to her home experiences.

Cindy Willey provides insights, as the head teacher of a nursery school, of the need to work closely with parents and carers of the children. The relationship is demonstrated to be interactive. The school staff learn from the parents about the children's experiences and knowledge. And the parents gain confidence in what they have achieved and in what they can provide in the future – for Amy, Richard, Tim and Emma. All of that requires a range of connections between the school and home which are described in this chapter.

The third section is devoted to language and literacy. First Tim Parke in chapter 12 explores talking and listening. There he demonstrates the importance of the interactions between the child and the adult which support language development. Using two and a half year old Mark, and later a group of children, as a guide, he shows how the interactions at home and in the early years setting may vary. But, each of the language interactions extend the children's language.

In chapter 13 Robin Campbell looks at literacy learning at home and at school. The importance of story readings and the need of children to have stories repeated so that they can gain ownership of meanings and words is debated. Other learning experiences such as using the print in the environment, singing songs and nursery rhymes, having opportunities to draw and write, looking at the alphabet and writing one's own name are considered. Five year old Alice's recipe for making a shepherd's pie exemplifies, and brings to life, some of that learning. In all of that the important role of the adult is made evident.

Pauline Minnis moves us forward, in chapter 14, to literacy in reception classes. How are five year old children best supported in their literacy development? In part that question is explored as we follow Kieran's literacy experiences during the course of a day. The variety of literacy activities which are provided in the reception class today for Kieran and other children are debated. We can follow the self-initiated explorations of the children and the more directed teaching which has become a feature of the reception class.

The final section explores other aspects of the curriculum, however it does so by noting how very young children are learning about that curriculum naturally at home before being directed towards that learning in early years settings. First in chapter 15 Patti Owens debates the interpersonal world of the growing child. She does so using Stern's model of infant interpersonal development. Patti helps us to understand that model as she observes ten month old Thomas at play and provides an analysis of his interactions with his father. The emphasis on this important area and the role of the adult as a support is appropriate before we move on to other early years 'subject' areas.

As a start Val Warren and Susan Westmoreland examine number in play and everyday life in chapter 16. Once again it is a young child who helps us to see the learning that takes place in the early years. Four year old Amber counts the crackers that she wants to eat, counts the number in her family using her drawing and writes out raffle tickets from one to ten. Using those examples, and others, the current emphasis upon counting in early years settings, developing from counting at home, is made explicit. Subsequently, that leads us on to the more directed interactive teaching of number suggested for the first years of schooling in England.

Exploring our world is the topic of chapter 17 by Peter Bloomfield, Max de Boo and Bernice Rawlings. They demonstrate that the curiosity of the child leads inevitably to a need to find out about the immediate and wider environment. The children are aided in that learning where the adults ask the appropriate type of questions which further the children's scientific and geographical thinking. Sara's drawing of her journey to the nursery suggests concepts still to be learned but it also indicates the value of exploration.

Encouraging children's creative expression is the subject of chapter 18 by Rosemary Allen, Tricia Lilley and Gill Smith. Particular emphasis is given to children's musical and artistic expression. They note how children use sound leading to song and rhyme. The creative use of sounds is valuable of itself and also contributes to other aspects of learning such as literacy development. In the same way making marks, drawing, painting and other forms of artistic expression enable children to represent and use their imagination as well as supporting mathematical thinking and the development of writing.

Finally Rosie Turner-Bisset considers meaningful history with young children. Five year old Harriet's question about the school gates inevitably leads to a response of a historical nature. History becomes part of the curriculum because of the nature of children's interests. And they can be helped by the type of questions that adults use to support the learning. The fact that Rosie argues for the use of stories and play to encourage historical thinking also links across to the messages conveyed in other chapters.

So this book is about children but it has been primarily written to support professionals in a variety of training contexts. It is therefore comprehensive in scope and takes account of recent policy initiatives. It reflects the themes of inclusion, partnership in early years education and care, the need for finding a balance between the educative and caring functions of provision, and the significance of particular areas of the early years curriculum in relation to an understanding of child development.

The children's voices and stories weave a powerful thread through the chapters and lead us to reflect on how we can lay firm foundations for all young children and their families in a diverse range of early childhood settings. We are reminded of the fundamental beliefs and principles which underpin our practice as early years practitioners and of the key theories about children's learning and development. We also recognise the crucial role of the adult in young children's learning. All of this makes a timely contribution to the professional debate as we enter the new foundation stage for young children in the England (QCA 1999a).

We believe that this book will be of interest and relevance to everyone working with young children in early childhood settings and particularly those training for qualifications in early years education and care. With the current focus on the early years, we aim to re-focus our readers' attention to the foundations of young children's learning and development and re-state the vital importance of early years practitioners.

References

Ball, C. (1994) *Start Right.* London: Royal Society of Arts.

Department for Education and Employment (1997) *Guidance 1998–1999: Early Years Development Plans and Partnerships.* Darlington: Department for Education and Employment.

Department for Education and Employment and the Department of Health (1998) *Consultation Paper on the Regulation of Early Education and Day Care.* Darlington: Department for Education and Employment.

Department of Education and Science (1990) *Starting with Quality*. London: HMSO.

O'Grady, C. (1998) 20/20 vision, Co-ordinate extra. January 2–4.

Qualifications and Curriculum Authority (1999a) *Early Learning Goals*. London: Qualifications and Curriculum Authority.

Qualifications and Curriculum Authority (1999b) *Early Years, Education, Childcare and Playwork sector: A framework of nationally accredited qualifications*. London: Qualifications and Curriculum Authority.

Chapter 2

Play as a foundation for learning

Linda Miller

The Guardian reported on 23 June 1999, on the review of the curriculum guidance for three to six year olds by the Qualifications and Curriculum Authority (1999a) under the headline 'Play is out, early learning is in' (Carvel 1999). This illustrates the dichotomy which exists in the debate regarding the role of play in young children's learning. The article goes on to quote the education minister at that time who argued that play should be 'purposeful' and that the days of toddlers 'colouring, cutting and pasting are over'. In contrast, the same article reports that 16 of the 18 nursery settings designated as 'centres of excellence' by the government, had protested that the proposed curriculum guidance, which sets out Early Learning Goals for three to six year olds, is unsuitable and that children under six should learn through play. It is encouraging to note that the final guidance includes a section on the value of both planned and spontaneous play (QCA 1999b). This chapter explores the play/learning divide through the use of case studies, in particular in two early years settings, using literacy learning as an example.

The emergence of literacy

In 1996, in a book about early literacy development, I brought together some recent research on how young children learn about literacy in mainly Western societies. I illustrated this development through an iceberg model (see Figure 2.1) to show the range of literacy experiences which many, but not all, young children experience in the home and surrounding contexts. In the submerged part of the iceberg are the literacy related activities which many parents and carers engage in with their young children. These unplanned learning experiences are part of what has been described as the 'hidden curriculum' of the home. In the tip of the iceberg the very visible signs of literacy development can be seen, i.e. the learning outcomes which arise from these earlier experiences (Miller 1996).

I advocated that the literacy curriculum in early years settings needs to build upon and link to children's home experiences, many of which are embedded in contexts which can be described as playful. This is illustrated by Robin Campbell

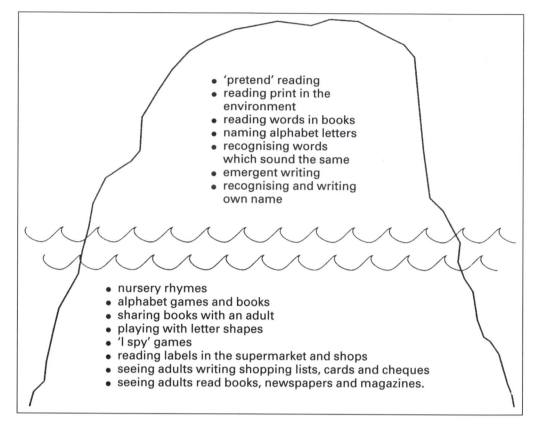

Figure 2.1 The tip of the iceberg

in chapter 13, where he discusses the opportunities for literacy learning which three year old Caitlin encountered in a single day at home. It is, however, important to note that such opportunities are affected by family circumstances, culture, lifestyle and parents' aspirations for their children. A common value system and common experiences cannot be assumed. It is important for early years practitioners to acknowledge the socio-cultural framework within which children play and learn (Woodhead 1998, QCA 1999b). For example, parents and early years practitioners may have diverse perspectives on what constitutes play and learning and their relative weighting within the curriculum.

At the time of writing the above mentioned book, I was experiencing a period of optimism. I believed that the view of early literacy development, described as 'emergent literacy', was becoming firmly rooted amongst early years practitioners. This term has replaced notions of 'reading readiness'. It encapsulates the view that there is no one point at which young children 'read' or 'write', but that these skills gradually emerge in the first years of life (Miller 1996). I believed that the notion that literacy development begins long before children embark upon formal schooling, was gaining acceptance and was indeed a watershed for early years practitioners .

However, developments in the United Kingdom over the last ten years have threatened this perspective. These were the introduction of a statutory curriculum framework for primary schools in 1988; a framework for early learning, which stressed the achievement of outcomes for five year olds (SCAA 1996); a related inspection system (Ofsted 1997) and baseline assessment for five year olds (SCAA 1997). These have had a knock-on effect on non statutory educational provision for children aged three to five. Even more recently the National Literacy Strategy (DfEE 1998a and b) has introduced a Literacy Hour into primary schools, including reception classes for five year olds (see Pauline Minnis's discussion in chapter 14). This practice has also been adopted by some nursery settings. The notion of an hour in the day when literacy may be taught and learned seems to be the antithesis of the iceberg model in Figure 2.1. This model suggests that literacy learning occurs at opportune moments throughout the day, supported by a sensitive adult, who is tuned in to the child's agenda. Whitehead (1999, p. 59) calls this '24 hour literacy' which she says begins with language and play and is rooted in meaningful contexts across cultures and languages.

Literacy practices in early years settings

Over a two year period, from 1997 to 1999, I carried out a small scale study which involved spending one day (a minimum of six hours) in each of 11 early years settings. They included five private nurseries, three playgroups, two of which offered inclusive provision for children with special educational needs, a nursery in a non maintained school, a workplace nursery and a voluntary aided nursery school. They were located in both rural and urban areas. All the settings were working within the guidelines for four year olds provided by the Desirable Outcomes for Children's Learning (SCAA 1996). Data was collected about the range and type of literacy provision through observations of the environment, resources, evidence from children's records of work and discussions with staff. The staff included six qualified teachers, five of whom were designated as teacher in charge or nursery manager. Three of the teachers were qualified for, and had experience of, working with the under fives. Other staff qualifications included nursery nursing diplomas, a Montessori diploma and a nursing qualification. Some staff were unqualified, but most had attended relevant short training courses such as those offered by Pre-School Learning Alliance. It is important to note that the settings varied in relation to the quality of the buildings, sources of funding available for equipment, staff salaries and training opportunities and also in parental expectations. All these factors had an effect on the experiences provided for the children.

Data from the settings showed that literacy practices varied widely. Like Browne (1998) in her study of provision for reading in nursery settings, I found that the qualifications of the staff were generally related to what has been proposed as 'developmentally appropriate practice'. Browne (1998, p. 9) summarises this as opportunities for children to:

- engage in purposeful and relevant learning;
- gain real understanding of new concepts;
- discover through active exploration;

- learn through experimentation;
- develop motivation and interest in what is learned;
- become confident learners;
- acquire dispositions towards life time learning.

However, Woodhead (1998) warns against blindly applying quality indicators across different contexts, without taking account of different conditions, cultural values and practices (see chapter 3 for further discussion).

In the settings where staff were not qualified early years teachers, there were examples of good practice as defined by Browne (1998) above. However, these staff were unable to articulate the principles and rationale underlying this practice and so had difficulty in implementing the changes required by the new curriculum guidelines, in a way which was developmentally appropriate.

The implications of this were evident in the two playgroup settings offering inclusive provision for children with special educational needs. One setting provided an inclusive curriculum based on well planned, well resourced play which was appropriately supported by key workers who worked with individuals or groups of children on a range of activities. There was good multi-disciplinary support for the children which included home visiting teachers, speech therapists, educational psychologists and physiotherapists. There was a specially equipped soft play room with cause and effect toys and sensory equipment. However, for twenty minutes each day this programme was set aside for the children to complete adult directed literacy activities in small groups. For example, chanting letter sounds, responding to words on flash cards and completing work sheet tasks, such as drawing round dot to dot letters of the alphabet. Some of these children had not yet developed spoken language and needed adult support to hold a writing implement. The staff had hastily implemented this literacy programme in good faith believing, 'It is what Ofsted wants'.

Similar practices were observed in the second setting. This play group offered rich resources for imaginative play and there was a strong emphasis on experiences which supported speaking and listening. However, in order to meet the requirements for literacy set out in the curriculum guidelines, individual or small groups of children were taken out of the main activity room in order to undertake adult directed activities such as writing patterns, copy writing and completing work sheets. The staff were unaware of the possibilities for developing literacy through the provision and resourcing of writing areas or role play areas such as shops or cafés. These are example of what Browne (1998, p. 10) describes as 'crudely interpreted' desirable outcomes.

In two of the private settings the children were being 'prepared' for conventional reading and writing. There was considerable emphasis on the use of reading schemes, worksheets and workbooks. In the record folder of one three year old, I read that his parents were concerned about his lack of progress in reading. This illustrates a dilemma for early years practitioners in settings where parents are paying substantial fees for their children's care and education. The teacher in charge was concerned about the parents' expectations of the child, but the ethos of the nursery was that reading and writing were of prime importance. Just three of the 11 settings offered a literacy curriculum which could be deemed developmentally appropriate, although all had pockets of good practice.

I had hoped that early years settings had moved on from the notion of a pre-school reading readiness curriculum, as evidence suggests that such activities have little pay-off for subsequent reading development (Adams 1990). Also, as Edwards and Knight (1994) discuss, the term 'pre' suggests that these activities are not quite reading or writing and that real literacy starts in school. It is possible that my previously described optimism stemmed from the fact that we do not have a clear picture of what literacy learning is like for some children in some settings. The following 'snapshot' descriptions, based on the above mentioned observations, attempt to cast some light upon the experiences of some four year old literacy learners in two contrasting early years settings.

Learning about literacy through play?

Setting A

Setting A is a private nursery based in a family house situated on a busy main road in a town. Six staff work with 19 four year olds on a rota system over five mornings each week. The manager qualified as a primary school teacher in 1968, but has, along with other staff, attended short courses funded by a limited training budget. The staff are proud of their literacy programme which places a strong emphasis on teaching letter sounds and letter formation. There is a reading scheme and the children take home a book from the scheme each day to share with the parents. The parents I spoke to are pleased with what the nursery has to offer.

The day of the observation was a literacy focus day. Other curriculum areas such as mathematics or creative activities are focused on, on different days. The curriculum is offered through a series of rotating, adult led groups over the morning. Each activity lasts for about 20 minutes. As the children enter the nursery they are able to select from a limited range of books in a comfortable seating area or may sit at a table to share a literacy based game or jigsaw puzzle with their parent, carer or another adult, as other children are arriving. Books are not available again until just before home time.

In one group the children sing songs and rhymes and listen to a story, all from the Letterland scheme. They continue with related activities which include responding to words on flash cards and answering questions about the letter of the day, for example, 'Who has a name beginning with. . .?' They become restless. There is considerable direct teaching and the use of 'display' questions such as 'show me . . .', 'tell me . . .' which feels exhausting to the observer. The session ends with a workbook activity which involves copying over the letter of the day. Many of these four year olds recognise their names and some of the letters in their names. Some children form their letters very well. The children's portfolios are full of copy writing, there is no evidence of independent writing.

The session finishes before the next adult is ready for them. This activity involves writing the letter of the day with their fingers in salt on trays. While they are waiting they are allowed to choose what to do, so four of the children move into the home corner. They become involved in imaginative play about their pending summer holiday. They talk about all the things they will need such as tickets, swimming costumes and sun cream. They share their experiences of going on an aeroplane and one child tells about being sick in the car. Three children start to pack a bag and some rich oral storying begins about a pending holiday. One child finds a scrap of paper and a pencil and begins to write a 'packing list'. They are absorbed and engaged in a way which contrasts strongly with the previously observed session. There are no resources or props to support literacy related play. The 'writing in salt' activity is in the same room. The adult in charge shows a passing interest and says 'Oh, you're going off on holiday', but this is the only acknowledgement of this play.

Comment on setting A

The above scene illustrates how opportunities for the children to engage in meaningful reading and writing were missed. This was due to the lack of adult involvement in the play and the absence of literacy related resources. Hall (1991) argues that when children are offered play experiences with literacy related resources they act in literate ways. Literacy is contextualised for them in similar ways to real life, for example helping to write a shopping list. There were opportune moments to encourage the writing of lists, postcards and messages. The holiday theme could have been developed the next day through related stories, the production of holiday photographs and holiday brochures. A travel agents theme, a hotel or a sea-side scenario could have been introduced into the home corner and appropriately resourced. In the curriculum guidance offered by the QCA (1999b p. 26) an example of literacy play in a café setting is included. In chapter 13, Robin Campbell, in his discussion of Alice's recipe for shepherd's pie, offers an example of this functional literacy, which involves reading and writing for a real purpose, Also, as he observes, it shows the learning Alice has yet to achieve. A skilful adult can build on this by:

- providing a model for literacy;
- offering further support;
- providing appropriate resources;
- giving direct instruction;
- allowing children to take further risks, i.e. encouraging them to 'have a go'.
(Miller 1996)

In setting A the message to the children is that only literacy which counts is that which the adult chooses to offer. Also, that you show what you know through a 'write and tell mode' (Bruce 1994, p. 194). Literacy is seen as a separately taught subject, under the control and direction of the adult. This has implications for what is noted and valued in relation to the children's literacy development. The emphasis on learning outcomes and products severely limits those opportunities which we know contribute to children's literacy development. For example, the chance for children to hypothesise or make 'good guesses' about what the printed word might say or how it might be written, in situations where there is no pressure to 'get it right'.

Setting B

Setting B is housed in an old village school and provides for 39 three and four year olds. It is staffed by two qualified early years teachers, a nursery nurse, an unqualified assistant and parent helpers. The central room is large, light and airy. Well labelled paintings, pictures and collaborative friezes made by the children adorn the walls. There is a small room leading off the main room which offers a well stocked and well used library area containing a small sofa and floor cushions. There is a listening corner with taped stories, books made by the children and a display of environmental print packaging brought in by the children. Another, larger room, is staffed by two adults and is resourced to provide creative experiences such as clay work, model making and painting.

As the children enter the nursery music is playing. In the middle of the floor an adult is sitting beside a long roll of paper in the centre of the room, drawing and writing messages. The children start to join in, later they talk about what they have drawn or written. Monty the Bear, who accompanies a child home each day, is returned with his suitcase and diary. Later, with the help of an adult, a group of children read in his diary about what he did overnight. There is a big alphabet mat on the floor and two children are jumping on and off the letters, a nearby adults says the letter sounds as they land. In the writing area the children have free access to a range of paper, envelopes, forms and writing implements. The provision of scissors, stapler, sellotape and a computer support the children in making their own books. Adults and children leave messages for each other on the message board.

The children have recently been to see an aeroplane and a project on flight is underway. At the back of the room an aeroplane, made up from rows of chairs, is ready for take off. The children take the passports which they have made to the airline desk, where forms are filled in and tickets are issued. As a visitor, I am offered a menu card so that I can choose my in-flight meal, which is eventually delivered on a tray. Related posters, displays and word labels provide a model for the children's independent writing.

Later in the morning two adult led activities develop the theme of flight. One group of children explore a large model aeroplane. They observe the movements of the wings as the adult demonstrates the controls, new vocabulary such as 'propeller' is introduced. A second group of children are excitedly guessing what a set of different sized suitcases might contain. They sort them for size and use vocabulary such as 'big', 'little'. The suitcases are weighed to see if they are too heavy to take on the aeroplane. Later, they are incorporated into role play. In the creative room a group of children making models of aeroplanes are helped to use reference books to explore the theme of flight.

Comment on setting B

In this setting there is no pressure on the children to meet learning goals set out in curriculum guidelines. Nevertheless, the children are guided towards the same outcomes as the children in setting A. The adults in setting B were articulate in defending their practice in the face of pressures to consider more formal routes to learning. Literacy is not seen as a separate subject, but as part of a of broad range of experiences within a curriculum which is based on well planned and well resourced play (QCA 1999b). Adults support and scaffold children in their learning. They provide models for literacy through the explicit use of, and making of, books and through reading and writing labels, messages, filling in forms and reading with the children from a variety of sources.

Play as a foundation for learning

In a lecture entitled 'Playing for Life: laying the foundations for lifelong learning', Guy Claxton (1999) talked about the need for 'relaxed modes of cognition', of 'slow ways of knowing' which start with what children do well. This suggests that children need time to learn. Bruce (1994, p. 196) has also referred to the ways in which young children in non western societies learn alongside adults through 'watching, playing, socialising and slowly doing'. In Miller (1998) I have described how young children learn about print in the environment through informal interactions with adults. This mode of learning is contrasted by Claxton with what he describes as 'the sausage machine of literacy', the fast route to literacy, which he believes damages children's capacity to develop the disposition to learn, i.e. the wanting to. Katz (1995) has said that we cannot teach children everything they need to know, therefore developing the disposition to learn must be a major goal of education. Developing 'positive attitudes and dispositions towards their learning' is stated as one of the aims for young children in the new foundation stage (QCA 1999b, p. 9). Concerns about setting specified time scales within which children will achieve specific learning goals have been voiced by Drummond (1997, p. 5). She notes that some children are reading conventionally at age four and some at age seven, but argues that we have no evidence to suggest that 'sooner is better'. She goes on to say, 'focusing on the end point, the attainment, distracts us from the true continuous process – the learning. And of the two, learning is the more important'.

Planning for literacy learning through play

In early years settings, particularly where a key worker system is in operation, i.e. where an adult takes particular responsibility for a group of children, well planned play experiences offer contexts for learning which embody the principles set out in this chapter. Edwards and Knight (1994) cite Munn's (1992) work on both literacy and numeracy, in what are described as educationally focused nurseries in Scotland. They discuss how Munn has shown the ways in which experienced practitioners 'operate with curricula' in everyday situations such as serving vegetables at lunch time or talking to a child as he or she completes a puzzle. The adults highlighted the features of the children's experiences which 'they as experts consider to be relevant to the children's needs' (Edwards and Knight 1994, p. 23). Munn's observations showed that adults and children were involved in often short conversations which took the children's thinking and ways of experiencing 'one step further' (Edwards and Knight 1994, p. 23). They go on to say, 'These children, far from developing pre-literacy or pre-numeracy skills, are engaging with the challenges of literacy and early numeracy within a familiar and goal-directed context which allows them to work slowly and safely towards agreed understandings' (p. 23).

Claxton (1999) offers evidence from research on the brain which he refers to as the brain's capacity for rough tuning. He suggests that the implications of this research for practitioners is that the young brain 'knows what it is ready for'. That teaching and learning in the early years should not be through a tightly pre-determined curriculum, but through a form of rough mapping. This does not imply a sloppy, *laissez faire* approach to planning the curriculum, but an approach which allows children to make choices, to take risks and to become independent learners, with appropriate and sensitive adult support. Government guidance on the curriculum should recognise the expertise of well trained and experienced early years practitioners and trust them to provide appropriate learning goals for young children (QCA 1999b).

Conclusion

Early years practitioners, particularly those working towards the Early Learning Goals with three and four years olds, must hold on to the fact that nowhere is it suggested in curriculum guidelines or in the inspection framework that settings should work in any particular way towards the early learning goals (Ofsted 1997, QCA 1999b). By putting pressure on children to demonstrate their knowledge through 'write and tell' activities, we are in danger of setting them up to fail and of turning them off literacy. Early years practitioners should seize the opportunity to protect the route into literacy, which for many children begins in the home, so that it remains playful and enjoyable. For those children who experience literacy in ways which are different to school, then as Robin Campbell says in chapter 13, early years settings must provide the foundations for literacy through contexts which relate to literacy in real life and which will promote life long literacy learning.

References

Adams, M. (1990) *Beginning to Read*. London: Heinemann Educational.
Browne, A. (1998) 'Provision for reading for four year old children', *Reading* **32** (1), 9–13.
Bruce, T. (1994) 'Play, the universe and everything', in Moyles, J. R. (ed.) *The Excellence of Play*, 189–98. Buckingham: Open University Press.
Carvel, C. (1999) 'Play is out, early learning is in', *Guardian*, 23 June 1999.
Claxton, G. (1999) 'Playing for life; laying the foundations for lifelong learning'. Paper delivered at BAECE Conference *Sure Start–Brighter Future*. Church House Conference Centre, Westminster, London, 9 June.

Department for Education and Employment (1998a) *The National Literacy Strategy: Framework for Teaching*. London: Department for Education and Employment.

Department for Education and Employment (1998b) *The National Literacy Strategy*. London: Department for Education and Employment.

Drummond, M. (1997) 'An undesirable document', *Coordinate*, January 7-8.

Edwards, A. and Knight, P. (1994) *Effective Early Years Education*. Buckingham: Open University Press.

Hall, N. (1991) 'Play and the emergence of literacy', in Christie, J. F. (ed.) *Play and Early Literacy Development*, 1–25. New York: State University of New York Press.

Katz, L. (1995) 'Multiple perspectives on early years provision'. Paper presented at RSA Conference *Start Right*. London, 20–22 September.

Miller, L. (1996) *Towards Reading: Literacy Development in the Pre-School Years*. Buckingham: Open University Press.

Miller, L. (1998) 'Literacy interactions through environmental print', in Campbell, R. (ed.) *Facilitating Pre-school Literacy*, 100–118. Newark: International Reading Association.

Munn, P. (1992) 'Teaching strategies in nursery settings'. Paper presented to the Education Section of the British Psychological Society Annual Conference, Wokingham, November.

Ofsted (1997) *Guidance on the Inspection of Nursery Education Provision in the Private, Voluntary and Independent Sectors*. London: The Stationery Office.

Qualifications and Curriculum Authority (1999a) *A Review of the Desirable Outcomes*. London: Qualifications and Curriculum Authority.

Qualifications and Curriculum Authority (1999b) *Early Learning Goals*. London: Qualifications and Curriculum Authority.

School Curriculum and Assessment Authority (1996) *Desirable Outcomes for Children's Learning*. London: HMSO.

School Curriculum and Assessment Authority (1997) *The National Framework for Baseline Assessment*. London: School Curriculum and Assessment Authority.

Whitehead, M. (1999) 'A literacy hour in the nursery? The big question mark', *Early Years: An International Journal of Research and Development* **19** (2) 51-62.

Woodhead, M. (1998) '"Quality" in Early Childhood programmes – a contextually appropriate approach', in *International Journal for Early Childhood Education* **6** (1), 5–17.

Chapter 3

Aspects of practice in early years settings

Linda Miller

Introduction

This chapter considers key aspects of practice in early years settings. Christopher Ball (1994) considers the nature of good practice. He sets out twelve fundamental principles of practice, derived from a range of sources, which underpin early learning (Bruce 1987, Early Years Curriculum Group 1992). Those principles were:

1) Early childhood is the foundation on which children build the rest of their lives. But it is not just a preparation for adolescence and adulthood: it has an importance in itself.
2) Children develop at different rates, and in different ways – emotionally, intellectually, morally, socially, physically and spiritually. All are important; each is interwoven with others.
3) All children have abilities which can (and should be) identified and promoted.
4) Young children should learn from everything that happens to them and around them; they do not separate their learning into different subjects or disciplines.
5) Children learn most effectively through actions, rather than from instruction.
6) Children learn best when they are actively involved and interested.
7) Children who feel confident in themselves and their own ability have a head-start to learning.
8) Children need time and space to produce work of quality and depth.
9) What children can do (rather than what they cannot do) is the starting point in their learning.
10) Play and conversation are the main ways by which young children learn about themselves, other people and the world around them.
11) Children who are encouraged to think for themselves are more likely to act independently.
12) The relationships which children make with other children and with adults are of central importance to their development. (Ball, pp. 51–3).

Children are at the forefront of this list. It is evident that as a minimum children require the opportunity for play, a variety of stimulating activities, meaningful and challenging contexts, and support from adults. Few early years practitioners would disagree with these fundamental principles and these aspects of practice are endorsed throughout this book.

However, whilst recognising the importance of the above principles as a basis for good practice in many Western contexts, this chapter takes a wider view. In chapter 4, Lyn Karstadt, Tricia Lilley and Linda Miller argued that early years practitioners need to be willing to reflect upon their practice and to challenge long held assumptions. They also contend that children need to be around thinking adults. In this chapter the reader is challenged to take a critical perspective in relation to some aspects of early years theory and practice. This will enable early years practitioners to answer the difficult 'why' questions when their practices and beliefs are challenged (Lally 1995).

A knowledge of child development

In 1990 the report *Starting with Quality* (DES 1990) outlined the knowledge and skills required by adults working with children under five. A knowledge of how young children learn was seen as a key feature. Surprisingly child development as a body of knowledge in its own right has only recently been recognised by the Teacher Training Agency (DfEE 1998) as an important element of training to work with young children This initiative has been welcomed by teacher educators who have spent many years lobbying for such a change. However, it is only relatively recently that questions have been raised about the social and cultural context in which this body of knowledge is applied. As Woodhead (1999) points out, the vast majority of studies of early child development and education have been carried out in narrow socio-economic and cultural contexts – mainly in Europe and North America. He cites Penn (1998) who notes that Europe constitutes only 12% of the world's population and North America a further 5%. However, Woodhead and Penn argue that the outcomes of such studies are often cited as the 'norms' to be universally applied to all children.

One example of the application of universal norms is the notion that young children require time and space of their own in order to learn properly (see principle 8 above). An example of this might be the amount of time which children spend alone or with others. Time alone and space to play and learn is dependent upon the social and cultural context within which childhood is lived. Helen Penn (1998) recounts how Nelson Mandela, in his autobiography, recalls that up to the age of seven he never remembers being alone. There were always other children present, of different ages and from different families. Penn (1998, p. 27) goes on to say, 'for most of the world's children, separation, privacy and individual ownership of possessions, things which we in the minority world take absolutely for granted, simply do not exist'.

The way in which childhood is experienced is what Kessen describes as 'domain specific', i.e. that what you are doing and why you are doing it is influenced by the context in which it takes place (Kessen 1983, p. 238 cited in Penn, 1998 p. 26). I recently gained a better understanding of what Kessen means during a visit to some Chinese kindergartens in Malaysia, where it was commonplace for one practitioner to have sole charge of groups of 40 three and four year olds. They were taught a range of subjects in preparation for the primary school curriculum, in three different languages on a rotating basis. This necessarily involved considerable whole class teaching and direct instructional methods, which would be considered inappropriate in the United Kingdom context. However, what you can do with a group of fifteen to twenty children is very different to what you can do with forty.

The drive to encourage individuality in children by encouraging them to become independent learners and to engage in conversations with adults (see principles 10 and 11) offers another example. Penn (1996, p. 15) argues that recent research suggests 'cultural expectations are an extremely powerful determinant of how children behave, and what is considered normal in one setting is regarded as abnormal in another'. For example, in chapter 10 Rose Drury describes how Nazma has difficulty in adjusting to the cultural expectations and norms of her nursery class, which have few links with her experiences within her family. Penn cites the example of young children in Western societies being encouraged to speak out and express their own viewpoints, as behaviour which would be regarded as immature in many African communities. (See also chapter 12 for a discussion of adults' interactions with children in Western Samoa.) So Penn and others are challenging the assumption that there is one type of childhood, one set of developmental norms and one way in which to implement early years practice.

Developmentally appropriate practice

The term developmentally appropriate practice (DAP) is outlined in a position statement in Bredekamp (1987). Central to the definition are the notions that the curriculum and learning experiences must be matched to the age and individual abilities of the child. Bredekamp argues for programmes based on the notion that children learn most effectively through a concrete, play oriented approach to the curriculum. Play is seen as the primary vehicle for development and learning. In a discussion of DAP Kelly (1994) says that the focus of the early childhood curriculum must be on the child and his/her development rather than on subjects and the acquisition of knowledge. He describes a developmentally appropriate curriculum as being based on:

- active forms of learning;
- enquiry and discovery;
- the process rather than the content of learning.

He argues that the curriculum should be framed in terms of activity and experience rather than knowledge to be acquired and facts to be stored. The principles outlined at the beginning of this chapter can be seen to underpin DAP. (See also Browne's (1998) summary of DAP in chapter 2.)

In chapter 2, whilst advocating an approach which recognises play as a vehicle for learning, it is also argued that the socio-cultural framework of the learning context must be acknowledged. Woodhead's (1998, p. 10) view is cited in support of this, that using DAP as a 'quality indicator' of good practice cannot be applied to all settings without taking account of the social and cultural context. Woodhead sets out the features of what he believes is a more contextually sensitive approach which includes:

- practice based on local variations in children's growth and change, age and individuality;
- the social context of their care;
- their roles and responsibilities within the family and the community;
- patterns of communication language;
- the recognition of cultural difference;
- the recognition that children learn in a variety of ways;
- the teacher's/carer's role is adapted to the resources available and the standards, values and social environment of the local community.

For example, Woodhead cites cross cultural studies which have taken account of parents' views on the curriculum. When a group of Venezuelan mothers and day care workers were questioned about the relative importance of play and discipline for young children's development, 8% of the mothers replied play and 52% replied discipline. The remainder thought that the two were equally important. The pattern of replies from the day care workers were similar, although they gave a little more emphasis to play and a little less to discipline. As Woodhead notes, these findings may seem surprising to those who have been educated to see play as pre-eminent in children's development. Similarly, Gregory (1993) has described how four year old Tony, from a Chinese family living in England, had difficulty in settling into school. Consequently, his teacher visited the home, where Tony's grandfather expressed his disgust to her about Tony's independent attempts to write his name in school as 'ToNy' saying 'This is rubbish'. The teacher was proudly shown an exercise book containing rows of immaculate ideographs which Tony had completed at Chinese Saturday school. Hence, parents and practitioners beliefs, values and priorities may not always be complementary even within Western contexts. Therefore, it can be seen that quality is not a unitary concept with a single set of indicators, which can be easily be applied to practice and agreed amongst early years practitioners.

Quality

Despite the subjective nature of quality, as argued above, objective measures are constantly sought, often through some sort of measurement scale. For example, the Effective Early Learning Project (Pascal and Bertram 1999) is admirable in its aims to 'evaluate and improve the quality of early learning in a wide range of education and care settings throughout the UK, Netherlands and Portugal' (p. 1). It attempts to quantify the quality of adult engagement in children's learning, through measures of sensitivity, stimulation and autonomy. Data from recent evaluations suggests that these levels have increased as a result of staff involvement in the action research programme. There is no doubt that encouraging practitioners to closely observe their own practice leads to heightened awareness. However, subsequent discussion of the presented findings (Pascal and Bertram 1999) at a recent conference, suggested that notions of sensitivity, stimulation and autonomy may be interpreted differently in different contexts and that consequently numerical scores of quality may not be reliable, or even useful, indictors. At the same conference Martin Woodhead and Thelma Harms, both distinguished researchers in this field, were unable to agree about who should decide what quality is in early childhood programmes – politicians, children, parents? They further disagreed about whether there can be universal measures of quality.

In England, in the last few years the Government has been striving to raise the quality and standard of early years and primary education. Literacy and numeracy strategies which aim to bring about improvement are discussed in chapters 14 and 16. In early years settings provision for four year olds is inspected to ensure that the educational component meets quality standards; this will soon be extended to three year olds. The inspection body OFSTED (1998) reported on the quality of education in early years settings inspected under the arrangements for funding nursery education. In the report a chart was presented which awarded stars to providers in a range of settings such as playgroups, independent schools and private nurseries; more stars equalled better provision. But what does this mean? To take language and literacy as an example, the private nurseries and independent schools were awarded three stars (the highest score) for indicators such as children recognising their own names and familiar words or writing their names with appropriate use of capital letters. This emphasis on the formal skills of reading and writing are the antithesis of the generally accepted view of developmentally appropriate practice, as discussed above. Playgroups, who have traditionally offered a play based curriculum and have placed a high priority on involving parents, received only one or two stars for the same items. Viewing quality through an imposed inspection framework will give only a partial view of what is provided. Checklists and rating scales necessarily capture those items which can most easily be observed and the choice of items for inclusion may be politically driven. Such narrow quality indicators may lead practitioners to seek hard evidence of measurable outcomes in the form of worksheets and written exercise, as discussed in chapter 2. Thus changes in practice become externally imposed rather than internally 'owned' by practitioners. There is a danger of the word 'quality' changing in meaning, without practitioners being sufficiently aware of the impact this may be having on their practice.

The language of early years education

Nutbrown (1998) argues that the language used by early years practitioners is crucial. The above section warns against drifting into the use of new language without noticing the change. For example, in a relatively recent move the former Pre-School Playgroups Association became the Pre-School Learning Alliance (PLA). Many playgroups subsequently changed their titles from playgroups to pre-schools. This move has largely been driven by external policy relating to the implementation of Government curriculum guidelines in these settings (School

Curriculum and Assessment Authority 1996). In their efforts to retain funding relating for four year olds, playgroups have been keen to emphasise their role in children's learning. This shift in terminology implies much more than a change in language but suggests a shift in both philosophy and practice.

The language of the set of principles outlined at the beginning of this chapter involves terms such as 'child initiated learning', 'active involvement and interest', 'confidence', 'time and space', 'play and conversation', 'independent action' and 'the centrality of relationships'. It can generally be said to describe the process of learning. Contrast this with the more recent language of early years education listed by Nutbrown (1998, p. 17) i.e. 'orders', 'standards', 'levels', 'stages', 'targets', 'outcomes'. Others could be added such 'goals', 'attainment', 'value added'. This language describes the outcomes of learning. Such a shift in terminology must not go unnoticed. Questioning the language of early years education can lead to a rigorous assessment of practice. Do we, for example, share with parents the same meanings in relation to words such as 'play' or 'learning'? (See the example of Tony and his grandfather cited earlier in this chapter). Do we talk about and articulate such meanings with colleagues?

We also need to consider the effects of the use of this new language on children and their parents. I was reminded of the time my 10 year old daughter came home from primary school after the receiving her SATs results and announced that she was 'a low four'. Consider how this made Katie and her parents feel? Clearly Katie has not met the required 'standard' for her age. Does this mean that she is substandard? As Drummond (1998) argues, the notion of a substandard child is totally unacceptable. Similarly Cindy Willey, who has written chapter 11 of this book, recounted a discussion with the parents in her nursery about baseline assessment scores. The parent of one child said 'How does a number tell me all the things I want to know about my lovely child' (personal communication). Drummond argues that language which shifts our focus on to end points, on to attainment and the achievement of goals, can detract from the process of learning, and of the two she believes the process is more important.

Respecting early years practitioners

Early years practitioners are, of course, concerned about standards and quality. As Drummond (1998) argues, we are concerned about high standards and quality of provision for our children. We want well trained practitioners and buildings and resources which are not part of the 'jumble sale' mentality and which are respectful of the children who play and learn in them. But what about the practitioners themselves? Rouse (1991) believes strongly that practitioners need to take care of themselves. She refers to the work of Elinor Goldschmied, a trainer and tutor, who asserts that quality provision is dependent upon adults being responsible for their own psychological well being – their welfare, care and health. This means having systems which allow time for planning, for talking in teams, for assessing and evaluating work collaboratively, issues which are raised in chapter 6. Rouse draws upon her visit to the Italian nurseries which follow the Reggio Emila philosophy. She describes how in the nurseries she visited the children had lunch followed by a one to two hour siesta. During this time cooks, guests and teachers had 'a relaxed and delicious meal' during which 'banter, news and views were exchanged' (p13). In addition six hours each week were set aside for in-service training. The work of these centres is renowned for the quality of the environment, relationships with parents and carers and pedagogic practices.

Hard pressed practitioners may view such practices with a degree of scepticism and doubt the possibility of transferring this philosophy to a UK setting. However at Penn Centre for the under fives and their families, now a Centre of Excellence, situated in the industrial town of Corby in Northamptonshire, similar practices can be seen. Margy Whalley (1996), who set up the centre states 'We believe staff have the right to a properly structured staff development programme which involves training, supervision and support, the majority of which should take place in work time' (p. 177). All staff, including ancillary, support staff and parents take part in training opportunities and international exchange programmes to other nurseries. Whalley acknowledges that there may be a temporary reduction in the quality of service when staff are attending courses and some inconvenience to parents and children, but as she says 'we inconvenience parents and children as little as possible' (p. 175). Such inclusive training opportunities and practices are a way of showing staff that they are valued and this in turn will contribute to their well being. Staff who feel good about themselves and their professional practice, will be in a position to provide challenging opportunities and experiences for the children in their care and will have the time, confidence and energy to respond to the needs of children and their families.

Linking home and early years settings: continuity and discontinuity

The needs of children are strongly intertwined with the social and cultural context of their families. Ball (1994, p. 43) states that 'Parents are the most important people in their children's lives. It is from parents children learn most, particularly in the early months and years'. Whilst broadly accepting this view, which is reiterated and exemplified throughout this book, it cannot be assumed that this is the case for all children. Earlier in this chapter I referred to Rose Drury's research in chapter 10, where she sensitively documents how, despite the best efforts of the nursery staff, assumptions were made about the continuity of experience from home to school for Nazma. Gregory (1993) although writing about bilingual children and literacy practices in schools, makes points which are pertinent to broader social contexts. She argues that we need to be as aware of discontinuities as we are of continuities between home and early years settings. She makes us aware that children from 'non mainstream' families need to learn to situate themselves in new and strange contexts with unfamiliar language and practices. Such continuities and discontinuities can either enhance or diminish children's life chances and the opportunity to 'do well' once formal schooling has begun.

Five year old Becky, was featured in a recent television documentary. At that time she lived in a dilapidated three bedroomed house on a run-down inner city estate with twelve members of her extended family. Becky is engaged in learning within her family, but not the sort of learning linked to everyday routines and focused around 'privileging academic, literate approaches' which Rogoff *et al.* (1998, p. 228) make us aware of. Becky is agile and physically skilful, as can be seen as she climbs onto abandoned cars outside. She is learning to taking sole responsibility for her younger brother, a toddler, when they go out to play unsupervised. She is developing good insights into the lives of adults. She knows that it is hard for her parents to get off drugs and drink and understands that a member of the family goes out stealing because he has no job. She has learnt that she doesn't fit in well with other children at school because 'she gets picked on' and is called a 'scruff'. She claims not to have been to school for two and a half months. Her account of a typical day includes watching soaps, going out to play, going to bed after midnight and getting up around midday. She is learning that it is OK to treat toys roughly and that you can engage in boisterous play fighting without adult interference.

Discussion

Ball (1994, p. 43) makes the point that there are many parents, like Becky's, who lack the 'permitting circumstances' to give children the best start in life. His answer in the *Start Right* report was to offer preparation for parenthood through education and support. However, a number of contributors to the report expressed their disagreement with these particular findings (p. 45). They contended that this suggests a deficit model of parenting and perpetuates the view that there is only one acceptable model. Becky will not have experienced those patterns of social and academic interaction which will make the transition to school easy for her. It is possible that projects such as Sure Start (Eisentadt 1999) referred to in chapter 9, will provide a more hopeful start in life for children like Becky.

Conclusion

Whilst endorsing the fundamental principles of good practice described at the beginning of this chapter, it has been argued that they need to be considered in relation to diverse social and cultural contexts. Throughout this chapter challenges and questions have been posed about the knowledge base for our assumptions about children, their families and the nature of childhood and the effects of this upon practice. Questions have been raised about the language used by early years practitioners in relation to their practice, for example how we define the term 'quality'. Practitioners have also been invited to consider the value they place upon themselves and to consider their own well being as an aspect of practice. As stated in the introduction to this book, we are working towards firmer foundations for young children and their families. The opportunity to challenge long accepted assumptions, practices and beliefs will strengthen rather than weaken those foundations.

References

Ball, C. (1994) *Start Right: The importance of early learning*. London: RSA.

Bredekamp, S. (ed.) (1987) *Developmentally Appropriate Practice in Early Childhood Programmes Serving children from Birth through Age 8*. Washington DC: National Association for the Education of Young Children.

Browne, A. (1998) 'Provision for reading for four year old children', *Reading* **32** (1), 9–13.

Bruce, T. (1997) *Time to Play in Early Childhood Education*. London: Hodder & Stoughton.

Department for Education and Science (1990) *Starting with Quality*. London: HMSO.

Department for Education and Employment (1998) *Teaching: High Status, High Standards*. Annex 1B (1) 2.3.1. 136 London: Department for Education and Employment.

Drummond, M. (1998) 'Warning: words can bite', *Coordinate* 4–5.

Early Years Curriculum Group (1992) *First Things First: Educating young children*. Oldham: Madeleine Lindley Ltd.

Eisenstadt, N. (1999) 'Sure Start: A new approach for children under 4', *Primary Health Care* **9** (6), 26–27.

Gregory, E. (1993) 'Sweet and sour Learning to read in a British and Chinese school' *English in Education* **27** (3), 53–59.

Kelly, V. (1994) 'A high quality curriculum for the early years', *Early Years* **15** (1), 4–6.

Lally, M. (1995) 'Principles to practice in early years education', in Campbell, R. *et al.* (eds) *Supporting Children in the Early Years*, 9–27. Stoke-on-Trent: Trentham Books.

Nutbrown, C. (1998) *The Lore and Language of Early Education*. Sheffield: University of Sheffield, Division of Education.

OFSTED (1998) *The Quality of Education in Institutions Inspected Under the Nursery Education Funding arrangements*. London: OFSTED Publications Centre.

Pascal, C. *et al.* (1999) 'The Effective Early Learning Project: The quality of adult engagement in early childhood settings in the UK.' Paper presented at the 9th European Conference on Quality in Early Childhood Education. University of Helsinki, 1–4 September, 1999.

Penn, H. (1996) 'Where white is still not right', *Times Educational Supplement*. 15 August 30.

Penn, H. (1998) 'Facing some difficulties', in Abbott, L. *et al.* (eds.) *Training to Work in the Early Years,* 26–38. London: Buckingham: Open University Press.

Rogoff, B. *et al.* (1998) 'Toddlers' guided participation with their caregivers in cultural activity' in Woodhead, M. *et al.* (eds) (1998) *Cultural Worlds of Early Childhood*, 225–250. London: Routledge/Open University Press.

Rouse, D. (1991) *The Italian Experience*. London: National Children's Bureau.

School Curriculum and Assessment Authority (1996) *Desirable Outcomes for Children's Learning*. London: HMSO.

Whalley, M. (1996) 'Working as a team', in Pugh, G. (ed.) *Contemporary Issues in the Early Years,* 170–188. London: National Children's Bureau.

Woodhead, M. (1998) ' "Quality" in Early Childhood programmes-a contextually appropriate approach', in *International Journal for Early Childhood Education* **6** (1), 5–17.

Woodhead, M. *et al.* (1999) 'Quality and early education: are notions of quality universal or culturally specific?' Paper presented at the 9th European Conference on Quality in Early Childhood Education. University of Helsinki, 1–4 September, 1999.

Woodhead, M. (1999) 'Towards a global paradigm for research into early childhood education', in *European Early Childhood Education* **7** (1), 5–23.

Chapter 4

Professional roles in early childhood

Lyn Karstadt, Tricia Lilley and Linda Miller

Introduction

Professionalism can be difficult to define. Some people might claim to know it when they see it, but ideas vary about what it is. Dictionary definitions suggest that it involves belonging to or being connected with a particular profession or demonstrating the skills relating to a profession. It is likely that in the field of early childhood education and care, early years practitioners will be at various points along a continuum of professionalism depending upon their age, stage in their career and level of training and qualifications. As Penn (1998) notes, work involving caring has traditionally been done by women; 99 per cent of those working in early childhood services are women. She cites a worrying survey by Penn and McQuail (1997) which revealed that women thought they brought a 'natural' talent to the job and felt that this aptitude was at least as important, if not more important, than training. Penn goes on to argue that such attitudes are problematic. Firstly, because they devalue the theory underlying professionalism. Secondly, they do a disservice to men wishing to enter the profession, as they suggest that men do not possess such aptitudes. Such attitudes create barriers to raising the status of the professional roles associated with early childhood practitioners.

Traditionally, training to work in the field of early years education and care has been practically based. However, the onset of early childhood studies degrees and the new training framework (QCA 1999a) should lead early years practitioners towards a new professionalism. The importance of training for practitioners is recognised in recent curriculum guidance from the Qualifications and Curriculum Authority (1999b). In this chapter we address some of the issues which have been a barrier to professionalism in the past. We also look to the future and consider the broadening role of the early childhood professional in early childhood settings. We do this through a consideration of training, the role of the early childhood educator, the health dimension, the important role of all adults who works with young children and finally, the importance of all early years professionals working together.

The national picture of training for working with young children

Traditionally, in the United Kingdom, we have a philosophical and structural divide between care and education provision. This has evolved as a result of administration by two different government departments – the Department of Education and Science (DES) (now the Department for Education and Employment (DfEE)) and the Department of Health and Social Security (DHSS) (David 1990). This has resulted in damaging differences in training routes, status, pay and conditions for those who care for and educate young children in early years settings. In a review of early years training Hevey and Curtis (1996) found that the majority of day care and pre-school services are staffed by 200,000 unqualified child care and education practitioners. Another survey showed that 65.7 per cent of qualified teachers working with children under eight had received no specific training for working with children under five (Blenkin and Yue 1994). As the numbers of young children in early years settings have increased, the question of who their carers and educators should be and what they need to know needs to be addressed.

In 1996 a group of early years trainers and advisers who met regularly at the National Children's Bureau published a report on Education and Training for Work in the Early Years (Pugh 1996). This presented a snap shot of training developments in the areas of teacher training, early childhood studies degrees and vocational training in childcare and education and outlined a value base and the underpinning principles for this training. This debate is further developed in Abbott and Pugh (1998) which includes a discussion of the issues relating to different training routes, diverse professional roles, the quality of provision and their impact on young children. In May 1999, the Qualifications and Curriculum Authority (QCA 1999a) published the response to a consultation paper on qualifications and training in the early years education, childcare and playwork sector. The consultation document set out a training framework for this sector and the underlying principles on which it would be based. It proposed that national occupational standards would form the basis of all qualifications in the framework and for all recognised training provision leading to those qualifications. A follow up document (QCA 1999b) describes the first phase of the framework. Although not yet part of a national plan, early childhood studies degrees are recognised as an important part of this training route alongside teacher training and vocational training. As Abbott and Pugh (1998, p. 156) acknowledge 'The ways in which early years workers become competent, knowledgeable and skilful will continue to be many and varied'.

The early childhood educator

In a critique of recent curriculum developments in England, Peter Moss (1998) referred to what he described as a factory model of learning, which has a centrally controlled curriculum and which emphasises learning goals, targets and outcomes. He considered the implications of this model for early years practitioners. He questioned whether the early childhood worker was, 'A technician, a neutral transmitter or reproducer of knowledge to young children' or 'a pedagogue, researcher and producer or coconstructor of knowledge with children'. Nutbrown (1994) argues for the latter definition. She describes all those who work with young children in a professional capacity as 'professional educators' and defines such people as 'adults who have some relevant training and qualifications and understand something of how young children learn, and who are active in their thinking and interaction with children in group settings'.

Later in this chapter we argue strongly that a key role of the adult in young children's development and learning, is to build upon the child's early experiences and so promote greater understanding. In order to do this, the adult needs to be skilled and knowledgeable and have a willingness to reflect upon his or her practice and to learn from this. Tiziana Filippini (1997), the pedagogue who accompanied The Hundred Languages of Children exhibition, which features the work of nurseries in the Reggio Emilia region of Italy, has said 'a nice lady is not enough' to ensure that this happens. Lilian Katz (1995) has also argued that children need to be around thinking adults. She has spoken about nurseries where 'all the adults are nice and kind . . . and lovely, but inside (i.e. the head, our brackets) there is nobody at home'. This may seem harsh and unkind, but we believe this statement underlines the need for professional training for early years practitioners as discussed below.

What does the early childhood educator need to know?

The debate about the content of and the knowledge base for training and qualifications for early years practitioners is ongoing (see Thompson and Calder 1998). What seems to be agreed, is that practitioners working with young children need to take a critical stance in relation to both theory and practice. The challenge for early years practitioners, who undertake further professional development after years of valuable practical experience, is to acknowledge that experience, and more importantly to analyse it. It is necessary for them to step back and to develop a critical perspective in relation to their practice, in order to see the familiar with a new, professional eye. One student on an early childhood studies degree course, who had worked for many years in early years settings, queried why the group needed to participate in a paint mixing exercise. The tutor's response was to ask, 'Why have you been mixing the paint with the children? How do you move children on from this? How do you know what they are ready to learn next?' Lally (1995) has said that practitioners who cannot give confident answers to 'why' questions about their practice will be weak on rationale and therefore vulnerable to outside pressures. Gibbs (1988) argues that to have an experience is not sufficient for learning to take place; there also has to be reflection on the experience or the learning potential may be lost and cannot then be used to inform new situations. The learner must make the link between theory and practice as illustrated by Tracey below.

Tracey is a mature student on an early childhood studies degree course. She is the parent of two children and is a very experienced practitioner. The following is an extract from her address to incoming students at the Open Day for her course, in which she reflects upon her experience of the previous year.

> As the course progressed, I began to look at myself in a different light. I looked much more closely at the way I worked, putting into practice a lot of the learning, but with the realisation that I needed to question myself a great deal more about the 'why' of doing things. I also began to come to the conclusion that much of what I learned came from what I was prepared to put in. Maybe the most poignant moment for me, were some words said to us by one of the tutors during a teaching session on creative expression. She said that we needed to look deeper at our own learning, under the surface of what was being taught. From that day these words stayed with me and I looked at the teaching and learning assignments in a different light, not just taking the modules for what they were, but questioning, thinking, reading and researching more about the subject concerned.

The health dimension

What early years practitioners need to be authoritative and knowledgeable about extends beyond the way children learn and how to structure that learning. As mentioned in both previous and subsequent chapters, it is difficult to study children in isolation from the families in which they grow and develop. Holistic ideology values the whole child and views each individual in the context of its family community and culture. Taylor (1998) reminds us that it is impossible to study discrete areas of early childhood without gaining at least some knowledge of other important and related areas.

When considering the development of the early years practitioner, relationships with small children are an important part of that development. In addition, however, one must also consider the relationships that such a practitioner builds with the significant adults in the child's life. Within many early years settings practitioners not only guide children in the way that they learn but also their parents with regard to their role in the day to day life of these children. Advice proffered is extremely important and must be professionally credible and not merely anecdotal. The example of Tracey is a powerful one and her attitude toward her learning fairly typical of such students. This changed attitude, enabling analytical consideration of her charges would surely have extended to their well-being, their health needs and the advice that she was offering to parents in her context as an early years professional.

The Department of Health publication *Health of the Young Nation* (DoH 1995) charges all those professionals who work with young children with the responsibility of enabling each child to reach and maintain optimum health. This may be done by working with the child in a guiding capacity or by working with the parent(s) who in turn, may then exert positive influences on the child's environment and experiences. Eisenstadt (1999) analyses the potential contribution of the 'Sure Start' initiative with its better co-ordinated services aimed at improving the life chances of young children in disadvantaged areas. Good quality play and learning as well as support for families are introduced as strategies to enable these desired improvements. Community ownership and parent participation are valued by this initiative which certainly views the child and family holistically.

Eisenstadt (1999) aims her analysis and subsequent discussion at Health Visitors, although much of what she says is applicable to all who work with children in the early years. Sure Start initiatives can be led by any appropriate professional and partnerships between voluntary agencies and health bodies are encouraged. Potential for the involvement of early childhood practitioners in association with health, social services, education and community or parent organisations is therefore great (QCA 1999c).

Our Healthier Nation (DoH 1998) cites good health as what everyone wants for themselves, their family and friends and as the supreme gift that parents can give to their children. Knowledge and expertise in this field can enable the early childhood practitioner to have a positive influence within the environment of the children in their care. As Drummond (1997, p. 7) has said 'The key to quality in early years provision is sustained, rigorous and disciplined training in early years practices and principles'.

The role of the adult in young children's learning

'Adults have the power to make a major difference to children's lives and their development by what they offer children and by how they behave towards them' (Lindon 1993, p. 75). Consider the power of the early childhood practitioner, to make that difference, not only in their direct contact with young children but in their support for other adults who know them, usually their primary carers. The importance of the adult in the development of children's learning and their well-being has been well documented in research on children's development (Bruner 1963, Vygotsky 1978) and the ways in which adults can use this potential power positively are discussed in this section.

Gura (1996) draws attention to the changing relationship between adults and children which has emerged in recent years following research on the importance of the social context in which children learn. She describes a shift towards a 'flexible repertoire of roles and relationships' (p. 32), acknowledging that learning is not always individual and internal but can also be influenced by a child's interactions with others. As the young child strives to become independent perhaps in feeding herself, in reading a favourite and often repeated story, or in taking her first few steps, the adult offers support, sometimes described as 'scaffolding', for the child's learning. Bruner (1963) regards scaffolding as one of the key roles of the adult who provides a kind of structure or series of steps for the child to explore a new experience successfully and add to her initial learning. The key for the adult is to know how to provide steps which are small enough for the child to gain success but challenging enough to motivate her and take her learning forward.

Bruner identified several ways in which an adult can provide this level of support or scaffolding by gaining the child's interest, ensuring that the required responses are achievable, giving plenty of feedback and encouragement to keep the child focused and by modelling the task for the child. The adult will need to be observant and know what the child can do already, building on this existing learning to support development in a structured way. The relationship between the adult and the child should be flexible. For example, sometimes the child might be seen as an apprentice working alongside the more experienced adult as they read a book together. At other times the relationship can become a loan arrangement, with the adult supporting or 'loaning' expertise to the child, for example by helping to cut food into manageable pieces or by providing a suitable plate to make the task easier for the child as she moves towards independence in using a knife and fork herself. Alternatively the adult and child can be partners playing alongside each other in a mutually supportive way (Gura 1996). Whatever the format of the relationship, scaffolding learning is one of the ways early childhood practitioners can make a powerful difference for the young child.

Vygotsky (1978) was particularly interested in the ways in which knowledge is passed from one human to another and much of his research on child development and communication focused on the effects of our social interactions on learning. He suggested that although we can all learn new skills and knowledge as individuals, it is through our interaction with others that our early experiences are extended. Vygotsky believed that it was very important for adults to identify what a child could do and knew already and then build on this existing knowledge to help the child to make sense of the world. He believed that if a child was left to explore something new on his or her own, such as some bricks, the ways in which he or she played and used the bricks could be described as the child's 'actual level of development'. However, if an adult interacted with the child, he or she may build a more complex structure with the bricks, perhaps finding different ways to position bricks and so build a taller tower. This extension of learning arising from skilful adult intervention was described by Vygotsky as the child working within a 'zone of proximal development' or, more simply, as a next stage of learning which could only be achieved with adult support. So by scaffolding or supporting learning, skilfully interacting with a child at appropriate moments in his or her learning, the adult could help the child to move into the next zone or stage of his or her development.

More recent research by Rogoff *et al.* (1998) extends the notion of a zone of proximal development to take account of guided participation where young children and adults are interacting in non-academic activities. They point to the limitations of Vygotsky's work which appeared to focus predominantly on language development and work within contexts of learning which were largely academic in nature. Rogoff *et al.* draw attention to wide cultural variations in the range of household activities that young children participate in and observe adults undertaking. Although many activities are common to children from different cultural communities, the range of role models, the types of activities, the extent of any scaffolding for learning provided by the adult and the accepted level of independence for the child is varied. As early childhood practitioners it is important to be aware of the differences that may exist in children's early experiences of guided participation.

Woods (1998) asserts that in the best early years provision education and care are not separated but are combined to produce the concept of 'educare'. This enables young children to be cared for sensitively and competently while their early educational needs are addressed by those responsible for that care. Healthy practices are promoted primarily when the adults act as role models to the children in their care. Good habits relating to personal hygiene, social skills and healthy lifestyle are all examples of desirable behaviours transmitted in this way. As with all other learning children often work in partnership with adults or more knowledgeable peers who guide their participation until they feel able to manage the task alone.

Bruner also placed particular emphasis on the adult modelling behaviour for a young child. In chapter 13, Robin Campbell describes the importance of adults modelling literacy for young children, reading stories or perhaps writing a shopping list. The power of example cannot be over-emphasised. Holt (1989) argued that it is through watching and listening and joining in with others, often adults, that a young child begins to make connections between experiences. He calls for adults to make their skills visible to young children, for example by modelling the ways in which they read, write, play, cook, shop, learn new things. Consider the powerful impact that watching someone at work has perhaps had on your life, your attitudes, your self-image. Adults have a responsibility to recognise the power of their influence as role models and use this opportunity to enhance learning. Other contributors to this book have made various references to the importance of the adult's role in a wide range of contexts across curriculum and developmental areas which will give you further insights into the significant contribution that skilful adult interactions make to a young child's development.

Working together

Wherever early years practitioners are on the continuum of professionalism and whether they are working in an education or a care context, with other early years professionals, or the multidisciplinary team, they must embrace a philosophy that recognises that each child is an individual with rights, that have recently been discussed and made explicit (DoH 1999). The development and well being of children is influenced by the relationship they have with their family, their environment and their individual health status. The interests of all parties within any given situation should be considered, remembering that the rights of the child are paramount (DoH 1990).

The authors would like to thank Tracey Alexander for her contribution to this chapter.

References

Abbott, L. and Pugh, G. (ed) (1998) *Training to Work in the Early Years.* Buckingham: Open University Press.

Blenkin, G. M. and Yue, Y. L. (1994) 'Profiling Early Years practitioners: some first impressions from a national survey', *Early Years* **15** (1) 13–23.

Bruner, J. (1963) *The Process of Education.* New York: Vintage.

David, T. (1990) *Under Five – Under Educated?* Buckingham: Open University Press.

Department of Health (1998) *Our Healthier Nation: A Contract for Health.* London: The Stationary Office.

Department of Health (1990) *An Introduction to the Children Act 1989.* London: HMSO.

Department of Health (1995) *Health of the Young Nation.* London: HMSO.

Department of Health (1999) *Convention on the Rights of the Child: Second Report to the UN Committee on the Rights of the Child by the United Kingdom 1999.* London: The Stationary Office.

Drummond, M. J. (1997) 'An undesirable document', *Coordinate* **57** 7–8.

Eisenstadt, N. (1999) 'Sure Start: a new approach for children under 4', *Primary Health Care* **9** (6) 26–27.

Filippini, T. (1997) *The Reggio Approach.* Paper delivered at The Hundred Languages of Children Exhibition Conference, The Picture Gallery, Thomas Coram Foundation for Children, London, 11 July.

Gibbs, G. (1988) *Learning by Doing: A Guide to Teaching and Learning Methods.* London: Further Education Unit.

Gura, P. (1996) 'Roles and Relationships', in Robson, S. *et al.* (eds) *Education in Early Childhood: First Things First.* London: David Fulton Publishers.

Hevey, D. and Curtis, A. (1996) 'Training to Work in the Early Years', in Pugh, G. (ed.) *Contemporary Issues in the Early Years: Working Collaboratively for Children,* 211–231. London: National Children's Bureau/Paul Chapman.

Holt, J. (1989) *Learning all the Time.* Ticknall: Education Now Publishing Co-operative.

Katz, L. (1995) 'Multiple perspectives on the right start'. Paper delivered at the *Start Right Conference* Barbican, London, 20–22 September.

Lally, M. (1995) 'Principles to practice in early years education', in Campbell, R. *et al.* (eds) *Supporting Children in the Early Years,* 9–27. Stoke-on-Trent: Trentham Books.

Lindon, J. (1993) *Child Development from Birth to Eight.* London: National Children's Bureau.

Moss, P. (1998) 'Young children and early childhood institutions: who and what do we think they are?' Paper delivered at the *Child at the Centre Conference.* NES Arnold/National Children's Bureau Conference, East Midlands Conference Centre, 16–17 July.

Nutbrown, C. (1994) *Threads of Thinking.* London: Paul Chapman.

Penn, H. (1998) 'Facing some difficulties', in Abbott, L. *et al.* (eds) *Training to Work in the Early Years,* 26–38. Buckingham: Open University Press.

Penn, H. (1997) Childcare as a Gendered Occupation and Research Report RR23. London: DfEE. McQuails.

Pugh, G. (ed.) (1996) *Education and Training for Work in the Early Years.* London: National Children's Bureau.

Qualifications and Curriculum Authority (1999a) *A Draft Framework for Training and Qualifications in Early Years Education, Childcare and Playwork Sector.* Suffolk: Qualifications and Curriculum Authority Publications.

Qualifications and Curriculum Authority (1999b) *Early Years Education, Childcare and Playwork: a framework of nationally accredited qualifications.* Suffolk: Qualifications and Curriculum Authority Publications.

Qualifications and Curriculum Authority(1999c) *Early Learning Goals.* London: Qualifications and Curriculum Authority.

Rogoff, B. *et al.* (1998) 'Toddlers' guided participation with their caregivers in cultural activity' in Woodhead, M. *et al.* (eds) (1998) *Cultural Worlds of Early Childhood.* London: Routledge/Open University Press.

Taylor, J. (1998) 'Working with young children and their families', in Taylor, J. *et al.* (eds) *Early Childhood Studies*. London: Arnold.

Thompson, B. and Calder, P. (1998) 'Early years educators: skills, knowledge and understanding', in Abbott, L. *et al.* (eds) *Training to Work in the Early Years*, 38-55. Buckingham: Open University Press.

Vygotsky, L. S. (1978) *Mind in Society*. Edited by Cole, M. *et al.* Cambridge, MA: Harvard University Press.

Woods, M. (1998) 'Introduction', in Taylor, J. *et al.* (eds) *Early Childhood Studies*. London: Arnold.

Chapter 5

Children in the family and society

Lyn Karstadt and Jo Medd

From the moment of birth human babies are dependent upon the families in which they are to grow and develop, not only for physical comfort and care but also for their psychological well being. Over recent years psychologists have ceased to study infants in isolation, but instead have chosen to study them in the environment in which that development is to take place (Schaffer 1996).

Early childhood studies demand that infants and small children be considered holistically. This is understood to mean a view of the whole child to include its social physical emotional and psychological well being in the context of all aspects of the environment. This is usually considered to relate to the context of health (Ewles and Simnet 1999), but in the context of this chapter is viewed as wider and applicable to all the child's potential and experiences.

As an early years practitioner one cannot consider the child in isolation from the family. Although some practitioners may focus their primary activity with the individual child in an educational or care context; because of the profound effect that each family has on its individual members; it would be foolish to consider the child in isolation. Instead, practitioners must endeavour to work in partnership with the child's family in an atmosphere of mutual respect (QCA 1999). This is well encapsulated by the philosophy of Casey (1988) who states that the care of all children is best carried out by their parents assisted as necessary by expert staff. Such partnership is dependent upon mutual respect and the valuing of parental acquired expertise.

This chapter sets out to consider the early experiences of the child within the family and to explore how those experiences interface with the role of the early years practitioner. The recently published Early Learning Goals (QCA 1999) inform us that practitioners must be able to observe and respond appropriately and that their responses should be informed by a knowledge of how children develop and learn. Much of this development and learning must be viewed in the context of society. There is no doubt that the factors that influence the development of individual children are incredibly diverse (Bronfenbrenner 1979). Initially the infant is usually party to a unique relationship with its mother or other primary care giver, Schaffer (1996) refers to this as a dyad. However as time and development progress he recognises that babies become involved in a multi-person world, with many interactions and relationships occurring beyond this initial pairing and he refers to this as a polyad. This polyadic approach encompasses, the family or significant others and in some instances the early years worker. Ball (1994) talks of a 'strong triangle' with the three points representing parents, professionals and the community, pointing out that all are needed in the ante-natal period, at the birth of the baby and as the child progresses to negotiate infancy, childhood and eventually adolescence.

This would echo the approach of Vygotsky and those psychologists who have embraced his principles. Vygotsky views the child as social from birth and sees that it is the individual's interaction with others that facilitates development (Meadows 1993). Vygotsky places the emphasis not only on interaction, but also on culture, suggesting that culture creates certain forms of behaviour and that interpersonal interactions can only be adequately understood when reference to history and culture is made (Tudge and Winterhoff 1993).

Pre-adaptation

There is a spectrum of opinion as to whether the human infant is pre-adapted or programmed with reference to surviving within a social world. Human infancy is usually viewed as a period of total dependence, during which time the infant is cared for, protected and nurtured while he begins to learn. This learning takes place within the mother–child relationship, the mother mediating the child's experience of his or her environment.

In contrast to this view point, Schaffer (1996) observes that infants demonstrate behaviours that appear specifically designed to bring them into contact with other people. It appears that infants arrive in the world especially attuned to the kind of visual and auditory stimuli provided by other people. They have a predisposition and tendency, which is pre-adapted to mediate the infant's interactions with its social environment. Schaffer (1996) also informs us that infants show a visual preference for qualities inherent in the human face. At first this is relatively unsophisticated and any object resembling a face will capture the infant's attention. With maturity, however, infants pay greater attention to all aspects of the face and by the latter part of the first year only particular faces will elicit a positive response. A similar pattern is described for speech like noises. (This is further expanded in the later chapter addressing creative expression.) The work of Ainsworth *et al.* (1991) further supports this idea, suggesting that infants are genetically biased toward interaction with other people from the beginning. They confirm that the infant's sensory equipment is responsive to 'people stimuli' and in this way infants are pre-adapted to a social world.

Although much of the infant's early behaviour is reflex like and not under conscious control, it is this behaviour that initiates, promotes and strengthens the infant's first social relationships. Such behaviours have survival value during the initial helpless phase and need to be recognised as such by parents, carers and early years workers. Pre-adaptation should guide those responsible for the environment of infants in the early days, to ensure that the stimuli encountered are people orientated. This is particularly pertinent when an infant is in an institutional setting, where routine and technology may mould the environment, making it less than facilitative.

Schaffer (1996) suggests that infant behaviour is structured in such a way as to enable co-ordination with a partner's behaviour. The social partner may be the mother, a substitute or a professional acting on the mother's behalf. If the infant is to progress as a full partner within social exchanges, then the acquisition of certain skills by the infant is pre-requisite. Kaye (1982) suggests that infants learn to play a variety of roles by being placed by adults in situations where the skills it lacks are performed for it. Carers keep up the essential features of their own role in the interaction and take the infant's role for it. Gradually as the infant develops and indicates an ability to do so, the adult relinquishes the infant's role.

It must be stressed that turn taking is a dyadic phenomenon, which tells us nothing about the infant's ability to take turns. Schaffer (1996) suggests that adults skilfully insert their contribution between those offered by the infant and allow the infant to dictate the pace, therefore taking the responsibility for converting the encounter into a dialogue. This process facilitates progression, as over a period of time the infant begins to take responsibility for its own part of the interaction. This is not however a true conversation as only one participant is aware of the rules.

When handling infants, parents and their substitutes skilfully but unconsciously allow such turn taking to dominate their interactions and observations would confirm that infants thrive in such situations. Parents or professionals, unable to synchronise their behaviour with that of the baby, have been shown to enjoy poorer relationships. If a lack of such synchronisation is simulated, then infants are shown to become agitated and difficult to handle. Kaye (1982) refers to such adult adjustment to an infant as a form of socialisation. Early childhood professionals interact with infants primarily but also in situations where mothers and babies form the focus of care delivery and should be mindful of this synchronisation when dealing with difficult babies or dissatisfied mothers.

Attachment

Even before the moment of birth the relationship between a child and its parents has begun to develop. Initially the emotional investment within this relationship is one sided with the parents having the active role. In the late 1970s much attention was focused upon the initial moments following birth. It was postulated by Klaus and Kennell (1976) that early contact between mother and baby was not only desirable but pre-requisite if a strong relationship was to be built up between them. Failure to establish skin to skin contact was seen to be catastrophic with possible long-term deleterious consequences. Bonding, as it became known, was a rapid process occurring soon after birth and was a process by which a mother became attached and committed to her infant. Although, able to distinguish its mother and indicating a preference for her company, within the first months of life, an infant will accept care from all who offer it. This neutrality, however, is short lived and by approximately eight months of age the baby will have formed a strong attachment to those closest to him (Bowlby 1965).

After this time, infants show a definite preference for their primary care giver, and recognition must be afforded to the importance of a secure attachment.

Although this assertion is not without its critics, it is generally well accepted. This is particularly because it portrays the infant as not merely an organism driven by inner needs and outer stimuli, but as quickly evolving with its own intentions and plans, so becoming capable of steering its own course (Schaffer 1996). During the latter part of the first year strangers will be treated with suspicion and intimate care will only be accepted from an established attachment figure. Recent studies have shown that children of this age can make multiple attachments (Ainsworth *et al.* 1991) and any one of these adults or older children can provide the security necessary in an alien situation. Early years practitioners often provide an attachment figure for the children in their care. The allocation of particular children to an identified practitioner, who is able to act as a key worker for that child, facilitates this and affords those children maximum security in any given situation.

In order to highlight individual differences in the quality of infant attachment Ainsworth *et al.* (1991) describe a standard procedure to elicit behaviour indicative of such differences. In a laboratory situation mothers were observed with their small children. Each child, while with its mother was confronted by a stranger. The mother then withdrew from the situation leaving the child in the presence of the stranger, who after a period of time also left. The child was then momentarily left alone before being reunited with the mother. On reunion a range of behaviours was noted in the children. One group, sought close contact with the mother, while a second group avoided her. The final group showed ambivalence. Only the first group was considered by the researchers to be exhibiting behaviour that confirmed they were securely attached.

This research and its findings is of particular interest to all early years practitioners, who will often, in their professional role find themselves in situations similar to that created within the experiment. The difference, however, is that generally speaking early childhood practitioners invest time and energy in building a relationship with each small child in their care; they are therefore not strangers. Tizard (1991) purports that children may make multiple attachments and that to consider the mother–infant dyad in isolation is artificial as children grow up with a number of social relations. Infants may be securely attached to their father or some other adult figure but not to their mother. Dunn (1983) suggests that infants can be securely attached to siblings and Tizard (1991) reports extreme cases where in the absence of appropriate adults have used their peers as a secure base. Evidence would suggest therefore that the presence of attachment is more important than the details when considering normal development.

Ainsworth *et al.* (1991) inform us that there is a dynamic balance between attachment and exploratory behaviours. Experimental studies confirm that infants will explore even unfamiliar environments while mother is present, although in her absence the child may not be so bold. While exploring, if the child becomes alarmed it will again seek closer proximity with the secure adult. A correlation has also been identified between infants who appear to be insecurely attached and those who do not exhibit exploratory behaviour in the usual fashion. It can therefore be postulated that a child who has a healthy secure relationship with a number of primary care givers, including early years professionals, will actively explore its environment allowing development to proceed at an optimum.

Working mothers must be reassured that such evidence suggests that young children are unlikely to suffer psychological damage if their mother goes out to work. Tizard (1991) evaluated a range of care environments concluding that if professionals were aware of the child's needs, with particular regard to attachment, then meaningful relationships would be fostered and children gain comfort and security from dedicated carers.

It is interesting to note that attachment theory as outlined above is a culturally specific model (Singer 1998), that describes a secure attachment to the mother or primary carer, that facilitates the exploration of the outside world. In this conception the mother has a central role in the child attaining skills relating to self regulation and self confidence. Singer (1998) goes on to inform us that this fits neatly only with western culture and that the model suggested here is not universal. In other parts of the world, practices differ quite considerably; in some parts of Africa, for example, it is not uncommon for two year olds to be abruptly separated from their mothers and their care assigned to older children within the community.

There would, therefore, seem to be clear evidence to suggest that child development is fundamentally a social and cultural process that is affected by the development of social relations within the child's particular cultural context. Sameroff (1991), however, informs us that both the individual child and its environment are necessary for any developmental process, and that the contribution of both factors are not only active but interactive and transactive. Early characteristics of the child are frequently overpowered by factors within the environment. The example given is that of an infant who has suffered severe perinatal complications, but has overcome adversity to achieve normal developmental milestones, when the family and cultural variables have been favourable (Sameroff 1991). Conversely such variables can also hinder development in instances where potential for development is good. Sameroff (1991) asserts that all development follows a similar model, where behavioural competencies are a product of the combination of an individual and his or her experiences.

On evaluating the contribution of nature and nurture, Sameroff (1991) considers both the individual and the environment to play an active part. The model developed is usually referred to as a transactional one, and describes the development of a particular child as the product of continuous dynamic interaction of the child and the experience provided by family social and cultural context. This model was originally seen as innovative due to the emphasis placed on the effect the child has on the environment.

Berk (1997) outlines a similar explanation as offered by Brofenbrenner, who suggests that different aspects of the environment may have an effect on the child's overall development. Both of these theorists acknowledge the importance of social and cultural factors, a dimension that historically was often ignored. Brofenbrenner describes the environment in terms of different layers that each have a powerful impact upon the child's development. Conversely, and congruent with Sameroff (1991) Brofenbrenner also suggests that the child has an effect on each layer. Early childhood practitioners, depending upon particular situations may fit either into the inner-most layer as a primary significant carer, the second layer with other members of the immediate family, or the third layer which pertains to the community in which the child lives. The fourth and outer layer refers to the values laws and customs of a particular context and can not be ignored or seen as irrelevant to the context of the early years practitioner. Brofenbrenner we are told, also recognises that the child changes over time in response to maturation and life events. Again this mirrors assertions made by Sameroff (1991) and suggests great applied significance since interventions at any level of environment can be noted to enhance or deter development.

Early childhood practitioners are an active part of the environment of young children in their care. Such practitioners must work in partnership with parents (QCA 1999) and the wider community sharing the responsibility to engineer that environment, in order to achieve optimum child development. Once a secure tripartite relationship has been established the environment must be made positive and nurturing allowing children and their families to be supported and cared for in such a way that relationships and thereby quality of life are maximised.

References

Ainsworth, M. D. *et al.* (1991) 'Infant–Mother attachment and social development: socialisation as a product of reciprocal responsiveness to signals', in Woodhead, M. *et al.* (eds) *Becoming a Person*. London: Routledge.

Ball, C. (1994) *Start Right: The Importance of Early Learning*. London: Royal Society of Arts.

Berk, L. E. (1997) *Child Development*. Englewood Cliffs, NJ: Prentice Hall.

Bowlby, J. (1965) *Child Care and the Growth of Love*. Harmondsworth: Penguin Books.

Brofenbrenner, U. (1979) *The Ecology of Human Development*. Cambridge Mass. and London: Harvard University Press.

Casey, A. (1988) 'A partnership with child and family', *Senior Nurse* **8** (4), 8–9.

Dunn, J. (1983) 'Siblings Relationships in Early Childhood', *Child Development* **54** 787–811.

Ewles, L. and Simnet, I. (1999) *Promoting Health: A Practical Guide*, 4th edn. London: Baillière Tindall.

Kaye, K. (1982) *The Mental and Social Life of Babies*. Chicago: Chicago University Press.

Klaus, M. H. and Kennell, J. H. (1976) *Parent–Infant Bonding*. St Louis: Mosby.

Meadows, S. (1993) *The Child as Thinker: the development and acquisition of cognition in childhood*. London: Routledge.

Qualification and Curriculum Authority (1999) *Early Learning Goals* London: QCA.

Sameroff, A. J. (1991) 'The Social Context of Development', in Woodhead, M. *et al.* (eds) *Becoming a Person*. London: Routledge.

Schaffer, H. R. (1996) *Social Development*. Oxford: Blackwell Publishers.

Singer, E. (1998) 'Shared Care for Children', in Woodhead, M. *et al. Cultural Worlds of Early Childhood*. London: Routledge.

Tizard, B. (1991) 'Working mothers and the care of young children', in Woodhead, M. *et al.* (eds) *Becoming a Person*. London: Routledge.

Tudge, J. R. H. and Winteroff, P. A. (1993) 'Vygotsky, Piaget and Bandura: Perspectives on the Relations between the Social World and Cognitive Development', *Human Development* **36**, 61–81.

Chapter 6
Working in teams in early years settings

Mary Read and Mary Rees

In all the many and varied early years settings there is perhaps one common characteristic: a number of adults work together to meet the needs of children. The likelihood of excellent early childhood provision is enhanced by the team's ability to work collaboratively, and being a member of an effective team is a source of satisfaction and support for many early years workers. The variable nature of settings and the range of people involved mean there is no guaranteed recipe for team success. An effective group of early years practitioners emerges as the result of an investment of time and energy by all concerned. If an effective team is valued as an essential part of quality early years provision, it is necessary to identify how this can be achieved. In many instances too little attention or status is given to either the skills of teamwork or to the process of working collaboratively. This chapter addresses these important areas. It encourages consideration of the role and skills of the early years practitioner and questions how these contribute to the efficiency of the whole team. It places the skills of teamwork in a management context, seeking to elevate the status of teamwork beyond a 'muddling through together' to a planned, professional activity.

In any early years setting there is probably a core team of adults who work together on an ongoing daily basis consisting of staff and volunteers, all with different roles and expertise. In a large organisation early years practitioners may work in a small core team which is only part of the whole. In either case the core team may form part of a wider team encompassing, for example, speech and language therapists, physiotherapists or professionals from social services. In reading this chapter it may be helpful to identify specific teams in individual contexts and reflect on current practice and professional development.

So how can effective teamwork be developed? A number of features characterise successful teams.

Finding time for professional dialogue

Finding time

Young children make continuous, challenging demands on the adults who work with them. Finding time to focus on adult needs can be difficult as there is a real danger of responding to children's immediate needs to the exclusion of all else. Looking at the daily or weekly programme to identify potential time availability for staff to meet is a vital step in team development. Finding an appropriate time which includes part time and hourly paid staff can be problematic, therefore solutions have to be found through open discussion and negotiation. Perhaps a monthly rota of short meetings is more viable than a weekly set time.

The Cherry Tree case study (Figure 6.1) shows how one large nursery faced the important issue of planning for children with special needs. The willingness to confront these problems and seek a workable situation provides a starting point for team commitment. Whalley (in Pugh 1996) documents an interesting approach to finding quality meeting time at Pen Green Centre for Under Fives and Families by freeing up Wednesday afternoons. Failure to secure an appropriate meeting programme involving everyone, may lead to individuals feeling marginalised and devalued. The potential contribution of some team members is lost and the cohesion of the team is damaged as a result.

Cherry Tree is a large nursery including several children with special educational needs. The specific needs of the children mean that the team felt it was important that all staff were familiar with the different programmes and targets necessary for their development. Many of the staff were paid on an hourly basis so meeting time was precious. This is how planning was coordinated.

- Monthly one-hour meeting for all staff defining main activities. All staff to attend, either paid or time off in lieu.
- Booklet for each session where all significant events are noted.
- Children's records open to all staff
- Assessment meetings to discuss individual children weekly on a rota basis. Minutes written up and available for staff who cannot attend.

Planning recorded (see below) so that all staff are familiar with learning focus of activities.

wk beg 3rd Oct			
activity	focus	specific children	comments
wet sand	tracing numbers for week	Kirsty – K Alan – say name as he traces	
water	vocab: full empty	Gary – talk to other children	
story	remember and repeat sequence	all	

Figure 6.1 Case study

Using time effectively

Valuable staff time needs to be used effectively. This is easy to say but rather more difficult to establish and maintain. A possible starting point is to keep a

meeting and purpose	no. of people	contribution	achievement	comments
A. weekly planning to establish outline of week's activities 1 hour	total 8 4 teachers and 4CAs (classroom assistants)	teachers 85% CAs 15% Miss X and Mrs Y (both CAs) no contribution	plan agreed mainly repeat of previous week 2 new activities	lacked focus; some useful evaluation; dominated by teachers
B. purchasing decision meeting – order for outdoor play equipment 1 hour	10 nursery manager + full-time and part-time staff	manager – majority others – questions	order not agreed	staff insufficient info. to reach decision. Lots of disagreement, staff raising alternatives – soft play, books etc.

Figure 6.2 Meeting log

brief log of meetings taking place over a week or two (Figure 6.2). The resulting information can then be shared within the team or raised with the manager. A log of this type can show whether the meeting time is well used or that there are areas for significant improvement. Meeting B could be probed further – was the manager meeting with staff when the decision had in fact already been taken? If so, why? Could the relevant information have been provided as a written proposal? How was the original decision to purchase outdoor play equipment reached?

The use of logs to investigate the efficiency of meetings has potential to be extended by two or more people comparing perspectives. Figure 6.3 shows the manager's view of meeting B. Manager and staff were at cross purposes, everyone was dissatisfied and the opportunity for agreement was lost. In this case the simple log would enable the team to focus on the real issues standing in the way of a team decision making approach, and make sensible changes rather than continue to set up frustrating experiences.

The log format can be adapted in a number of ways to access the desired information: the length of meetings; the cost (number of people x number of hours x hourly rate of pay) and the contribution of individual or particular categories of staff. The decision to investigate meeting efficiency through logs or other methods needs to be openly shared with all team members and the

meeting and purpose	no. of people	contribution	achievement	comments
purchasing decision meeting – order for outdoor play equipment identified by OFSTED as priority for upgrading 1 hour	10 nursery manager + full time and part time staff	little contribution from staff	order not agreed	staff reluctant to use outdoor play area – especially through winter. Suggesting alternatives based on personal preference.

Figure 6.3 Meeting log – manager's perspective

outcomes discussed. This ensures real use of the material and preempts any sense of seeking someone to blame.

Setting the agenda

A clear agenda is a key tool in ensuring that meeting time is well used. The list of items commonly provided has limited value. It gives only the area of discussion and provides no clue about key questions or issues, parameters for the discussion or desired outcomes. Meetings, particularly those where crucial decisions are necessary, have greater potential for success if everyone attending has the opportunity to consider the critical issues beforehand. Figure 6.4 illustrates an agenda which has this purpose. It allows participants to think about the items and be ready to offer a view. A meeting which is structured in this way helps to avoid the pitfalls of participants changing their mind afterwards or feeling that they have been pressured into a course of action without time for thought. Ideally all team members should leave a meeting feeling satisfied with the decision making process, even if they have had to make some personal compromises.

The agenda should also give the timing for the meeting, perhaps for the individual items, but essentially for the start and finish. The quality of contributions deteriorates rapidly if staff are worrying about collecting children from the child minder or wondering how much longer they will have to sit there.

Minutes of meetings can be very useful in recording decisions made and action agreed, although it should not be assumed that they are always necessary. It is very rarely useful to record the detail of discussion, particularly as this is a time consuming and tedious task. A rotating responsibility with a standard proforma provided can be a simple solution. The proforma need be nothing more than a version of the agenda with a column for decisions, dates and responsibilities.

Staff meeting agenda
3.30   tea available
3.45 – 5.00   meeting in large staffroom
Minutes   Susan's turn

1. Update on calendar
2. Use of equipment fund
£500 available. Various possibilities
      a) outdoor equipment (catalogue marked with possibilities on staffroom noticeboard – please look) Storage is an issue
      b) replacement sand/water equipment for Red Room
      c) new book stock
      d) other suggestions
NB: money has to be spent by end of this month so decision required at meeting
3. Open Day
Date? Needs to be Tuesday or Thursday in February. Please come with suggestions. Particular idea/events to be included? Foyer display – suggestions?
4. AOB
Unless just brief announcement please notify to manager in advance.

Figure 6.4 Agenda

Forging and maintaining professional relationships

Building the team

Successful teamwork requires a group of individuals to share the daily working experience in a positive and proactive manner. Over time the members of a team develop ways of working with each other, responding to the needs and idiosyncrasies of colleagues, recognising strengths and weaknesses, and valuing the complementary contributions that each makes to the team effort. Handy (1990) summarises teams as a:

> collection of individuals gathered together because their talents are needed to perform a task or to solve a problem. If the team wins, all those in it win. If the team loses they all lose. There is a common purpose, and the sense of camaraderie that should go with a common purpose. (p. 128)

The challenge for the team is to have a shared understanding of the common purpose so that team members can act confidently and with a clear understanding of their individual role. Handy (1990) also puts forward an analysis of the stages of team growth, using the headings 'forming, storming, norming and performing'. He suggests that all teams have a period in which they are finding their own identity – the forming stage. Then comes a period of challenge (storming) when individuals begin to assert themselves, moving into the norming phase as they settle to new ways of working. The final phase comes when the team is mature and able to perform at high levels of efficiency. Part of this process in Handy's view is about the establishing of the trust which has to build over time to allow a team to work efficiently.

Trust and shared understanding cannot be merely agreed upon in a meeting or laid down in a set of policies. They grow through the daily occurrences in the work place, the discussion between individuals and the decisions that are made. Teams that have been working together over time develop their own forms of verbal short-hand to share ideas and suggestions, and are able to ground their discussion in an understanding formed through day-to-day communication and awareness of each other's views. This can be an unnerving experience for a new team member who may feel shut out or de-skilled by exchanges which he or she cannot follow. For example in planning an event an established team draws upon the knowledge and experience of all the previous events of this type; making tacit assumptions and using abbreviated references to occasions, incidents, successes and disasters. Individuals who have collaborated with one another in an ongoing situation are able to rely upon each other's skills, making allowance for personal preference or dislike for particular tasks.

Positive communication

As the days and weeks pass the early years team members will communicate with each other on a myriad of subjects and with thousands of interactions. The key feature for success is the quality of this communication, rather than the quantity. The notion of positive communication is a helpful one in that it contains several strands. Being positive, in the sense of ensuring our communication includes plenty of praise and affirmation, is an important aspect of working successfully with others. It is important to reflect honestly and ask questions such as . . . .how often do I communicate praise to my colleagues? . . . to a volunteer or part time worker? . . . to a parent? . . . to my boss? The expectation that the manager will praise the subordinates sometimes leads to disappointment and frustration if workers feel their manager does not give sufficient recognition to their efforts. The successful team member looks for opportunities to communicate positively with support, praise and even delight throughout the daily interaction with colleagues. Honest and sincere positive feedback oils the wheels of the daily task and enables all team members to benefit from both giving and receiving affirmation. The valuing of the contribution is key to team success.

Another strand of positive communication is that of the locking together of team thinking. To operate effectively the various individuals needs to mesh ideas and actions. Where two or more colleagues are working together there should be clear communication with specific instructions as necessary. This requires time for individuals to check their understanding with one another and perhaps even to have written clarification. The key issue is that team members need to understand the importance of appropriate communication and the need for others to question and seek clarification. A team which is able to communicate openly and clearly avoids wasting time on frustration and misunderstanding. Look at this example and see whether it could happen in your setting.

> 'The other day the class teacher said "I want them to paint rainbows. Paint rainbows using as few colours as possible." So we mixed colours and talked about it and painted rainbows. And then she said "Oh, you could have done it this way". And I thought "Oh knickers, she didn't say that, she wasn't that specific." That's happened a few times and I feel I haven't just got the wrong end of the stick, I've got the wrong stick!'
> (Classroom assistant talking about her experiences.)

Managing conflict

It is important not to have an over-optimistic picture of the effective team. An established ability to work together does not deny the possibility of conflict or disagreement. A good team will also develop strategies for dealing with those occasions on which agreement is not easily reached. In fact some teams may thrive and operate extremely efficiently with an element of argument or challenge which pushes the team forward. Continual agreement may indicate a team that is complacent or bored. Teams tend to have a productive period and then need to be challenged or changed (Handy 1990) to reinvigorate and remotivate them.

One of the vital aspects in managing conflict is the separation of the disagreement and the person. It is possible to disagree completely with a colleague's view of how to manage a child's difficult behaviour and yet continue to work with them in a professional and appropriate manner. Goleman (1998) summarises the paradox: 'On one hand, the wisdom holds that the more freewheeling and intense the debate, the better the final decision; on the other hand, open conflict can corrode the ability of a team to work together.' (p. 220). The ability to listen to colleagues is a key feature in avoiding conflict. There is a significant difference between merely listening to the words used and trying to actively understand meaning and feelings. The team that values listening to one another and devotes precious time to exploring feelings and concerns is likely to avoid the potential descent into disagreement and acrimony. Pedler and Boydell (1994) put forward the useful notion of 'supportive listening' and give some strategies for practicing this skill with a 'speaking partner' in order to help your development. If this is an area which is relevant some of these ideas could be tried by the early years team.

A clear understanding of roles and responsibilities

We have established that there is a great diversity of expertise within the early years team. This is a strength of the team, as children need to mix with a variety of adults who relate to them in different ways. The different skills of individuals all add to the strength of the team if recognised and deployed sensitively. It is also important to take careful account of the current employment legislation, legal requirements and best practice in the appointment and management of staff; these are dealt with comprehensively by Reason (1998) elsewhere.

Establishing roles

In order to operate effectively within a team, each member needs to know where they fit in, how their own role relates to that of others, their particular responsibilities and, equally important, what tasks should be referred to others in the team. Each team member needs the confidence of understanding where the pieces of the jigsaw fit in. However in any setting which is flexible and responsive enough to meet the changing needs of children, there are bound to be grey areas where responsibilities are not always clear or there is a degree of overlap.

Roles and responsibilities are often implicit in an established team. Staff seem to instinctively work with each other. However, when there is a new member, it becomes more difficult to explicitly describe current working practice . There are occasions when a team can become too stagnant, when the different roles become too rigid to allow for personal and professional growth. Thus it would seem to be part of an effective team's responsibility to make roles and responsibilities more explicit, understood by everyone and regularly reviewed, perhaps as part of the staff development or appraisal process.

Role definitions

Roles and responsibilities often operate on two levels, the formal and the informal. For example, it may be a particular team member's responsibility to organise the mid morning drink for children. This is a routine task which is understood by all. However, there may be different aspects of the role which are less explicit but none the less important to the efficiency of the team, for example who takes responsibility for dealing with lost property. The shared understanding of the parameters of individual responsibility is crucial; we all need to know that our individual contributions are important and valued.

Job descriptions provide a formal definition of roles and responsibilities and need to be as clear and precise as possible. In Figure 6.5 the working

---

Job description

Post title

Department   Post grade

Location   Post hours

Purposes and objectives of post

Accountable to

Immediate responsibility

Working relationships

Duties and responsibilities

Support for children

Support for staff

Support for unit/setting

Other duties

Agreed by the post holder

Agreed by the supervisor   Date

Adapted from Lorenz (1998)

Figure 6.5 Job description

relationships section describes how the member of staff relates to others in the team, for example who works with whom at different times. The duties and responsibilities clarify in as much detail as possible the boundaries of the post and provide a clear starting point for the formal role and responsibility of staff. However, the remit of the early years setting is so wide that such descriptions cannot entirely capture the reality. Job descriptions are sometimes couched in very general terms and try to encompass every eventuality. They do not always relate directly to the day to day pattern of work. Informal allocation of duties is an important function and needs to recognise the different strengths of individuals. Members of the team may have particular strengths in the following areas:

- relating to parents
- dealing with children's tantrums
- diffusing potentially problematical situations
- having new ideas for craft activities
- displaying children's work
- observing children
- settling new children in
- remembering key dates
- working together.

It is important to consider how these skills be exploited within the team. Members tend to grow into these roles rather than be allocated to them. In deploying staff, individual strengths should be recognised and valued.

Opportunities for change

There are of course occasions when acquired roles, formal or informal, seem impossible to amend or to shed. For example, does a particular member always clear up, look after the sick children or tend to work with those children who need extra help? The more roles are reinforced by continuing to perform duties that fit with it, expectations to adhere to those roles will be placed upon particular members of the team. This may be perfectly acceptable or it may limit the skills of individuals who are unable to extend and develop their practice beyond certain parameters. A skilled manager will give the team opportunities to develop by varying the tasks that they perform. Confident team members will be flexible enough to extend their practice through new challenges. The balance between using individual strengths and extending personal and professional development is important.

Team skills: personal and professional development

How does this relate to individual team members in a specific context? How can everyone in the team be encouraged to take responsibility for the development of their personal skills? Is there shared ownership of team building and working together to achieve goals? The questions below may be used to analyse current practice and identify ways forward.

- Are all staff active team members? Do they accept and act upon their own responsibilities when working with others? How often do they put forward ideas or actively respond to other people's suggestions? Small improvements can be equally as important as major innovations. Are staff at all levels encouraged to put forward good ideas, and are there positive opportunities for these to be shared and acted upon?
- Does everyone in the team take an active part in meetings? Are there main contributors? A meeting log is a useful way to find out. Can everyone contribute to the agenda for meetings? Is it possible for staff to suggest items that they consider to be important?
- Are all contributions (including your own) valued? How is this demonstrated? Do all staff take responsibility for praising and supporting others? Put yourself in another team member's position and think about whether they feel valued.
- Do all staff communicate directly and sensitively with others in the early years team? Do they actively listen to everyone's contribution? Is communication always clear and unambiguous? Often people think they are clear but give quite another signal to the listener. One way of checking communication skills is for colleagues to pair up and give each other feedback.

Our final message is that working with other adults should be an enjoyable aspect of being in an early years team. Using some of the strategies suggested in the chapter may enhance team skills and foster real professional benefits from interaction with colleagues.

References

Goleman, D. (1998) *Working with Emotional Intelligence.* London: Bloomsbury.

Handy, C. (1990) *Inside organisations.* London: BBC Books.

Lorenz, S. (1998) *Effective In-class Support: the management of support staff in mainstream and special schools.* London: David Fulton Publishers.

Pedler, M. and Boydell, T. (1994) *Managing yourself.* Aldershot: Gower.

Reason, J. (1998) *Good to work for.* London: National Early Years Network.

Whalley, M. 'Working as a team', in Pugh, G. (ed.) (1996) *Contemporary Issues in the Early Years Working Collaboratively for Children.* London: Paul Chapman/National Children's Bureau.

Chapter 7

Supporting children with communication difficulties

Joy Jarvis and Sue Lamb

Introduction

All children are developing their communication skills during the early years. Some, however, may have particular difficulties with this aspect of their development. Crystal (1984) suggests that perhaps one in ten children has a language difficulty significant enough to cause concern to his or her carers. Some of these children will be simply delayed in their development of language while others will have a specific difficulty which will need to be addressed. For professionals working in early years settings it can be difficult to know whether a child has a language difficulty or whether he or she is inhibited by a context outside the home. Some children will not speak for some time in a new setting but will chatter away happily at home telling parents about their experiences. Any concern regarding communication needs to be shared with parents so that it can be clarified whether or not it is a context-specific problem. Early identification of children with communication problems is crucial due to the key importance of language in development.

Language is important for social development, for emotional development and it is part of cognitive development through the linking of concepts and words and the ability to use language internally for thinking. Language is a large part of how adults interact with children and how children are given information and explanations. It is the main medium of teaching and how, to a considerable extent, children's learning is assessed. Without appropriate communication skills children will have difficulty developing and learning in early years settings.

The reasons for children having communication difficulties fall into three categories.

Firstly they may have a condition that interferes with language development such as a hearing loss. Many children have middle ear problems during the early years (Watson *et al.* 1999). This results in reduced and inconsistent levels of hearing so that listening to spoken language is difficult and unrewarding. Comprehension of what is heard may be limited and the child's speech may be unclear. It is important that hearing loss is eliminated as a causal factor when communication difficulties are being investigated. Other conditions which may result in communication difficulties include visual and physical impairments and a range of syndromes with associated language problems.

Secondly, the child may have a specific language difficulty. All aspects of development are appropriate apart from the child's communication. The cause is likely to be unknown but may be due to minimal brain dysfunction and it may be genetic. Difficulties may be evident when the child is young, perhaps at age two there is no evidence of understanding or producing speech, or they may not become apparent until the child is older. In the latter case the child may have good basic communication but may fail to understand more complex uses of language such as words that have more than one meaning or non literal meanings such as a teacher giving the instruction; 'Walk back to the hall' which the child interprets as walk backwards. This older child may also be showing difficulties with literacy, particularly with understanding the text. It is important, therefore, that any child who has problems learning to read should have his or her underlying language competency investigated.

The third type of reason for a difficulty with communication is that the child's environment has not been supportive of language learning. Work by Wells (1986) and Tizard and Hughes (1984) suggests that it is rare for a home not to provide an environment in which a child's language can develop appropriately. However, the home language may be different in type and use from that expected in some early years settings, particularly schools. So, for example, children may not have learnt to listen for key information or to give reasons and explanations. Their vocabulary knowledge may not be related to activities undertaken in an educational context. These children will need support to extend their range of language structures and usage. Other children who do not have language difficulties as such but who may be having communication problems in an early years setting are children for whom English is not their first language. These children may be at an early stage in their development of English and will need strategies discussed in chapter 10 to support their communication and their learning of an additional language.

This chapter will explore two aspects of working with children with communication difficulties. Firstly, identification, and how early years professionals can work with others to identify and assess communication difficulties, will be described. Secondly, strategies which can be used to support the communication skills of these children will be discussed in relation to case studies representing children with different types of communication problem.

The identification of children with communication difficulties

Some children will come to an early years setting with an already identified communication problem. In this case parents, health visitors and other professionals and practitioners will need to collaborate to assess a child's needs within a particular context and provide appropriate support. In the case of other children a parent or professional may raise concerns which require investigation. All concerns regarding communication need to be responded to, for while they may be resolved quickly they may be indicators of a long term problem. If a baseline of skills is established early then progress can be monitored and intervention can take place at a later date if appropriate. There are three main ways of identifying and assessing a child's communication: observation, collecting data from parents and other professionals and using published assessments.

Observation

Observation is a powerful tool which is often used very effectively by early years practitioners. There are different ways of observing children including timed observations which can build up a picture of a child's abilities within an identified time frame and more focused observations which may look at a particular aspect of development, for example, how does the target child use turn taking in different contexts? In relation to observing communication there are three main areas of focus: firstly, the difference between verbal and non verbal skills, secondly, the child's skills in different contexts and thirdly the aspect of language being observed. So, for example, a concern may be expressed about a child's ability to concentrate. Observations could show that there is a difference between the child concentrating in a non verbal context, such as completing a jigsaw puzzle, when he or she can concentrate for up to thirty minutes compared to listening to a story when he or she loses concentration after about three minutes. Further observations looking at different contexts, could show that s/he concentrates for a similar length of time in both group sessions and in one to one interaction with an adult. This could suggest that this child has a particular problem understanding language and therefore he or she shows limited concentration during language-based activities.

In order to observe different aspects of language behaviour we need to have a framework for our observations. A model of language which is used frequently for this purpose is the form – content – use model devised by Bloom and Lahey (1978). Using this approach each aspect of language can be looked at separately, although of course they interact with each other. Each aspect can be investigated in terms of both comprehension (what the child understands) and expression (what the child uses). (See Table 7.1)

Form

Form is the structure of language, the speech sounds and the grammar. We can observe whether the child can identify differences between speech sounds, 'boat' and 'goat', for example, and can produce the speech sounds appropriate for his or her age. The acquisition of speech sounds is gradual and mastery of most speech sounds would not be expected until the age of six.

It is possible to observe a child's expression of grammar by seeing how many words he or she is putting together. Is he or she using single words only or are there two word phrases ' dog gone', three words, 'dog gone now' or four word phrases 'big dog gone now'. Structures such as negatives from the simple 'dog gone no' to the more complex 'dog hasn't gone' can be noted.

Also noticeable is the child's overgeneralisation of grammatical rules such as 'mouses', 'tooken' and 'goed'. These are positive aspects of language development, showing evidence of learning the rules, and examples are likely to be used by even ten and eleven year old children, particularly with unusual vocabulary, i.e. 'It overshooted the runway.'

With regard to comprehension it is possible to see how many sentence elements a child can respond to. Which parts of the instruction do they follow? 'Fetch your *beaker, spoon,* and *bowl*', '*Sit* in the *hoop* and put your *hands* on your *head*'. The key words needed are often referred to as Information Carrying Words (ICWs). The first instruction has 3 ICWs and the second 4. Additionally, the ways in which children respond to different question forms can be noted, e.g. 'when', 'where', 'why', 'how' and to negatives such as 'You mustn't go on the grass'. Observing comprehension can be difficult. A child who doesn't respond appropriately to the last instruction, for example, may still understand it!

Content

Content is what is being talked about. Vocabulary is a key element and observation needs to be undertaken to discover the range of the child's comprehension and expression of vocabulary.

Topic words and words used in daily routines of the particular early years context need to be checked. A range of meanings for words need to be explored to see whether the concept has been generalised, 'corner' for example, does not just mean the book corner. Some children may struggle to produce vocabulary and use 'thing' or 'that one' rather than the name of the item. A child with this difficulty may have a word-finding problem. In this case the child has the knowledge of the word but can't recall the name quickly enough. Sometimes a similar item is recalled, 'brother' instead of 'sister' for example. This can be extremely frustrating for the child and can lead to adults underestimating his or her knowledge or ability. When observing a child's vocabulary it is necessary to check comprehension, for example by asking him or her to find toy animals named by an adult, and then check the ability to express these words by asking the child to name the same animals.

Use

The use of language involves a whole range of communication skills both verbal and non verbal. These include the desire to communicate with other people and the ability to do this by the use of touch, eye gaze, gesture and language. Children in early years settings would be expected to initiate communication and to respond to the initiations of others. They would be expected to understand the role of turn taking in conversation and show increasing understanding of staying on the topic of conversation and the need to clarify information for the listener. Using and responding to questions and greetings, refusing, teasing and arguing are all examples of language use and children's understanding and use of these can be observed and recorded.

Table 7.1: Summary of normal speech and language development

Comp. = Comprehension
Exp. = Expression

Age 2	Form	Content	Use
Speech	Sentences		
Comp. Perceive differences between most speech sounds	Understands 2 ICWs Follows simple instructions out of context	Understands basic vocabulary related to their own world	Understands gestures, such as pointing
Exp. Produce a range of vowel sounds and some initial and final consonants	Uses two word utterances	Vocabulary consists mainly of nouns	Words used to gain attention, request, reject, greet and name

Age 4	Form	Content	Use
Speech	Sentences		
Comp. Perceive differences between all speech sounds	Understands 4 ICWs Follows more complex instructions	Understands a wide range of vocabulary including words related to space, time and emotions	Beginning to rely less on context for comprehension
Exp. Speech intelligible All consonant clusters not developed	Uses sentences with two or more clauses Uses plurals, possessives and some past tense structures	Uses nouns, verbs, adjectives, adverbs, prepositions and pronouns	Uses language to give information and to talk about past and future events

Age 6	Form	Content	Use
Speech	Sentences		
Comp. Perceive differences between all speech sounds	Understands complex sentences including passives	Understands that words can have more than one meaning	Beginning to understand non-literal language and jokes
Exp. Most consonant clusters used Articulates polysyllabic words in full	Uses complex sentences Expresses sequences of events	Can sort words into categories Quickly learns and uses new vocabulary related to topics	Communicative intentions include negotiation, expressing emotions

Collecting information from others

Principled observations should result in a profile of the child's communication strengths and weaknesses, however, observation will have generally been made in only one context. Parents and other professionals can help build a more complete picture of the child's communication, either through discussion or in writing, by completing a check list, for example. Health visitors and social services professionals may be able to give a wider perspective on the child's abilities and educational psychologists can give information regarding the child's non verbal skills. Language focused assessments can be undertaken by speech and language therapists who are likely to select from a range of published assessments.

Language assessments

Many types of assessment are available. Some may be used by anyone working with a child, while others are restricted to professionals with particular qualifications. Some assessments involve using a check list and can produce a profile of a child's skills while others are norm referenced and will give an age equivalent score for a particular aspect of language development.

Prior observation will indicate which particular assessments would be useful in an individual case. Table 7.2 gives some examples of published assessments which may be used by professionals to investigate language:

Table 7.2 Speech, language and communication assessments

Test	Age Range	Purpose	Publisher
Action Picture Test	3 to 8 yrs	Assesses age levels of information content and grammatical usage	Winslow Press
Word Finding Vocabulary Test	3 to 9 yrs	Assesses word finding skills	Winslow Press
South Tyneside Test of Phonology	3+ yrs	Screening assessment of child's speech sound system	Winslow Press
AFASIC Language Checklists	4 to 10 yrs	Screening test to help mainstream teachers identify speech and language difficulties	Winslow Press
Reynell Developmental Scales III	15 months – 7 yrs	Provides a standard measure of children's expressive language and verbal comprehension	NFER – Nelson
Pragmatics Profile of Everyday Communication Skills in Children	9 months – 10 yrs	Through a structured interview for parents/carers and teachers the Pragmatics Profile assesses: Communicative functions Response to communication Interaction and conversation Contextual variations	NFER – Nelson
British Picture Vocabulary Scales	3 – 16 yrs	Assesses receptive vocabulary	NFER – Nelson

Examples of individual assessment

The following two short case studies of children indicate how observation and assessment have been undertaken by professionals and parents. The aim is to see how use has been made of the Bloom and Lahey (1978) model, of observation and of assessments if appropriate. The two children are in different early years contexts and illustrate common types of language difficulty. Later in the chapter the way in which the children were supported will be described.

TOM

Tom is three years old and attends a day care centre with his twin sister. His mother, a single parent, was concerned that at age two neither child was talking, although they used a lot of non-verbal communication. Now, however, Tom's sister appears to be developing language appropriately but all the adults involved are concerned about Tom. Observation was undertaken by day care staff as follows:

Table 7.3 Observation of Tom

	Form		Content	Use
	Speech	Sentences		
Comp.	Understands differences between similar sounding words i.e. big/pig	Understands sentences with two ICWs i.e. get a *bucket* and a *scoop*	Understands a range of vocabulary including names of people and play equipment, verbs including run, jump, sit down, sleep, cry. Also concept words: no, yes, gone, big, red, green, yellow, in, on, and questions 'what do you want?' 'Where's the . . . ?'	Understands and follows short instructions, requests and 'what' and 'where' questions. Responds using gesture, pointing and actions, i.e. taking an adult to an object.
Exp.	Uses a range of vowels Plus p, b, d, g, m, n, w	Uses two single words plus one symbolic noise: 'nee naw' for a fire engine	Uses only 'no' and 'mum' consistently	Initiates communication non-verbally with eye gaze, gesture and touch
Other Observations	Tom can concentrate on an activity of his own choosing, such as a construction toy, for up to thirty minutes without adult support. He enjoys listening to stories in a small group. He joins in with the actions during action songs. He gets frustrated at times when he can't make himself understood.			

Tom's mother completed the Pragmatics Profile of Communication Skills (Dewart and Summers 1995) which confirmed that while he had a range of skills in terms of use of communication and his comprehension and vocabulary were developing appropriately, he had problems with expressive language. No other professionals were involved at this time. The observations had provided a base line and a clear indication of the area needing development. Strategies were developed by the day care centre staff and Tom's mother and these will be discussed later in this chapter.

KIA

Kia is five years old and has been in a reception class for half a term. She had been assessed by a speech and language therapist at the age of three due to concern regarding her limited communication. She had attended some pre-school group language development sessions at the health centre. Observations and assessments produced a picture of her communication behaviour as in Table 7.4.

The profile indicated a child with particular difficulties in the area of comprehension. Targets and strategies, which will be described later, were developed by Kia's class teacher, the special needs co-ordinator, a speech and language therapist and Kia's parents. Her progress was reviewed, by all involved, at the end of her second term in school.

Both these children had language difficulties which caused concern to themselves and to adults. In both cases parents and professionals collaborated to gain a clear picture of the children's communication skills. How assessments can be used to develop individual programmes, and how children can be supported by the use of appropriate strategies will be discussed next.

Strategies to support children with communication difficulties in early years contexts

Strategies to support children with communication difficulties can be divided into two types: those which provide a facilitative language learning environment for all children and those which are targeted on a particular area of language difficulty.

General strategies to support language development

All children will benefit from an environment that supports language development. Key aspects would appear to include:

- sustained one to one interactions with an adult;
- the adult responds to the child's communication attempts and follows his her interests;
- the adult's language is related to the child's level of understanding;

Table 7.4 Observation of Kia

	Form Speech	Sentences	Content	Use
Comp.	Distinguishes between all speech sounds i.e. nose/toes	Consistently follows instructions with 2 ICW's but not 3. Comprehension assessed by speech and language therapist using a standardised test. Assessment score – 2.11 yrs at 5.00 yrs	Limited knowledge of topic vocabulary	Understands the function of questions, instructions and explanations. Understands basic non-verbal communication
Exp.	Uses all speech sounds appropriate for her age	Very long sentences but often echoes adult speech. Expressive language assessed by speech and language therapist using a standardised test. Assessment score – 3.06 yrs at 5.0yrs	Uses a range of nouns and verbs but inconsistent use of pronouns. A few adjectives used i.e. 'pretty', 'naughty', 'good' and 'silver'	Finds turn-taking difficult, interrupts other people's conversations

Other Observations	Kia can sustain concentration on visual-only tasks for 20 minutes. She always selects construction tasks at free choice times. She often wanders aimlessly around the classroom after tasks have been given out. She is skilful in PE but copies the other children's activities. Adults observed that Kia had few friends in the playground and was upset when she could not follow rules of games initiated by the other children.

- the adult does not correct the child's grammar but responds to the meaning of what has been said;
- the adult 'models' appropriate language, i.e. in response to the child saying 'Mummy home now' the adult could respond 'Yes, Mummy's gone home now' and maybe extend this to include 'She'll be back later.'

When children are in group situations it can be difficult for adults to interact individually with them to support their understanding and use of communication. Twins generally show delay in their development of language because their parents have less opportunity to engage with them as individuals (O'Keefe 1999). In early years settings with young children, such as day care centres, it is crucial that adults spend time communicating individually with children and are not distracted by care, safety and other considerations so that talking time becomes fleeting and limited. Timetables and record keeping systems need to ensure that communication needs are planned for and met.

Once children enter nurseries and schools the language environment is likely to be less facilitative of communication development than when they are in smaller group contexts. This is partly due to class size and also to the instructional role of teachers. Teacher language in particular is generally involved with management and with instruction and is usually directed at groups rather than individuals. There is a high level of questioning and children are usually expected to follow the teacher's train of thought. Children tend to produce shorter utterances in their interactions with teachers than with parents, they initiate less and ask fewer questions (Wells 1986). Communication can be fostered through interaction with peers but group 'talk' needs to be planned for carefully, otherwise children with difficulties in this area can be marginalised.

The role of 'other adults', i.e. non-teachers, in the classroom is very important in the provision of a good language learning environment. Children may communicate more confidently and freely with nursery nurses or classroom assistants, for example, who may in turn have the opportunity of working with individuals and small groups. If these opportunities are used to support children's language, rather than for the adult to dominate the communication exchange, then this can enhance language development. 'Other adults' can offer children a responsive listener who is able to be a more equal partner in conversation, thereby allowing children to initiate, ask questions, seek clarification and show a wider variety of uses of language in their talk. In this way 'other adults' can play a complementary role to teachers. If this is to happen both teachers and 'other adults' need to understand how adults support children's development of communication and the role of each other in this process. If the 'other adults' model themselves on teachers in terms of language use then they will be denying children the advantage of different types of talk partner. As Hughes and Westgate note it is important 'to recognise the established relationship between the quality of pupils' progress and pupils' contact with all adult talk partners'. (1997, p.7)

Supporting specific aspects of language development

For children with communication difficulties the provision of a good language learning environment is vital but it is unlikely to be sufficient alone to accelerate development. Generally these children have had a good language learning context at home and have not developed appropriately because they have a problem with an aspect, or more than one aspect, of language. In this case additional strategies need to be used. Tom and Kia, the children discussed earlier in this chapter, both have identified language difficulties. The strategies used by their parents and the professionals involved in their care and education will be described. These case studies show how early years professionals can effectively support children with communication difficulties in different contexts.

TOM

Three year old Tom has good comprehension but virtually no expressive language. At first this was attributed to 'twin delay' but his twin sister now has language appropriate for her age.

Following the assessment described earlier, Tom's mother, a speech and language therapist and the staff of the day care centre met to develop a plan to develop his communication, as in Table 7.5.

Table 7.5

Objective	To develop Tom's expressive communication
Targets:	Tom to use gesture to request and name objects and actions; Tom to use more symbolic sounds, i.e. 'moo', 'baa', 'brm brm'; Tom to use objects and pointing at pictures to explain what he means when he can't make himself understood.
Strategies	Adults to use natural gesture at home and in the day care centre. This would include pointing and the use of gestures for verbs such as eat and drink, and for activities such as going in a car (pretending to drive) or playing with the sand (a digging action); mother to ask her sister to visit some evenings a week so that the twins can have individual bath times. Mother to talk about toys and activities in the bath and model sounds such as 'splash' and words such as 'bye bye' (to the bath water); mother and day care staff to name animals and objects and the sounds they make. Staff and mother to record Tom's attempts at copying these sounds and names so that items can be reinforced in both contexts; staff to make a book with Tom using photographs and pictures of items of equipment used in the day centre so that Tom can use this for choosing and recalling activities; staff and mother to respond to Tom's use of gesture and any verbal initiations.

Comments

Tom's mother was initially concerned that the use of gesture could inhibit his use of verbal language. She was reassured when she was told that gestures are used by all children as part of their communication development. At the suggestion of the speech and language therapist Tom's mother joined a Hanen Parent Programme group in her local area (see References). This programme is designed to help young children communicate through family focused early intervention. Parents/carers attend a series of group sessions to discuss how to foster their child's communication and learning during everyday routines, conversations and play. Videotaped sessions allow adults the opportunity to observe and discuss their own interactions with their children. Tom's mother found these sessions stimulating and useful and she was also able to link with other parents with children with similar difficulties. After a few weeks Tom started to use a few gestures consistently and was using 'bye-bye' in appropriate contexts. He was also using a number of symbolic sounds. After six months he used approximately 50 words and new targets for putting two words together were initiated.

KIA

The observation and assessment indicated that five year old Kia has a language comprehension problem. Her parents, class teacher and Special Needs Co-ordinator (SENCO) developed the following programme:

Table 7.6

Objective	To develop Kia's comprehension of language.
Targets:	Kia to follow instructions with 3 ICWs; Kia to rehearse instructions to aid recall; Kia to understand identified vocabulary related to the class topic and to class routines.
Strategies	Where possible adults to give instructions to Kia individually, limiting them to containing three pieces of information and modelling verbal rehearsal so that Kia can use this to help her to remember the important information; teaching staff to identify key vocabulary used in the classroom and list this to share with parents and other involved adults. Comprehension and generalisation work to be undertaken at school and followed up at home by parents; staff to help Kia to demonstrate sequences of movements in PE lessons so that she listens to instructions in a practical situation where she shows skill.

Comments

In addition to work in school Kia also attended a group session run by a speech and language therapist once a week at the health centre. By the end of term she demonstrated comprehension of most of the targeted vocabulary. She used more active listening skills and could respond to three simple ICW instructions. Her comprehension difficulties were still inhibiting her learning and the SENCO asked the speech and language therapist to help with the development of an Individual Education Plan (IEP) for the next term.

Discussion

This chapter has shown that practitioners working in early years contexts can, and need to, take an important role in identifying, assessing children with communication difficulties. Key aspects would appear to be an understanding of the normal process of language development and a clear approach to observing children's language comprehension and use. The families of children with communication difficulties are an essential part of the assessment team. The keeping of appropriate, shared records is also part of the assessment and monitoring process. Early years practitioners have a crucial role in supporting the development of communication skills in all children in their care and this needs to be planned for in all settings. Individual support programmes can be developed by a team which may include a range of professionals. Advantages and pitfalls of working in a team are explored in chapter 6 and the importance of clarifying roles, who is liaising with the parents, for example, must be kept in mind. It is important that early years staff, who may not feel that they have expertise in the area of language, develop confidence in their ability to observe, record and support children's communication. Through working with other professionals and with the families of these children an appropriate environment for the development of communication skills can be provided.

References

Bloom, L. and Lahey, M. (1978) *Language Development and Language Disorders.* New York: John Wiley and Sons.

Crystal, D. (1984) *Language Handicap in Children.* Stratford upon Avon: National Council for Special Education.

Dewart, H. and Summers, S. (1995) *The Pragmatics Profile of Everyday Communication Skills in Children.* London: NFER-Nelson.

Hughes, M. and Westgate, D. (1997) 'Teachers and Other Adults as Talk Partners for Pupils in Nursery and Reception Classes', in *Education 3 to 13* **25** (1) 3–7.

O'Keefe, J. (1999) 'Language Development in Twins', in *Twins and Multiple Births Association Magazine* **10** (2), 11.

Tizard, B. and Hughes, M. (1984) *Young Children Learning.* London: Fontana.

Watson, L. *et al.* (1999) *Deaf and Hearing Impaired Children in Mainstream Schools.* London: David Fulton Publishers.

Wells, G. (1986) *The Meaning Makers: Children Learning Language and Using Language to Learn.* London: Hodder & Stoughton.

Useful address:

The Hanen Centre, 1075 Bay St., Suite 403, Toronto, Ontario, Canada, M5S 2B1
Tel: (416) 921-1073 Fax: (416) 921-1225
e-mail: info@hanen.org Web site: www.hanen.org

Chapter 8

Inclusive education in the early years

Alice Paige-Smith

Introduction

In this chapter I will firstly consider who are the children with 'special educational needs'? The assessment and identification of these children and the involvement of their parents will be explored. Ways of dealing with the barriers to inclusive education will be considered through the experiences and views of parents of young children with learning difficulties or disabilities. The parents, whose views are presented, have been active in promoting inclusive education for their children. The notion of inclusive education will then be linked to a human rights perspective on education and society. The ways in which early years settings and mainstream classes can adapt the curriculum will be explored and linked to a commitment to the inclusion of all children.

Inclusive education – policy and practice

In October 1997 the Department for Education and Employment produced the Green Paper entitled 'Excellence for all Children – Meeting Special Educational Needs'. In this Green Paper there was a commitment to the inclusion of children considered to have 'special educational needs' within mainstream schooling 'wherever possible' (DfEE 1997, p. 5).

When considering inclusive education it is important to consider 'who ' is being included – who are this group of children with 'special educational needs'? Are they a specific, well defined group, and how does this group recruit its members, has this changed over time and will it change in the future? The membership of this group can be related to the assessment process, provision for children with learning difficulties or disabilities, and parental involvement.

In 1978 the Warnock Report identified that 20% of the school population could be considered to have a 'special educational need' at some time during their school life (Audit Commission Report 1992, p. 7). Pupils with special educational needs are considered to be children who have a learning difficulty (which is greater than the majority of children of the same age) or a disability that calls for special educational provision (DfEE 1997, p. 12).

In January 1997 18% of pupils in schools (1.5 million pupils) were considered to have special educational needs (DfEE 1997, p. 12) It has been estimated that nearly 3% (233,000) of these pupils have a statutory assessment of their needs resulting in a statement of their special educational needs (DfEE 1997 p. 35). According to the 1997 Green Paper statements are used to: define a child's needs; specify provision to meet those needs; and co-ordinate this provision by saying who will do what (DfEE 1997, p. 35)

There has been a rise in statemented pupils since 1992 when there were 168,000 pupils with statements in England and Wales (2.1%) (Audit Commission Report 1992, p. 8). The 1997 Green Paper *Excellence for all Children – Meeting Special Educational Needs* (DfEE 1997) suggested that secondary school age pupils with special educational needs should move closer towards 10% rather than the 18% estimated in 1997 (DfEE 1997, p. 12). This change in the amount of pupils identified as having special educational needs is to be bought about, according to the Green Paper, 'as our policies take effect' (DfEE, 1997 p. 12).

There is clearly a policy commitment from the DfEE to change the experiences of pupils categorised as having 'special educational needs'. The importance of early intervention and helping children through the early identification of their difficulties is recognised by the DfEE as improving through the early excellence centres, early years development partnerships, the £452 million Sure Start programme, and the implementation of baseline assessments. The DfEE also states that the national literacy and numeracy strategy should help all children 'achieve their potential' (DfEE, 1998a, p. 12).

However, how will these policy changes affect the educational experiences of pupils with learning difficulties or disabilities? Will the number of these pupils be reduced over the next few years as a result of policy changes to tackle literacy and numeracy problems at an early age? Will the growth of pupils requiring a statement of their special educational needs decline? Can this be perceived to be a positive development or could some children with statements lose their legal entitlements to support provision?

Parental experiences and concerns can be considered to be a central part of the assessment process, in the decision making over how a child is perceived as having 'special educational needs' and the educational provision they receive. The Early Learning Goals (QCA 1999) recognise the role of parents in the identification of the progress of the future learning needs of these children. The statementing process was introduced by the 1981 Education Act and was reformed by the 1993 Education Act. The 1993 Act recognised parents' rights to express a preference for a school and the parental choice of school had to be written onto the child's statement. This indicated a recognition of conflicting views on education provision between parents and professionals (the local education authority (LEA)) during the statementing process. The Act also set up the special educational needs tribunal where parents could appeal to a tribunal, independent from the LEA, about their child's special educational needs and provision.

In 1994 the DfEE Code of Practice on the assessment and identification of children with special educational needs was set up to provide guidance on the assessment process and how and where children categorised as having special educational needs should be educated. This was an attempt to consolidate differences between local education authorities that had been recognised in the 1992 Audit Commission Report which stated that there was a

> lack of clarity about what constitutes special educational need and about the respective responsibilities of schools and LEAs. (Audit Commission Report 1992, p. 51)

An example of the early experiences of one child, Paul, shows how he was integrated into his local mainstream school, until the demands of the National Curriculum were used to justify his exclusion to a special school. Alan was in the same class as my daughter and I conducted a piece of action research with his family. He was also written about in a report by SCOPE (then the Spastics Society) on integration (his name has been changed). Here is a summary of the experiences which show how inclusion can be affected by assessment, parental involvement, the wishes of the LEA and attitudes of school staff towards integration:

> Mrs Baldwin's son, Paul, had attended integrated nursery and subsequently mainstream infants school, but after resistance from the headteacher had had to leave mainstream junior school, along with the two other children who together comprised the first disabled children in the school. The head teacher's reason was that the prescribed welfare assistance was not forthcoming and that without it the three boys with special needs constituted a 'safety risk' . Although the family are pleased with the special school Paul now attends, his mother still hopes to achieve integrated secondary schooling for him, so that his chances of living and working independently will be greater . . .
>
> Mrs Baldwin felt she could not go through with an appeal against 'dis-integration', because of all she had to cope with generally (she had recently had a nervous breakdown). The family pinned their hopes on re-integration later, with the support of a local campaign for integrated schooling. (Leonard 1992, p. 18).

Paul's experiences illustrate how the attitudes of professionals, in this case the head teacher, are important for the sucessful inclusion of children into mainstream school. Alan's special educational provision changed when he was excluded from his local primary school. The DfEE policy document *Excellence for all children* (DfEE 1997) states that the inclusion of children would be supported 'wherever possible', in the following section I will consider how barriers to inclusive education may be overcome.

Enabling inclusive education and overcoming barriers

There was a process of consultation after the Green Paper on Excellence for All (DfEE 1997) was produced and comments were invited. In June 1998 the Special Educational Needs Update was produced from the 3,600 responses to the Department of Education and Employment which stated that: 'The great majority of comments supported the principle of inclusion but expressed reservations about the practicalities.' (DfEE 1998b, p. 1). In particular the barriers to inclusion were perceived as: inadequate funding, staff training and physical access, the need to change culture and attitudes (DfEE 1998b, p. 1). The Early Learning Goals (QCA 1999) suggest that there should be a focus in the early years to remove barriers, although the emphasis here is on preventing learning difficulties from developing through the use of effective strategies.

Parents may experience prejucial attitudes towards disability or learning difficulty when they try to secure a place for their child in a mainstream school (Paige-Smith 1996). Diana Simpson is the parent of a child with a learning difficulty, she became involved with the group Parents for Inclusion when it began in the early 1980s as a parents' campaign for integrated education. She described the difficulties facing parents who want integration:

> What parents of children with 'special needs' find is all the prejudice which anybody with a disability finds, and of course parents know that and that's why they want integration. Because they feel that their children should be a part of everything . . . by going to their local school and all the rest of it . . . Parents are desperate for their children to be welcomed in the world and the people who have any energy left to do the fighting want to make the world more responsive for their child. So they go for integration and they fight for it and they put as much energy into it as possible to make it work.
> (Diana Simpson, Parents for Inclusion in Paige-Smith 1994)

According to Diana the hidden ingredients required for parents to be able to fight for what they want are conceptualising disability as a 'social model' and being supported by others who don't subscribe to the dominant view of disability in education and society, as she explains:

> If you are actually supported by people who also are very much into the deficit mode – 'how awful it is' and 'isn't it going to be terrible' then that doesn't help. But if, by chance you are supported by people who can help you see over that, then you begin to feel indignant that your child isn't welcomed . . . not being totally overwhelmed by the fact that this child is going to be difficult.
> (Diana Simpson, Parents for Inclusion in Paige-Smith 1994).

Diana's perspective is that parents need support to enable them to get beyond a 'deficit' view of disability alongside an acceptance of their child by others. This negative view of disability is not considered to be a part of 'inclusive education', as Len Barton, an educator who has written an article on 'The politics of education for all' (1995) and has attempted to define inclusive education suggests: 'Disablist assumptions and practices need to be identified and challenged in order to promote positive views of others'. (Barton 1995, p. 157).

Mathew Carpenter, aged 16, has written about his experiences of being a brother to Katie who has Down's Syndrome in a chapter called 'Our Family' in a book entitled 'Families in Context'. He explains how other people regard his sister and that changing attitudes towards disability is about acceptance:

> She is not 'retarded', 'ill' or 'dumb' or whatever other names people wish to classify her under. She has Down's Syndrome: this makes her different but nothing more. If those people who try to classify Katie could be more accepting and trusting like Katie then the world would be a better place. (Carpenter 1997, p. 8.)

Research on 'full inclusion' in Canada was carried out by Stainback *et al.* (1992) on a school with kindergarten classes. This research found that teachers and students felt anxiety and fear when the full inclusion of disabled, non-disabled and students with 'severe disabilities' in the same classes occurred. However, in the kindergarten classes where children were included since the beginning of their school life, anxiety and fear were not noted. The reason for this is identified that these young pupils had been included since the beginning, so no changes had occurred for them (Stainback *et al.* 1992, p. 310).

Barton (1995) describes inclusive education as a 'part of a human rights approach' that is concerned with the well-being of all pupils, and that schools should be welcoming institutions. He identifies issues of social justice, equity and choice as 'central' to inclusive education. (Barton 1995, p. 157). The DfEE in the Green Paper *Excellence for all Children; Meeting Special Educational Needs* (1997) supports the United Nations Educational, Scientific, and Cultural Organization (UNESCO) Salamanca World Statement on Special Needs Education 1994. This statements 'calls on governments to adopt the principle of inclusive education, enrolling all children in regular school, unless there are compelling reasons for doing otherwise' (DfEE 1997, p. 44).

Mukhtar is the mother of Sophia who has been integrated throughout her pre-school and school life and is now in the sixth form with one A grade GCSE in Art. She was interviewed alongside other parents of children with learning difficulties or disabilities who had been involved in parents groups in England (Paige-Smith 1996). Ensuring Sophia has had access to mainstream pre-school and school has been difficult as she has the label of 'Down's Syndrome'. Mukhtar stated that she preferred the inclusion of her child:

> Because she is a human being. She is a human being. If she is not like a human being she should be in the cage or she should be just pushed away from the community, from the ordinary people. She is ordinary herself, so what if she is born with the label.'
> (Mukhtar in Paige-Smith 1994)

In 1992 I visited Canada to carry out research with parents on their experiences of inclusive education for their children. In particular I was interested in how the experiences of parents who wanted inclusion in Canada were similar or different to the parents in this country. I interviewed mothers who were members of parents' groups. In Canada there is a voluntary organisation called the Canadian Association for Community Living (CACL) which brings together the 400 local parent associations that have a commitment to the aim of the true and full participation in their communities for all individuals' and in 1958 CACL adopted and promoted the normalisation principle – that is based on the recognition of human rights and the principle of inclusion. Sindy was a member of her local CACL parent organisation and her child was in a mainstream primary school with support. She lived in a rural location where there was no access to special schooling.

Sindy did not experience major barriers against the integration of her daughter apart from the occasional 'bumpy' or 'stormy' meeting:

> I went to the school and they were concerned because Karen wasn't toilet trained, so they were a little concerned about toileting. My husband built a little stool so that she

could reach the toilet and at home we were working on toileting and decided it might happen before school started. They had a support worker that would meet her needs and change her if need be, but as it happened she was toilet trained before she went to school. This year we had to look at how to change how they treated Karen, because Karen was getting frustrated because other students were doing things that she couldn't possibly do. Karen has difficulties with fine-motor skills, she cannot hold a pencil whereas the others are writing. They adapted the curriculum so that she is still a part of the group. She will hand out the papers, she's very good at cutting, so she will cut, or glue so she participates where she can participate. We've looked at what she is good at. I sit on an identification placement review committee and I am a part of that and twice a year we sit down and talk about Karen's placement and we review what happened with her, and where she's going, her goals and our expectations. (Sindy in Paige-Smith 1994)

From the example above of Sindy's experiences as a parent she talks about her concerns; these are toilet training, her child's frustration at not being able to do the same things as her peers, and her child's difficulties with fine motor skills. The way that these concerns were dealt with by her involvement in the education of her child were through working with the school, with the staff – they 'sit down and talk' about her child's placement, review goals and discuss expectations. She also mentions how the staff adapt the curriculum so that her daughter can participate in the curriculum of her peers.

Tricia David *et al.* (1997) have written about curriculum development within the inclusive nursery, and point out that the role of the pre-school teacher should be to visit the family in the home and that this provides an opportunity for the pre-school teacher to listen to the parents, observe the child and ask questions, rather than professionals parading what they perceive to be their knowledge and expertise. Ellis (1995) makes a similar point in her chapter on an inclusive curriculum within a nursery school where support for the child begins with the sharing of information about the child's knowledge, skills and achievements and the context in which they have been acquired (Ellis 1995, p. 114). As she states: 'Because of the close involvement between staff and parent or carer it is possible to both establish our starting point for the curriculum, and to ensure continuity through an ongoing dialogue and sharing of information' (Ellis 1995, p. 114)

A profile of a child's development can be compiled through liaison between home and pre-school, these are considered to be helpful when forming children's individual education programmes (David *et al.* 1997). In one nursery school access to the curriculum for children with disabilities or learning difficulties is considered to be provided through a system of observations and record keeping (Ellis 1995). Observation notes are analysed, and then further action is planned for the individual children (Ellis 1995). In another nursery David (1997) describes how planning cards can be used to provide access to the curriculum as the children with learning difficulties can become involved in self-initiated planning with some adult support.

> The nursery is divided into 12 distinct play areas . . . At the beginning of each session, children are given the opportunity to plan their own activities, and the plan is stored in a clear, plastic wallet. (David *et al.* 1997, p. 143)

This method of curriculum adaptation recognises the individual needs of individual children and how they can be incorporated into the curriculum of their peers, with support. When I was working as a support teacher I provided the mother, at her request, with a copy of all the individual programmes, and equipment used in the class to teach her daughter to read. The mother reinforced the reading programme implemented at school with daily sessions at home – a lotto game was made out of the words. I showed the mother in school how she could play this game with her child at home, and asked her to show me how she could play the game. Within a few weeks her daughter was reading the words and making sentences from them. I had listened to the mother's insistence that her child should be improving by liaising with her over the curriculum of the child that then became part of her time at home when she played with her daughter. The child's improvement was celebrated at home and at school. The mother had asked for this and I had listened to her request and responded to it. She had the expertise, as a parent, to know that her child would flourish through effective home–school liaison for this aspect of her learning. The Early Learning Goals (QCA 1999) recognise the importance of parental knowledge and expertise necessary to promote children's learning in the section on parents as partners.

Stainback and Stainback (1990) suggest that the key to inclusive education is 'the willingness to visualise, work for and achieve a mainstream that is adaptive and supportive of everyone' (p. 17). Ellis (1995) alongside Stainback *et al.* (1992) who have both written about inclusive education and pre-school, suggest that succesful inclusion occurs alongside a strong commitment to full inclusion, the valuing of each child and a recognition that they are a part of the community to which they belong.

References

Audit Commission (1992) *Getting in on the Act.* Her Majesty's Inspectorate. London: The Department of Education and Science.

Barton, L. (1995) 'The politics of education for all', in *Support for Learning* **10**, (4), 156–160.

Carpenter, M. *et al.* (1997) 'Our Family', in Carpenter, B. (ed.) *Families in context: Emerging Trends in Family Support and Early intervention.* London: David Fulton Publishers.

David, T. *et al.* (1997) 'Curriculum issues in early childhood: implications for families', in Carpenter, B. *Families in context: Emerging Trends in Family Support and Early intervention.* London: David Fulton Publishers.

Department for Education and Employment (1994) *The Code of Practice on the Identification and Assessment of Special Educational Needs.* London: DfEE.

Department for Education and Employment (1997) *Excellence for all Children – Meeting Special Educational Needs.* Suffolk: DfEE.

Department for Education and Employment (1998a) *Meeting Special Educational Needs – a programme of action.* Suffolk: DfEE.

Department for Education and Employment (1998b) *Special Educational Needs Update.* London: DfEE.

Ellis, M. (1995) 'An inclusive curriculum within a nursery school', in Potts, P. *et al.* (eds) *Equality and Diversity in Education; Learning teaching and managing in schools.* London: Routledge.

Leonard A. (1992) *A Hard Act to Follow.* London: The Spastics Society.

Paige-Smith, A. (1994) Choosing Inclusion – The Power of Parents in Special Education. PhD Thesis. The Open University.

Paige-Smith, A. (1996) 'Choosing to campaign: a case study of parent choice, statementing and integration', in *European Journal of Special Needs Education* **11** (3), 321–9.

Qualifications and Curriculum Authority (1999) *Early Learning Goals.* London: Qualifications and Curriculum Authority.

Stainback, S. and Stainback, W. (1990) 'Inclusive Schooling', in Stainback, W. and Stainback, S. (eds) *Support Networks for Inclusive schooling.* Baltimore, MD: Paul Brookes.

Stainback, W. *et al.* (1992) 'Concerns About Full Inclusion, An Ethnographic Investigation', in Villa, R. *et al.* (eds) *Restructuring for Caring and Effective Education.* Baltimore, MD: Paul Brookes.

Chapter 9

Promoting child health

Lyn Karstadt and Jo Medd

In recent years it has become increasingly evident that agencies need to develop in their ability to work together, with the term 'partnership' becoming one of the key words of the current government (Department of Health 1998). Hall (1996) makes it clear that the issue of improving child health is not simply the concern of health care professionals, in fact it is suggested that all people working with young children should be aware of their health needs, being equipped to offer support and advice relating to child development, behaviour and nutrition. In order to explore the role of the early years practitioner in promoting child health it is necessary to first consider some of the definitions of health and the factors that influence a child's health during the early years. Two case studies will be used to illustrate the discussion.

Definitions of health

When we try to identify the meaning of health it soon becomes apparent that it is not an easy concept to define. We each have our own ideas about what being healthy means for us, yet to express this verbally can be remarkably difficult. The World Health Organization (WHO) provided a definition in 1946 which has been subject to extensive criticism and has since been revised. The first definition stated that: 'Health is a state of complete physical, mental and social well-being and not merely the absence of disease.' The main objection to this definition is that it suggests that there is some kind of utopian state of health that can be achieved, when in fact the majority of people would never be able to say that they are completely well. Seedhouse (1986) is particularly critical of this definition and provides a detailed discussion of why a more realistic view of health is needed. However, it should also be said that this early definition of health was important because it could be said to be 'holistic', which means that it includes all aspects of a person's health – our mental and social well-being as well as our physical state.

The later definition of health provided by the WHO (1984), describes health as

the extent to which an individual or group is able on one hand to realise aspirations and satisfy needs; and, on the other hand, to change or cope with the environment.

> Health is, therefore, seen as a resource for everyday life, not the objective of living; it is a positive concept emphasising social and personal resources, as well as physical capacities.

This identifies health as a much broader and realistic concept with the inclusion of personal and social development and the acknowledgement that there may be limitations which require people to adapt. Ewles and Simnett (1999) describe the different dimensions of health which make up this holistic approach as including emotional, spiritual and societal aspects in addition to the physical, mental and social. Seedhouse (1986) also provides a very broad definition, suggesting that

> A person's optimum state of health is equivalent to the state of the set of conditions which fulfil or enable a person to work to fulfil his or her realistic and chosen biological potentials. Some of these conditions are of the highest importance for all people. Others are variable dependent upon individual abilities and circumstances.
>
> (Seedhouse 1986, p. 76)

This definition clearly recognises that there are conditions which are required for, and factors which significantly affect, health. It acknowledges that we are all individuals and that we each have potential which may or may not be fulfilled. Seedhouse sees health as existing on a continuum, with different degrees of health being reached at a given point in time. He describes a set of central conditions and suggests that the degree to which these conditions are met will provide a foundation for the achievement of our potential. These conditions include food, drink, shelter, warmth, purpose in life, access to information about factors which affect life, the ability to use this information, and an understanding that we live and exist within the context of our environment and community.

Factors affecting health

From the discussion so far we can see that health is indeed a complex concept and just as there are many facets of a person's health there are also many factors which will have an influence upon it. In chapter 5 we considered Bronfenbrenner's ecological systems theory of child development. In the same way that this theory acknowledges the influence of both nature and nurture on the development of a child, the biological and environmental factors which affect health also need to be considered. Every child is born with a certain genetic make-up which will determine many of his or her biological features. Some of these will be immediately evident such as the sex of a child, whereas others may result in a predisposition to certain tendencies, for example the development of allergies or asthma may be subject to both genetic and environmental influences (Cross 1998, Caldwell 1997). Other factors may be purely environmental, such as the effects of poverty (Reading 1997).

A number of authors discuss the range of influences on health (Department of Health 1998, Ewles and Simnett 1999, Luker and Orr 1985, Seedhouse 1986). These have been adapted and combined to produce Figure 9.1, which illustrates possible influences on the health of a child. The model is based on the work of Ewles and Simnett (1999) who suggest that there are three levels of influence.

The inner ring represents factors at an individual level, the second ring represents factors within the immediate social and physical environment, and the third ring represents the wider social and political environment.

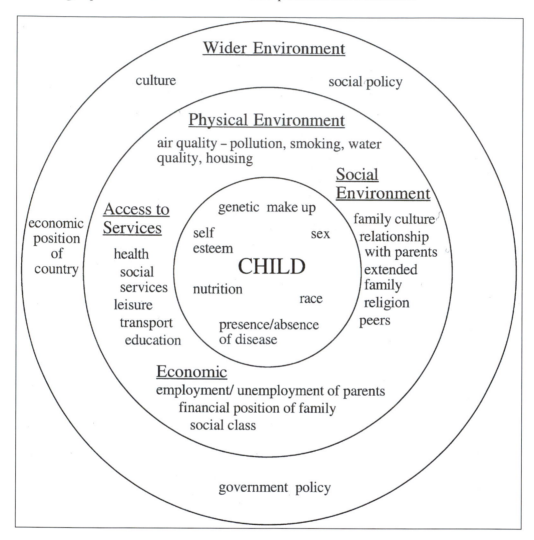

Figure 9.1 Factors influencing child health

The complexity of the many factors influencing health is acknowledged by the Government in its consultation paper *Our Healthier Nation: A Contract for Health* (Department of Health 1998). The significance of these factors can be seen in the fact that there are widening inequalities in the health of people according to their economic position, i.e. the worst off in society have a much higher incidence of ill health than those who are better off. The following case studies have been devised to provide examples of how some of these factors might influence a child's health.

Case Study 1 – Gemma

Gemma is 3 years old and is the only child of Robert and Sue, a couple in their thirties. The family live in a four bedroom house with a garden in a London suburb. Robert is an accountant and Sue is a management consultant. Gemma attends a local nursery from 8am until 12.30pm 5 days per week. Sue's parents live locally and care for Gemma in the afternoon. Gemma was born at 41 weeks gestation and weighed 3.8 kg. Sue was well throughout her pregnancy and there were no complications at delivery. Gemma was breast-fed for the first 6 months and then had a follow-on formula milk until she was a year old. As a toddler Gemma became a 'fussy eater' and still eats only a limited range of foods. She loves going to burger restaurants for a treat and eats a lot of crisps and chocolate biscuits. She will eat fruit if encouraged but says she doesn't like vegetables. Gemma has breakfast cereal in the morning before going to nursery. Although Gemma has opportunity to run around at nursery, she gets very little exercise apart from this as she tends to travel everywhere by car. At her three year development check the health visitor reassured Sue that Gemma's development was appropriate for her age, except for her weight which was above the normal range for her birthweight.

Case Study 2 – Lucy

Lucy is 3 years old and is the only child of Sarah, a single mother in her twenties. They live on the second floor of a council block in a one bedroom flat. Sarah worked in a local restaurant prior to having Lucy but has not worked since. She receives income support and housing benefit but is keen to either go to college or get a job once Lucy starts school. Lucy has just started going to nursery in the mornings and Sarah says that this has made a difference to her, although it takes quite a while to get to the nursery as it is a long walk or bus journey. There are no members of the extended family in the area. Lucy was born at 41 weeks gestation and weighed 3.0kg. Sarah was well throughout her pregnancy, although she continued to smoke, and there were no complications at delivery. Lucy was bottle fed from birth and had cow's milk from 6 months. Lucy eats most foods that she is offered and enjoys fruit and yoghurts, but her favourite food is chips. Sarah doesn't always have time for Lucy to have breakfast before going to nursery because of the journey. Lucy suffers from recurrent chest infections and her GP thinks that she is asthmatic and has referred her to the local hospital. Sarah has taken Lucy to the accident and emergency department a few times over the last couple of years, once when Lucy took some of Sarah's iron tablets and at other times for minor injuries from accidents within the home. Lucy gets lots of exercise as she and Sarah often use the stairs and walk to nursery when the weather is fine. Her development is within normal limits, although she is small for her age in relation to her birthweight.

Factors at the individual level

It is evident from the case studies that there are significant differences in the environment in which these two children live. However, even if they had experienced a more similar environment their genetic make-up would still have resulted in some differences, for example, Gemma may still have been bigger than Lucy, and Lucy may still have had asthma because of genetic influences even though these aspects of health are also influenced by the environment (Reading 1997).

Nutrition has increasingly been recognised as the most significant factor influencing child health worldwide (UNICEF 1998) and it has been placed in the centre of Figure 9.1 for this reason. Gemma is clearly not malnourished and yet her nutritional state is of concern. Given the limited range of foods that Gemma will tolerate and with such a high percentage of fat in her diet, Gemma may be developing eating habits that leave her at risk of obesity and heart disease as she gets older (Department of Health 1996). If she continues to gain excessive weight her self esteem may also be affected.

Lucy's diet may lead to iron deficiency anaemia, an increasingly common condition in children in the UK, with an estimated 1 in 8 young children suffering from it (Gregory 1995). The fact that Lucy had cow's milk from 6 months and often doesn't eat breakfast are factors which increase the likelihood of iron deficiency anaemia, whereas Gemma had breast milk and follow-on formula and also eats breakfast cereal every day, which offers some protection from this condition (MacDonald 1999).

Although race has not been mentioned in relation to the case studies it should be noted that particular groups are predisposed to certain conditions, for example girls of Indian ethnic origin are more likely to have iron deficiency anaemia than other groups (MacDonald 1999), and children of black African, black Caribbean, Asian or Mediterranean origin are more likely to have sickle cell disease (Thomas and Westerdale 1997). Guy (1998) suggests that families from ethnic minorities also have poorer access to health care provision, another factor contributing to child health which is considered in the following section.

Environmental factors – physical, social, economic and access to services

There are many aspects of the environment which could have an impact on a child's health yet they are often related and have a cumulative effect. For example Sarah is an unemployed single parent with few social support networks, which has resulted in her living in council accommodation which is cramped and basic. Lucy has therefore spent much of her time in a small flat with her mother, who has had to care for her alone without the resources to buy proper safety equipment. Given this situation it is hardly surprising that Lucy has suffered from several accidents and minor injuries which are more common in the lower social classes (Department of Health 1998). This illustrates the relationship between the physical, social and economic environment in which Lucy lives. Access to services also has an impact, as Sarah could not afford to send Lucy to nursery before she received state provision, nor could she afford to make use of local leisure services on a regular basis. Sarah smokes and she and Lucy live in an area of high pollution, affecting the physical environment. These factors will act as triggers for Lucy's asthma (Caldwell 1997). It should also be acknowledged that access to state benefits means that Sarah and Lucy are at least provided with the basics required to live, such as food, warmth and shelter. However, some would argue that this provision is so basic that Sarah and Lucy effectively live in a state of poverty (Reading 1997).

In Gemma's case her parents are financially secure and have a supportive social network which includes the extended family. They live in a large house with a garden, providing lots of space for Gemma to play, and they have the resources to provide a safe environment for her. The family have their own car and easy access to leisure, health and education services. These factors contribute to Gemma's relatively good health, but as we have already identified, Gemma's diet has resulted in her being overweight and this is exacerbated by her lack of exercise. This raises the issue that access to a positive environment does not automatically result in it being utilised. For example, Gemma's parents can afford to provide her with a well balanced diet, yet this is not what she eats, Gemma has access to a garden yet makes little use of it and hardly has any exercise. It seems ironic that through lack of transport and living in a second floor flat Lucy has much more exercise than Gemma. Family culture, lifestyle and the attitudes of parents have a major influence on the child, not least because in the early years it is the parents and family who will direct a child's activities. The interplay between these factors is significant because it also influences how we approach seeking to improve a child's health as we will see later.

Wider social and political factors

The overall economic position of a country has an impact on the health of the population because it affects so many of the factors which influence health (UNICEF 1998). Government policy, legislation and social policy all can have a direct influence on the health of children. One such example is the new Sure Start initiative through which the Government aims to improve the life chances of young children in disadvantaged areas. Each programme will provide outreach and home visiting, support for parents on parenting skills, good quality play, learning and child care, primary and community health care for parents and children, and support for families with special needs (Eisenstadt 1999). The opportunity to participate in such a programme would certainly be of benefit to Lucy. At a more general level, legislation and policies related to issues such as pollution or physical exercise in schools will affect both Gemma and Lucy.

Health promotion

Having considered the definitions of health and the factors which influence it we now turn to the subject of promoting health. Downie *et al.* (1996) suggest that health promotion is essentially about both preventing ill health and encouraging positive health. It is now widely accepted that this cannot simply be a job for people employed for the task. Just as the Government recognises the complex factors affecting health, it also acknowledges that there are a number of levels at which health promotion should take place. For example at a national level there is a role for legislation, the development of policies which will have an impact on the factors which influence health and national advertising campaigns. At a local or community level there is a role for ensuring provision of accessible health, leisure and education services and the development of initiatives to establish healthy workplaces, schools and neighbourhoods. At an individual level people need to be able to respond to the opportunities made available to them and take some responsibility for their own health (Department of Health 1998).

Hall (1996) outlines the recommended provision of child health services, including immunisations, development checks, screening and health education. It is noted that the term 'child health promotion' has replaced 'child health surveillance' in order to acknowledge the increased emphasis on activity which prevents ill health and encourages positive health, rather than simply detecting problems. As identified earlier, Hall suggests that all people working with children have a role in promoting their health through being equipped to offer appropriate support and advice. We would argue that this role could be even further expanded so that positive health is actively encouraged through the curriculum, health education, and role modelling of a healthy environment as suggested by the Department of Health (1998).

For early years practitioners in early years settings there are many opportunities to provide information for both parents and children in relation to subjects such as nutrition, exercise, accident prevention and access to health services. In addition to this, and perhaps more importantly, there is the opportunity to provide a healthy environment through the provision of nutritious food, ensuring that all children engage in regular physical activity, and observing safety regulations. The modelling of positive relationships is important in encouraging children to develop a high self esteem, which is not only important to their emotional, mental and social health, but will also influence their attitude towards their physical health (Strecher *et al.* 1986). In addition to their influence on the child and their immediate environment, the early years practitioner can act as an advocate at a community and national level through being aware of the many factors which affect a child's health and speaking out when policies and legislation may have an influence (e.g. in relation to provision of free milk or school meals, access to nursery places).

Health promotion in practice

We return to our case studies to consider what promoting child health in practice might look like. Both children have needs related to improving their diet and could benefit from beginning to learn about healthy eating through activities at their nurseries. However, for any health education to be effective in bringing about change in behaviour, the people to whom it is directed need to reach a point of being ready to change and to then follow this through (see Ewles and Simnett 1999, pp. 263–5 'Stages of changing behaviour'). As we suggested earlier, parents exert so much influence over their child's activities and lifestyle that it is crucial that any health education is addressed to both the child and the parents.

Gemma has lunch with her grandparents and dinner at home, so it is not only Gemma's parents but also her grandparents who will influence her diet. If the whole family tends to have a high fat diet it is important that they are all prepared to modify their eating habits. If it is unrealistic for Gemma to walk rather than travel by car, she could join some kind of activity club, such as swimming or dance. Gemma could also be encouraged to join in with some of the more physical activities at nursery. The health visitor may already have advised Gemma's parents about a healthy diet and the need for more exercise, but this could be reinforced by nursery staff. Gemma and her family may benefit from some advice from a dietician, which could be arranged through the GP. It is important to recognise that there is a multi-disciplinary team of people who could be involved in promoting Gemma's health and to ensure all members work together. If Gemma's parents were keen for her to adopt a new eating and exercise pattern it may be appropriate for the health visitor or dietician to discuss this with the nursery.

In Lucy's case one simple change which would have an impact on her overall nutritional state would be to have breakfast, as a significant amount of iron, vitamins and minerals are contained in breakfast cereals. If it is not possible for Sarah to provide this, perhaps the nursery could consider starting a breakfast club (Department of Health 1998). The provision of health education to both Lucy and her mother may not necessarily result in a significant change, as their diet may also be limited by cost and access to shops with affordable healthy food (Lang and Caraher 1998). This would therefore require change at a local and national level, in order to address the underlying poverty experienced by the family (Lang and Caraher 1998, Reading 1997). One way of increasing the family budget for food would be if Sarah could give up smoking, although the complexities of this should be acknowledged (Reading 1997). It is likely that Sarah would need considerable support through her GP, Health Visitor and friends if this were to be achieved, however she has attempted to give up before and may be willing to try again.

Finally, involvement in a wider scheme such as Sure Start which seeks to provide a high level of support from health, education and child care agencies may well provide Sarah and Lucy with the capacity to make some significant improvements in their health. This illustrates well the need for early years workers to contribute to an intergrated approach to health promotion for young children, working in partnership with other agencies.

References

Caldwell, C. (1997) 'Management of acute asthma in children', *Paediatric Nursing* **9** (6), 29–32.

Cross, S. (1998) 'The foundations of allergy', *Paediatric Nursing* **10** (1), 37–41.

Department of Health (1996) *Key Facts on Health of the Nation and Young People.* London: HMSO.

Department of Health (1998) *Our Healthier Nation: A Contract for Health.* London: The Stationery Office.

Downie, R.S. *et al.* (1996) *Health Promotion Models and Values.* Oxford: Oxford University Press.

Eisenstadt, N. (1999) 'Sure Start: a new approach for children under 4'. *Primary Health Care* **9** (6), 26–27.

Ewles, L. and Simnett, I. (1999) *Promoting Health: A Practical Guide*, 4th edn. London: Baillière Tindall.

Gregory, J. (1995) *National Diet and Nutrition Survey: Aged 1.5 to 4.5 Years. Report of the Diet and Nutrition Survey*.1. London: HMSO.

Guy, I. (1998) 'Equal opportunities, welfare and child health: a review', *Journal of Child Health Care* **2** (2), 76–79.

Hall, D. (1996) *Health for All Children. Report of the Third Joint Working Party on Child Health Surveillance,* 3rd edn. Oxford: Oxford University Press.

Lang, T. and Caraher, M. (1998) 'Access to healthy foods: part II. Food poverty and shopping deserts: what are the implications for health promotion policy and practice?', *Health Education Journal* **57,** 202–211.

Luker, K. and Orr, J. (1985) *Health Visiting.* Oxford: Blackwell Scientific Publications.

MacDonald, A. (1999) 'Iron deficiency in infants and children', *Primary Health Care* **9** (6), 18–24.

Reading, R. (1997) 'Poverty and the health of children and adolescents', *Archives of Disease in Childhood* **76**, 463–467.

Seedhouse, D. (1986) *Health: The Foundations for Achievement.* Chichester: John Wiley & Sons.

Strecher, V. J. *et al.* (1986) 'The role of self efficacy in achieving health behaviour change', *Health Education Quarterly* **13** (1), 73–91.

Thomas, V. N. and Westerdale, N. (1997) 'Sickle Cell Anaemia', *Paediatric Nursing* **9** (5), 29–34.

UNICEF (1998) *The State of the World's Children.* Oxford: Oxford University Press.

World Health Organization (1948) Constitution

World Health Organization (1984) Health Promotion: a WHO discussion document on the concepts and principles. Summary report in: *Community Medicine* 7 (1) 73–76, 1985.

Chapter 10

Bilingual children in the pre-school years: different experiences of early learning

Rose Drury

Introduction

All the principles for early years education set out in the Early Learning Goals (QCA 1999) have important implications for practitioners working with bilingual children. For example, while the precept that no child should be disadvantaged 'because of his or her race, culture, religion, home language' (p. 5) will not be new to early years educators, the explicitness of the statement will lead many practitioners to review their provision. Similarly, the principle that within a carefully stuctured early years curriculum there should be 'provision for the different starting points from which children develop their learning' (p. 5) has particular significance for bilingual children.

These principles are reinforced in the aims set out for the new foundation stage for early learning. A central aim is to 'foster personal, social and emotional well-being' through 'promoting an inclusive ethos and providing opportunities for each child to become a valued member of that group and community so that a strong self-image and self-esteem are promoted' (p. 9). This statement, like the other aims for early learning at the foundation stage, may be seen in the light of the government's intention for education to be 'inclusive' and to provide equality of opportunity. The phrase 'each child' therefore includes children from all social and cultural backgrounds, 'different ethnic groups' and 'diverse linguistic backgrounds' (p. 13). In the United Kingdom approximately 8.5% of children in primary school have English as an additional language (EAL) and they present a wide diversity of linguistic, cultural and learning experiences when they enter formal schooling.

This chapter explores the implications of this key aim for those bilingual children who are at a very early stage in their learning of English. It contrasts the different experiences of early schooling for a monolingual and a bilingual child by focusing on three significant aspects of their early learning: first their experience is viewed in the light of their need to learn about the expectations and procedural rules in early years settings; second they are seen in the context of learning that enables them to build on their home experience; third, opportunities for language learning are considered. The monolingual child, who conforms to the expectations, is used as a reference point and her experience is contrasted with a bilingual child who is at an early stage in her learning of English. The differences in the experience of the two children suggests that early years practitioners need to take into account the distinctive learning situation of bilingual children if they are to ensure inclusive education on the basis of equality of opportunity.

The presentation of the two children draws on data which is part of a wider ethnographic study of young bilingual children learning in nursery and at home (Drury 1997a, 1997b, 2000). Both children attend a multi-ethnic primary school in Watford, Hertfordshire, where approximately 30% of the 266 pupils on roll are bilingual and mainly of Pakistani background.

Nina

One of the two children used to highlight different experiences of early schooling is Nina, whose mother tongue is English. She is four years old, and the second and youngest child in her family. Her mother is a single parent who works full-time. Nina is looked after by her grandmother before and after school and she previously attended a local playgroup.

Nazma

The second child is Nazma who is nearly four years old. There are six children in the family and they all attend the same nursery and primary school. Nazma is the youngest child in the family. Unlike Nina, she has not attended a playgroup or any other pre-school setting. Her family originates from Azad Kashmir which borders North-East Pakistan, and her mother tongue is Pahari (a Punjabi dialect spoken in this area). Nazma uses Pahari with all members of the family. She was born in Watford and entered nursery as a developing bilingual child who did not share the language or culture of the school.

The expectations and procedural rules in the nursery

Parallel to the explicit language and learning curriculum, children are expected to understand and operate within a set of procedural rules (Street and Street 1993). The learning context is 'constructed' and structured by cultural norms and rules. In a case study of a nursery, Cochran-Smith (1984), describes and analyses the nursery school day according to the norms expected in the organisation of time and space. Firstly the nursery session is structured around periods of activity often called 'times', for example, 'story time', 'tidy up time'. Secondly, there is consistent use of materials and activities in different special areas of the nursery, for example, the use of small imaginative play materials on the carpet area. Cochran-Smith states that 'children came to expect a particular set of rules for each kind of activity at the nursery school, and became accustomed to using different interactional and interpretive norms for different activities.' (1994 p. 70)

As Nina and Nazma enter nursery, they encounter the rules and expectations of their new social world. Haste (1987) states that 'in acquiring these rules, the child learns the basis for interactions with others, and the shared cultural framework for making sense of the world' (1987, p. 163). The acquisition of these rules, the ability to interact with others, and the understanding of the shared cultural framework represent very different tasks for Nina and Nazma.

Nina

The following extract is taken from a two-hour recording session in the nursery. It may be taken as typical of the way Nina is able to engage in the setting not long after she has entered the nursery.

Key: N: Nina. S: Sara (one of the children Nina is playing with).
[Nina is playing at the sand tray with 3 boys, including Ben and Joe]

1 N:	I'm putting in sugar
2	sugar, milk
3 S:	sugar
4 N:	can I have a bit of the milk?
5	thank you
6	you can have a bit of sugar
7	there we are
8	there's some sugar
9	now, we're putting juice, OK
10	we're putting juice on our cake
11 S:	I made a pie
12	I made a pie
13 N:	that's good
14	there's juice in our cake
15	scrubeddy dub
16 S:	dub dub
17 N:	dub dub scrubeddy dub
18	what's that?
19	this is milk?
20	some milk in
21 S:	margarine
22 N:	now, I need margarine in first
23	putting in margarine my cake
24	a little bit of water
25	shall we put some sand in water?

From this transcript, we can see some of the implicit rules which children are expected to understand and follow in the early years setting. One expectation is that children can play independently and with others, learning about the importance of sharing and co-operating and discovering things for themselves, as cognitive development takes place through 'active learning'. They are learning about operating within the culture of the early years setting which for many children like Nina will be close to their home culture. Then they are expected to choose an activity. Nina knew immediately what to choose and said, 'I want to play in the sand.' They are also expected to be able to participate in the play activities. In the sticking example, Nina joins in and has the confidence to ask and pick up what is expected. Lastly, children are expected to understand the rules of the early years setting. Nina knows that only four children are allowed to play in the sand at one time. At one point in the recording she asks, 'shall we put some sand in the water?' and knows that they are not allowed to put water in the dry sand. Her friend replies, 'no, I'll be told off'. Nina is very much at home in the culture of the nursery. We can see that she is able to engage and she has self-motivation. The tasks are consistent with her knowledge of English and with her existing experience. She is doing what is expected.

Nazma

The vignette presented below is a composite picture of events over several weeks when Nazma first joined the nursery.

Nazma enters nursery holding her sister's hand. Her sister, Yasmin (aged 4½), moves over to the large carpet where the children sit with the nursery teacher at the beginning of every session. Nazma follows her, chewing her dress, staying close to her sister and watching everything. She stopped crying during the fifth week at nursery and she now comes every afternoon. The children listen to the teacher talking about caterpillars and many join in the discussion in English. Nazma is silent. Mrs Raja, (Bilingual Classroom Assistant), enters the nursery. She gathers a small group of Pahari-speaking children together to share a book. This activity had been planned with the nursery teacher and was linked to the current topic. The children switch into Pahari for this activity. Nazma listens and points to a picture of a dog (kutha) and cat (billee) in an Urdu alphabet picture book, but does not speak. They go outside to play. Nazma stands on the outside watching the other children and holds Mrs Raja's hand. She has learnt the climbing frame routine and repeats the climbing and sliding activity several times. The children go inside and choose from a range of play activities. Nazma watches. She stays at an activity for one minute and moves on. This is repeated several times. She then wanders around the room sucking her fingers. It is story time on the carpet. The children sit and listen to the story of 'The Very Hungry Caterpillar' (Carle 1986). Nazma sits close to her sister and watches. Their mother appears at the door and they go home. (Drury 1997b)

What are the factors that affect Nazma's limited engagement in the early years setting after five weeks in nursery? From a sequence of observations made over this period, the following points were noted:

- there is no evidence of co-operative support for her from other children;
- there is no evidence of any one-to-one contact with the teacher;
- engagement is wholly dependent on the presence of Mrs Raja who enables her to listen to Pahari although she does not speak herself;
- she listens to English in use in the context of a general discussion and of a story: however there is no evidence of understanding or of any support for her through English;
- there is no evidence that the cultural assumptions made in the nursery are being made explicit to Nazma.

For Nazma, the acquisition of procedural rules, the ability to interact with others, and the understanding of the shared cultural framework, which are essential for successful engagement in the early years setting, are dependent on her acquisition of English. At the same time her learning of English depends upon being able to interpret the rules and the culture of the nursery, and upon being able to interact with her peers. Tabors (1997) refers to this situation faced by many developing bilingual children as a 'double bind'. The learning tasks that Nazma faces are interdependent. Moreover all are necessary for cognitive development to take place in the context of the early years setting. In emphasising the role of the interpersonal social process, Vygotsky (1978) encapsulated the inter-relationship of these aspects of learning. He argued that the 'social' world operates at two levels. 'Firstly at the *interpersonal level* at which the child, through the *medium of language* as well as through *action*, experiences *concepts*-in-practice . . . and the sociohistorical system within which cultural meaning develops over time.' (1978, p. 173)

Match or mis-match: building on home experience

Nina

In the sand play example we can see that Nina is able to draw on her home experiences and knowledge of cake making. Firstly, she knows the ingredients for the cake and the appropriate lexis (margarine, milk, sugar, eggs) and knows that you 'stir' cakes. Secondly, she is able to use chunks of language from home (for example, lines 4–10). She is able to engage fully in the imaginative play over a sustained period of time (approximately 25 minutes for the whole sand play sequence) and exploit the learning experience. Thirdly, as can been seen in the following example, she is able to draw upon her knowledge of traditional stories ('The Gingerbread Man') and she knows about written language. As she engages in her 'writing' about the gingerbread man, her oral language reflects the language 'the gingerbread man is running away and he is not coming back'.

[Nina plays in the home corner with two Gujerati speakers]

1. Ch.1:that's a gingerbread man
2. Nina:I need to get one of these and get the mouth out and nose and get two eyes out and get the hair out and I need to get the legs out
3.   there we are
4.   now I need to get the arms out
5.   I just put in the oven
6.   we need to put some meat in my oven
7.   I need to put something down
   [Nina starts 'writing']
8.   the gingerbread man is running away and he is not coming back
9.   hello, I writing something about a gingerbread man and he's not going to come back from his home, he's running away from the home and he is not coming . . .

Nazma

Nazma's limited engagement at this point in time may not only be caused by her inability to use English: a further mismatch for her is between her home experience and the early years setting. The following information, drawn from interviews, provides some insights into what discontinuity might mean for Nazma, and shows that the school and the parents have different perspectives.

Nazma's early learning experiences have focused on playing with her siblings, and other members of the extended family who visit frequently. She enjoys dressing up and taking part in role play activities with siblings at home. She also watches, helps and talks to her mother when preparing and cooking food. Both her grandmother and mother tell her stories from their childhood, drawing on an oral tradition which is not recorded in written form. She has heard her older siblings talking in English and seen their school reading books at home. She has watched them preparing for Koranic classes, reciting verses in Arabic after school and seen the Arabic primers and Holy Koran read by all older members of the family. From the family's perspective, Nazma's mother has high aspirations for her daughter and wants her to achieve well in the education system. She has very little understanding of how children learn by play at nursery; and she relies on the school to give Nazma the educational skills she requires.

The school expects parents to understand and respond to its communications, to support what it is trying to achieve with the curriculum and to assist their child's learning at home. From the school's point of view, Nazma's mother is unable to communicate in English and she is not seen as supported in her school learning at home. The difficulties she and her siblings experience at school are explained in terms of cultural and language difficulties.

When Nazma enters the early years setting, she does not have the necessary English language knowledge and skills to engage with the social and learning experiences, and the cultural norms and behaviour implicitly expected by the nursery are different from Nazma's home experiences and difficult for her to interpret and understand. This point is underlined by the fact that, although she takes part in role play with confidence at home, she is unable to engage in the learning activities, including role play, in the early years setting. However, the potential for Nazma to engage and to learn in a similar way to Nina is shown in the following extract taken from tape recordings of Nazma at nursery during her first term. Mrs Raja and Nazma discuss a counting book in Pahari.

Mrs Raja:	What's this?
Nazma:	lemon, yuk I don't like that [making a face]
Mrs Raja:	Don't you like it, because it's sour?
Nazma:	yes
Mrs Raja & Nazma:	1, 2, 3 green apples [counting together]
Mrs Raja & Nazma:	1, 2, 3, 4 pears [counting together]
Nazma:	We eat them, we like them
	we get them, we go to a shop and we buy apples and pears . . .

Nazma:
We went to the shops with mum and Hasnan
and we bought lollies.
We had Hasnan's birthday.
We went in a big 'mosque' and there were lots of people,
[the 'mosque' is in fact a hall]
friends and everybody there.
There was cake.
I went with Hasnan to the shops.

(Drury 1997a)

The interaction with Mrs Raja, the bilingual classroom assistant, illustrates the importance of drawing on Nazma's home experience. It enables her to talk about her family and to retell significant events from her home life with an adult who shares her linguistic and cultural background.

Language and learning

Nina

In all of this learning, language is crucial because the use of language goes hand in hand with Nina's cognitive development. Firstly, there is a considerable amount of repetition, and her language, because it is her mother tongue, is freely available to her as a non-conscious resource to draw on. There are plenty of opportunities for the practice and extension of language itself and for directing and shaping thinking. She uses language as a kind of commentary on what she is doing and that is why it reinforces and lends purpose to what she is doing, for example in the Home Corner (lines 2–8). Secondly, language reinforces the activity, creates order for her and lends purpose to what she is doing, for example in the sand play, 'now I need margarine first'. It also enables her to respond to other children and to adapt her imaginative scenario as she goes along. She picks up on 'margarine' from another child adapting to this new idea. Nina interacts freely with her friends at the sand play, often leading the conversation and asking questions. Thirdly, the language helps to structure the activity, as in the sand play example, enabling her to progress in a sequence (sugar, juice, milk, margarine). She can also play with the sounds of the language (for example, 'scrubbeddy dub') while she stirs the cake. Lastly, Nina initiates interactions with adults in the early years setting as the following example shows.

[Nina comes up to nursery nurse (NN) and asks about the sticking activity]

1. N: what's she doing?
2. what's the person doing?
3. NN: making a house, a picture of the house to go in the home corner
4. we're making the home corner into the 3 bears' cottage
5. we're going to do a nice picture on the wall
6. N: can I do one?

In this example, she is able to ask the appropriate questions to enable her to begin to participate in the activity. She has learned what is required to take part in such interactions and exploits these learning opportunities successfully.

Nazma

The interaction with Mrs Raja illustrates the importance of providing opportunities for the use of mother tongue in the nursery. The conversation enables Nazma to talk about her family and to retell significant cultural and religious events from her home life. The opportunity to share a book with Mrs Raja provides the appropriate context for Nazma tell her personal story with fluency and at length. She knows that Mrs Raja will be able to interpret the meaning of her stories and she is able to express her thoughts and extend her mother tongue use. The crucial role of bilingual staff in the nursery is highlighted here as this is the only occasion when Nazma is able to show that she can meet some of the expectations of speaking and listening in the Early Learning Goals set out by QCA (1999). For example she is able to 'use talk to organise, sequence and clarify . . . . events' and she can 'speak clearly and audibly with confidence . . .'. However Nazma is dependent on the presence of a bilingual classroom assistant for this and there is no other evidence of support for her acquisition of competence in English during this period.

Nazma's early socialisation has taken place in her mother tongue. So, when she enters nursery, there is an abrupt change of both language and cultural expectations. In an English language environment, she is effectively dispossessed of her ability to communicate and the effect of this on a four year old can be profoundly disturbing. Indeed, if Nazma happened to attend a session when the bilingual classroom assistant was not present, she would be left largely to her own devices. In making this provision her school is meeting the expectations set out for the foundation stage that 'practitioners should help children who are learning English as an additional language to make the best possible progress' by 'building on children's experiences of language at home and in the wider community', by 'providing bilingual support in particular to extend vocabulary' and by 'providing opportunities for children to hear their home languages as well as in English . . .' (p. 16)

We have already seen the 'double bind' for Nazma of needing to socialise in order to learn English, and at the same time of having insufficient English language knowledge to enable interaction with other children to take place. She needs to progress in her English language development quickly in order to be able to benefit from a formal education context. Paying attention to English language learning goes hand in hand with finding ways of building on home experience and of developing first language knowledge.

Conclusion

This chapter has highlighted the differential impact of the rules and expectations in early years settings through the contrasting experience of two children. It has shown that there is a mutual dependency between the expectations built into the culture of the early years setting, the match between home and school experience and opportunities for language learning. The process is complex. First, the culture of the nursery is embedded in its rules and expectations (Haste 1987), and these in turn are part of the culture of the wider society (Vygotsky's sociohistorical system). The norms of the culture in the early years setting are not necessarily made explicit and come to be understood through patterns of behaviour, and the language used to express approval or disapproval, often through subtle and indirect forms which are difficult for a developing bilingual child to interpret. Second, the ability to engage positively is also dependent on building on known experience and on being able to interact with people who share and understand this experience. Third, social interaction through the medium of English is central to learning in the nursery. Fourth, cognitive development is stimulated by the learning that takes place through activities which are supported through language use (as we saw with Nina's monologue in the Home Corner), on social interactions with peers, and on listening and responding to adults. The use of English is central to these four aspects of learning in the early years setting. For Nazma, all represent discontinuities for her development. But while she is not able to engage through English, we have seen the contrast when she is able to interact with a bilingual adult. If she is to experience any success at this stage, such interaction is vital for her linguistic, cognitive and social development. It is equally important that the process of learning English takes place as quickly as possible.

In order to meet the aims of the foundation stage for all children, practitioners need to ensure that the provision is genuinely 'inclusive', and to consider what equality of opportunity towards these aims might mean for developing bilingual children. Genessee (1995) sums up changing attitudes towards the difficulties faced by minority ethnic pupils in terms of moving from a deficit view to one which accepts their background 'as simply different'. This is still essentially a negative characterisation of the learners 'which calls for changes in the children and their families if the matches between home and school are to be reduced and redressed'. He argues that 'we must get beyond simplistic notions of difference. We must come to know and understand the backgrounds of these learners in the same ways and to the same extent as those of majority group learners.'

Implications for practice

The issues raised for bilingual children like Nazma in this chapter have implications for early years practitioners as well as for policy makers. The following features of good practice would make for a more effective response to the distinctive needs of bilingual children at an early stage in their learning of English. They offer some steps towards interpreting the implications of the principles of the Early Learning Goals and the aims of the foundation stage for bilingual children.

- Through home visits, parents' involvement in the early years setting and discussion with bilingual adults, staff are able to draw on some of the bilingual child's home experiences and interests. Activities which are familiar to the bilingual child are included.
- Bilingual staff, or other bilingual adults, spend time on a planned basis using mother tongue for routine classroom interactions.
- There are activities to encourage other children in the setting to interact with the bilingual child and assist in her developing social and language skills.
- The aims and expectations of the early years provision are made explicit to the bilingual child and her parents, and the parents' views and expectations for the education of their child are sought.
- Bilingual staff build on the bilingual child's cognitive development in the home context and extend the child's range and use of her mother tongue.
- All adults are clear about when and why mother tongue is being used because it is included in the curriculum statement and is the subject of the ongoing planning of provision.
- An informed knowledge of the development of English as an additional language in young children underpins the educational provision for the bilingual child.
- Planning takes place to exploit language development opportunities in early years activities and there is a focus on language objectives in all areas of the curriculum.

References

Cochran-Smith, M. (1984) *The Making of a Reader*. Norwood, New Jersey: Ablex Publishing Corporation.

Drury, R. (1997a) 'Two Sisters at School: Issues for Educators of Young Bilingual Children', in Gregory, E. (ed.) *One Child, Many Worlds: Early Learning in Multicultural Communities*, 33–46. London: David Fulton Publishers.

Drury, R. (1997b) 'Bilingual Children in the Pre-school Years: Desirable Outcomes for Learning?', in Leung, C. and Cable, C. (eds) *English as an Additional Language: Changing Perspectives*, 65–76. Watford: National Association for Language Development In the Curriculum

Drury, R. (forthcoming) 'Bilingual Children in the Nursery: A Case Study of Samia at Home and at School', *European Early Childhood Education Research Journal*, **8** (1).

Genessee, F. (1995) *Growing up Bilingual: Language Development in the Preschool Years*. Plenary talk at the TESOL (Teachers of English to Speakers of Other Languages) Conference at Longbeach, CA. 1995. Audio-tape: Virginia, U.S.A.: TESOL.

Haste, H. (1987) 'Growing into Rules', in Bruner, J. and Haste, H. (eds) *Making Sense: The Child's Construction of the World*, 163–195. London: Methuen.

Qualifications and Curriculum Authority (1999) *Early Learning Goals*. London: Qualifications and Curriculum Authority.

Street, C. and Street, B. (1984) 'The Schooling of Literacy' in Murphy, P., *et al.* (eds) *Subject Learning in the Primary Curriculum: Issues in English, Science and Mathematics*, 75–88. London and New York: The Open University and Routledge.

Tabors, P. (1997) *One Child, Two Languages: A Guide for Preschool Educators of Children Learning English as a Second Language.* Baltimore, MD: Paul Brookes Publishing Co.

Vygotsky, L. (1978) *Mind in Society: The Development of Higher Psychological Processes.* Cambridge, Mass: Harvard University Press.

Children's book

Carle, E. (1986) *The Very Hungry Caterpillar.* London: Hamish Hamilton.

Chapter 11

Working with parents in early years settings

Cindy Willey

Introduction

Parents are children's first and most enduring educators. When parents and practitioners work together in early years settings, the results have a positive impact on the child's development and learning. Therefore each setting should seek to develop an effective partnership with parents (QCA 1999, p. 17).

Working with parents demands a commitment of time and energy which some maintain would be best spent directly with the children. This chapter explores one nursery school's approach to developing parental involvement and argues that as parents and carers are the key players in children's lives, early years practitioners can best promote children's development by working closely with parents.

My first experience of nursery education was as a parent rather than a practitioner. I had taught for five years in primary schools, having trained as an infant/junior teacher. The schools I had taught in had no nurseries. Parents bringing their children to school were asked to leave them in the playground and wait behind the fence. The bell went at 8.55 and children lined up to go into class. At the end of the school day parents collected their children from the playground. Parents were invited into school for assemblies and once a term for 'parents' evenings' when teachers told parents how their child was progressing. Some parents were invited into school to help with practical tasks like cutting paper and washing paint pots. There was an understanding among staff that there were only a few parents who could fulfil this role and fit into the school without being intrusive.

As a young and inexperienced teacher I accepted this pattern of contact without question. I knew that the home environment had an important influence on the child's learning and saw 'good' parents as those who heard their child read daily, in line with the school's policy. Communication between home and school was largely formal, consisting of letters informing parents of school events that they were invited to support, and notes from parents to explain their child's absences.

When my son was three, I took up a part time post in a primary school. The nursery class attached to the school was happy to accept him while I was teaching. I had expected that I would hand Matthew over at the door and retreat quickly, but I was welcomed into the nursery and stayed while he settled to play. I was overwhelmed by the purposeful way the children were engaging in play and by the staff's interest in my perspective. Staff listened as parents talked about family events, ranging from visits and holidays to how their child wouldn't get dressed this morning and the row that ensued. Staff, armed with information about the detail in children's lives, responded to children sensitively. They matched the experiences they planned for children at nursery using their knowledge of children's lives.

My own experience as a parent gave me a different insight into children's learning and Matthew's nursery demonstrated a different way of communicating with parents that acknowledged their role in their child's education. I was caused to reflect on the procedures in place in my previous schools that prevented parents from participating in their children's education. I recognised that I needed to develop my understanding of young children's learning and how parents and practitioners can work together to help children learn.

Working with parents at Wall Hall Nursery School

Learning is a lifelong journey. Twenty years later, having been at Wall Hall Nursery School for the last twelve years, I am still looking for ways of developing work with families. In sharp contrast with my early teaching experience, working with parents is integrated into every aspect of the nursery as the description of Elizabeth's session demonstrates.

Elizabeth jumps down from the bus saying to Yvette, the nursery nurse greeting the children 'My mummy's here today, it's my mummy's turn!' Tracey, Elizabeth's mother, helps the children take off their seatbelts and gather their bags. In the nursery, Elizabeth sits on a big chair, saving the one next to her for her mum, while the rest of the children sit on the carpet for large group time. Tracey relays the messages from other parents at the bus stop and looks through the children's bags while the nursery nurse fills in the register. Tracey asks Yvette if Elizabeth has been all right at nursery because her brother is having difficulties at school and the morning routine has been disrupted. Yvette assures her that Elizabeth has been fine but the nursery staff will be particularly vigilant in observing her responses during nursery. Tracey and Yvette then sit down to look at Elizabeth's nursery diary. There are photos of Elizabeth in a variety of dressing up clothes and one of her work with playdough which she had layered into a basket, covering the top with tissue paper and there is a sheet of paper covered with blue paint. Tracey comments 'she's still covering things at nursery as well then'. She describes the game Elizabeth plays every day where she takes off all the cushions from the furniture and builds them around herself and her dolls. Tracey has brought the card Elizabeth made for her dad's birthday, heavily covered with black pen. 'She drew a lovely picture then scribbled all over it, I was really upset, then I remembered how she'd been playing at nursery and I asked her why she covered it, she told me so daddy couldn't see it, is for a surprise'. Yvette asks Tracey if she would like to sit with a group of children rolling out pastry to make jam turnovers or if she would prefer to be alongside Elizabeth for the session. Tracey agrees to make pastry 'if I know Elizabeth, she'll be there, covering up the jam!' Tracey works alongside the staff and children through the session, giving time to Elizabeth when she needs it. At the end of the session Elizabeth passes round the bowl of apples to the children and sits on mummy's knee for the story.

Tracey plays an important role in the nursery when she comes in with Elizabeth. She helps practically with aspects of the nursery routine, she helps children in their activities and shares her daughter's nursery session. She knows who Elizabeth plays with and what she enjoys most. Tracey feels able to talk about home issues that she is worried about, recognising the possible impact on Elizabeth. She has an understanding of the framework the nursery uses for observing children (using schemas, referred to later in the chapter), she knows that Elizabeth is exploring an enveloping pattern and this has helped her support Elizabeth's learning.

After many years of staff working together at Wall Hall Nursery School, we feel we have found a way to work effectively with parents that fits with the constraints of our setting. We are able to talk openly with parents about their children's learning. Parents usually come to nursery with their own agenda for discussion. This dialogue enables staff to understand more about child and the parent to understand more about learning. Children benefit from this enhanced awareness of their learning 24 hours a day, whether cared for by parents or practitioners.

There is no single model for working with parents that would meet the needs of every setting. However I hope that by looking at the details of the approach developed at Wall Hall Nursery, important elements will emerge which can be used to inform other settings. The tradition of working closely with parents at Wall Hall Nursery School has been made easier because children are brought to the nursery by coach and parents form a rota to supervise children on the journey to and from nursery. The University campus on which the nursery is sited is distant from areas of housing and parents need to stay at nursery for the whole session. Staff and parents do not have the benefit of daily contact, but effective relationships are quickly established with all families. Some parents may not initially see the benefits of being involved in a nursery session, but all parents recognise the necessity of looking after children travelling to school by coach. Working parents make considerable efforts to come into nursery and childminders, grandparents or other adults significant to the child sometimes attend.

Two developments have been particularly significant in enabling the parents and practitioners to share understanding. The first, a practical issue, was the development of a vehicle for recording children's learning, the nursery diary.

The nursery diary

Highly skilled nursery practitioners have always maintained a tradition of careful observation of children, discussion with other members of staff and planning the environment to take forward children's learning. While regular discussions with parents were useful, parents and children did not have access to the process through which staff planned for children. After looking at different models for recording, we decided to use an informal diary approach for each child. An A4 card file/scrap book was made and photographs, children's work and observations written by staff and parents were recorded in it. The diary provides a child centred focus for staff/parent discussions. Photographs provide evidence that the child is learning through play in a variety of different areas.

Staff comments draw out important aspects of the children's learning and parents sometimes bring in pictures the child has done at home. The diary provides a record which children can read and reflect on their achievements. Summaries of each term's achievements are recorded under the desirable outcomes headings (SCAA 1996), on a 'focus sheet' with an added paragraph describing the child's attitudes to learning. Planned learning targets are discussed with parents, who make verbal or written contributions to the 'focus sheet'. Parents usually come into nursery every three weeks and staff ensure that recent observations are recorded to discuss with parents on their visit. Parents usually take it home to look at with partners, friends and family members.

Schemas

The second development was brought about by using schemas as a framework for observing children. Chris Athey (1990) described how observable patterns in children's play could be identified and used to promote their learning. Athey asserts that while children's play may seem like random, anarchic behaviour, by observing their actions it is possible to recognise patterns which underlie their activities and connect them. The nursery had always used observation as a basis for analysing children's development, but observations tended to focus on how the child was making meaning of the world rather than noticing their physical actions, as the following observations of Emma and Tim demonstrate.

Emma

Emma went straight to the home corner and *put on* a long dress and hat. She *put* a doll, a telephone, pens and paper *in* a pram and *covered* them up. Emma painted a house and *covered* her picture with a layer of black paint, 'its night time', she explained.

Before our awareness of schema theory we would have regarded Emma's play as role play based on the home. We would have provided more experiences to help extend her home based play, e.g. encouraged her to notice the doll's house, invited visits from a parent with a baby. The words in italic, in the observation, describe the actions Emma performs and indicate the schema she is exploring: enveloping. With this insight we would now encourage Emma to look at other forms of covering that will extend her range of interests, e.g. making pies or looking at creatures that live under the ground.

Tim

During a nursery session, Tim played with the small cars, fiercely guarding the cars with trailers and articulated lorries. He *put together* a complicated train track that went under tables and chairs but managed to *join* it to make a closed shape. In the garden he rode a bike to which he had *connected* a trolley with string. Later he *sellotaped* the large plastic blocks *together* saying 'its to stop people going through'.

Tim is clearly interested in vehicles and transport but the way he is using them indicate his schema: connection. Tim connected the vehicles with trailers inside and outside in the garden. We gave Tim opportunities to use string, sellotape and staples and introduced a pulley and crane in the outdoor area. Tim used the materials with absorbed concentration and developed a refined understanding of their properties.

The parents

Many parents recognise their child when we describe a range of schemas. They are often delighted that the behaviour they found hard to understand demonstrated their child's learning focus. One parent said 'I was really worried when Alex started to tie up all his play people, I thought he was reacting to the new baby!'

Talking with parents about schemas promotes a shared understanding of what children are focusing on in their learning. Parents are often the first to recognise the development of a new pattern and their insight helps staff to provide experiences to take the children's thinking forward.

Meetings with parents

We plan a range of meetings that constitute the 'formal' (nursery initiated) contact with parents.

- Pre-admission meeting
- Home visit
- Child's first nursery session and subsequent rota visits
- First term parent's meeting, meetings focusing on different issues important to families
- 'Father's day'
- Fund raising events and days organised to improve the nursery environment – gardening etc.

Pre-admission meeting

An evening meeting is held before the child starts nursery. It is set up so that two or three parents sit with a member of staff to look at arrangements for the child's admission and discuss thoughts and concerns parents may have about this important change in their child's life. In this fairly informal setting we offer to visit the child at home before she starts nursery, if parents feel it would be useful. Parents usually see the benefits for their child and only very rarely have parents asked to have time to chat at nursery instead.

Home visit

A member of staff visits the child at home just before the child starts nursery. The home visit provides a unique opportunity to be alongside a child in his or her home setting. We let parents know that although we bring books, games, pens and paper the agenda for the visit is the child's. Our first aim is to get to know the child and for him or her to feel more comfortable at nursery, having had a member of staff as a guest in his or her home. The child is usually delighted to play with the things we bring and the observations from this visit provide invaluable information about what and how the child is learning. The notes are written as a formal record that provides 'baseline' information and becomes part of the shared nursery diary. This visit is an important starting point in our relationship with parents. We can acknowledge the child's achievements and the parent's role in promoting them.

Parent rota visits

We hope, as a staff, we are sensitive to the feelings of parents sharing a nursery session with us, particularly on their child's first day or on later rota turns. We assure parents that we want them to choose to be alongside their child if they wish to, engage in play with the children, help with the routine jobs, e.g. preparing paper, covering books or to have some 'quiet' time. All staff have time to engage with the parent, however briefly and the member of staff recording observations of the child is able to spend 10 to 15 minutes focusing on what is important to the child, discussing important family issues and determining how best to promote the child's learning.

First term meeting

While the aims of the nursery are referred to at the pre-admission meeting, staff are aware that usually parent's main concerns are with the practical issues this new placement will have for them and their children. After the child has been at nursery for a few weeks parents are much better placed to reflect on the child's process of learning and the nursery's approach. Parents are asked to indicate areas of interest for discussion at this meeting and usually choose their own child's development and progress, early literacy and the nursery's approach to learning. Parents are introduced to the 'literacy jigsaw' (Weinberger 1990) and schemas are discussed.

'Father's Day'

We aim to open the nursery on one Saturday during alternate terms so that adults, who are significant in the child's life and who cannot come into nursery as part of the rota, can share a nursery session with the child. Many fathers who work during the week come to this session but also mothers who work full time, grandparents, uncles and aunts frequently attend. Young children live life in the present. They are often unable to share an experience by exploring it through talk. Sharing a nursery session with the important people in their life makes it possible to engage in a meaningful way about the day.

Fund raising events

Some parents want to contribute to the nursery but do not enjoy working with children. On their rota visits, they often prefer to engage in a practical task, like covering books or cutting paper. Many parents want to contribute to sustaining the nursery provision and fund raising events can offer a vehicle for organisational skills and provide opportunity for developing relationships in informal situations as well as building funds for the school.

Developing the relationship

Some parents immediately respond to the nursery's approach and enjoy the recognition of their vital role in their child's education. Other parents are more reticent. Their response may be affected by their own childhood experiences. If school was an uncomfortable place for them as children, they may retain their feelings of discomfort. Others may be in an English school setting for the first time, their own experience of education may have been very different (see chapter 10). In my experience all parents have wanted the best for their child and have been delighted to listen to observations of their child. Good relationships with parents depend on the development of trust and respect, as clearly articulated in principles of partnership (Early Childhood Education Forum 1998) and in the Early Learning Goals (QCA 1999) Practitioners need to actively listen to the parent's perspective as well as helping parents to understand the nursery's approach. Tina Bruce gives a series of examples of how sensitive staff found ways of working with a variety of parents, e.g. those who only drop off their children and avoid other contact with staff and parents whose expectations are very different from the school's. The examples demonstrate that, with careful reflection, regard for the circumstances of each family and commitment to achieving positive relationships, resourceful nursery staff can develop strategies to reach all families (Bruce 1997).

Why work with parents?

Schools, nurseries and pre-school settings have different attitudes and approaches to parents. There are many factors that make working with parents difficult. The working pattern of families has changed, increasing numbers of adults, who are responsible for the care of young children, are in full time employment. Factors identified in an NFER survey in 1980 (Cyster and Clift) such as lack of parental interest in schools are still cited by some practitioners today.

Brain studies

We now have a growing body of evidence that makes working with parents in the early years imperative. Brain research has provided scientific evidence of the crucial importance of the first six years of life. A study produced for the government of Ontario found that 'There is powerful new evidence from neuroscience that the early years of development, from conception to age six, particularly the first three years, set the base for competencies and coping skills that will affect learning, behaviour and health throughout life.' (McCain and Mustard, 1999 p. 5). The study further describes how different aspects of the brain develops at particular times. This has important implications for the care and education of children. 'There are critical periods when a young child requires appropriate stimulation for the brain to establish the neural pathways in the brain for optimum development. Many of these critical periods are over or waning by the time the child is six years old' (McCain and Mustard, 1999 p. 5–6). Other evidence indicates the sort of environment in which young children thrive. John Brierley, (1987) drawing from his work in brain study, identified the factors that produce the most favourable conditions for optimum learning. These included the opportunity for active and child initiated learning and the importance of play.

Between birth and six years formal education plays a relatively insignificant part in a child's life. Children are generally at home or being cared for by family, childminder or in day care settings. The child admitted to school at five is already coming to the end of the period of the brain's most rapid growth. There are critical periods for learning and optimum development will only be achieved if the child receives appropriate stimulation. The early years practitioner is uniquely placed to work with the child's carers, sharing their professional expertise, while the carer contributes the personal details of the child's life, so that learning can be optimised. 'The closer the links between parents and nursery, playgroups or childminder, the more effective the learning becomes'. (Ball 1994, p. 43).

Effectiveness of parental involvement in early years education

Research has also demonstrated that early education that has a high degree of parental involvement has important beneficial, lasting effects for children. (Consortium for Longitudinal Studies 1983) One such piece of research was the Froebel Educational Institute Project, reported by Chris Athey (1990). As a condition of inclusion in the project parents were required to sustain a high degree of involvement. The research focused on identifying children's schemas, with staff and parents providing experiences to help the children explore them. The project proved effective in raising children's IQ's.

These studies and others (Easen *et al.* 1992 and Pugh 1989) have been instrumental in developing a wider understanding of the need for high quality care and early education for all children. The three main political parties have expressed their commitment to extending good quality services to families with young children. The current administration has initiated the 'Early Excellence Centre' programme which aims to develop models of good practice for early years settings with parental involvement as an important element. Primary schools are also settings in which younger children are admitted in increasing numbers but here the educational potential of parent–teacher partnerships has not yet been fully realised; 'teachers struggling with curriculum and assessment workloads and with new forms of accountability … the deepening of partnerships with parents to support pupil learning was not a national priority' (Pollard 1996). Parents are seen as consumers of a service and their role is in danger of being reduced to fulfilling the terms of the home/school contract issued by the school.

Conclusion

There is compelling evidence that working with parents in the early years is not only desirable but a necessity. The role of parent in today's society has become increasingly difficult. Extended families providing reassurance, advice and child care for parents with young children are rare in this modern age. The acknowledgement of the parents' role in the education of their children can be an extra pressure. Parents are exhorted to buy work books promising to prepare their children for school through paper and pencil tasks often inappropriate for young children. Early years practitioners understand that children learn through active manipulation of the world around them. They recognise the vital role that parents play in developing their children's learning spontaneously by being in tune with their interests. Practitioners can help parents recognise that by responding to their children, they are providing appropriate learning opportunities so that parents develop confidence in their role as 'first educators – and most important influence in their child's life' (Ball 1994, p. 42).

References

Athey, C. (1990) *Extending thought in young children*. London: Paul Chapman.

Ball, C. (1994) *Start right: the importance of early learning*. London: RSA.

Brierley, J. (1987) *Give me a child until he is seven: brain studies and early childhood education*. Lewes, East Sussex: The Falmer Press.

Bruce, T. (1997) *Early Childhood Education*. London: Hodder & Stoughton.

Cyster, R. and Clift, P. 'Parental Involvement in Primary Schools', in Craft, M. *et al. Linking Home and School* (1980) London: Harper & Row.

Consortium for Longitudinal Studies (1983) 'As the twig is bent: the lasting effects of pre-school programmes'. in Clark, M. M. (1988) *Children under five: Educational Research and Evidence*. London: Gordon and Breach Science.

Early Childhood Education Forum (1998) *Quality in diversity in early learning*. London: Early Childhood Education Forum and National Children's Bureau.

Easen, P. *et al.* (1992) Parents and educators: dialogue and development through partnership, *Children and Society* 6(4), 282–96.

McCain, M.N. and Mustard, J.F. (co-chairs) (1999) Early Years Study Final Report for the Ontario Government *Reversing the brain drain*.

Pollard, A. (1996) *The social world of children's learning*. London: Cassell.

Pugh, G. De'Ath, E. (1989) *Working towards partnership in the early years*. London: National Children's Bureau.

Qualifications and Curriculum Authority (1999) *Early Learning Goals*. London: Qualifications and Curriculum Authority.

School Curriculum and Assessment Authority (SCAA) (1996) *Nursery Education. Desirable outcomes for children's learning*. London: DfEE.

Weinberger, J. (1990) *Ways of working with parents to promote early literacy development*. The University of Sheffield.

Chapter 12
Talking and listening

Tim Parke

Introduction

In the present chapter, I will first introduce the contemporary debate on the mechanisms by which children acquire language. I will then give a detailed analysis of an excerpt from a conversation to illustrate patterns of interaction in the home. Analysis of a second excerpt, this time from an early years setting, shows how children are expected to adapt to different demands on their use of language and what opportunities may be beneficial in helping them to do so.

Two positions in the debate on language acquisition

For a number of years, there has been a fierce debate between language researchers about how language is acquired by very young children. It is a genuine conflict between people who are unlikely to agree. We will not try to settle the debate here, but we will try to show how people working with young children can take evidence and arguments from each side which will throw light on the language-learning task for the child.

The two positions can be summarised, perhaps too simply, as *innatist* and *interactionist*. Innatists, associated mainly with the name of the American linguist Chomsky, claim that language develops primarily as a means for the individual child to express ideas which are the same wherever that child is born, into whatever society, and however socialised. That is, they are universal. For these people, language develops in very much the same way whatever the environment, and is unaffected by the type or quality of language that is going on around the learner. They imagine an in-built device, Universal Grammar (UG), being triggered by language going on in the environment. Once triggered, this device 'runs all by itself' (Gleason *et al.* 1989, p. 183). Individual language structures, such as the verbs and nouns of a particular language, are acquired in a predictable order simply because that is the way the mind develops: for example it moves from simple structures to complex ones, from the here-and-now to the abstract.

This view could be fairly dismal news for teachers, parents, and anybody else who believes that what they do, and especially what they say, might have an effect on a child's learning. Such well-researched practices as Child Directed Speech – the style of speech parents/carers use in talking to young children (Snow and Ferguson 1977) – are a waste of effort, because almost despite the quality of the language that surrounds the child, his or her language will inevitably develop according to its own agenda. The child is so primed to communicate, so much has developed prior to birth to predispose him or her to learn, that almost any interaction will be enough to trigger the process.

But the 'triggering' is the key, and it leads us to the opposing position, that of the interactionists. For them, communication, which is, after all, what language is mainly about, takes place in an environment. Cook and Hewson (1996) have pointed out that thinking about how much of UG is 'in place' before birth has made us realise how important the environment is. No environment, no trigger – so no language. It is only because we interact with children that UG has a chance to get going. In a way, it is only what children *do* with language that gives us any proof that there is such a thing as UG in the first place. To be convinced of this, we have only to consider those children who are totally neglected at birth, as in the well-documented but happily rare case of the Californian girl Genie (see Yule 1985 for a brief account). Such children fail comprehensively to develop language. Moreover, they find it impossible to retrieve the process even when they escape their isolation. In the same way, deaf children initially begin to develop speech in the same ways as their normally developing peers, and, like them, go through the stages of babbling and cooing. They fall silent when the reinforcement from parents/carers does not penetrate their auditory system. So to be talked to, as well as to be able to hear, is an essential prerequisite for acquiring speech.

A further argument for the interactionist case comes from considering how language acquisition works in other societies and cultures. This includes cultural variation within *our* own society. The studies show enormous variation. The most often quoted contrast is that revealed by Ochs (1982), who, writing of Western Samoa, reports on adults' wholesale neglect of what children may be attempting to communicate:

> children are explicitly told what to say and are instructed in providing socially appropriate utterances: for instance, a child is typically told to repeat after the adult appropriate greetings, social questions, and so on. (Ochs 1982, cited in Gleason *et al*, 1989, p. 182).

Even within societies closer to our own, there are the strong contrasts between different ethnic and class groups in North America as reported by Heath (1983), which affect literacy habits as well as speech. Again, children raised in bilingual and bicultural contexts in the UK are experiencing sharply differing oral and literacy practices. How children speak, including which language they choose, varies according to the age of the person they are addressing, who else in the room knows that language, the topic of the conversation, and so on. Even within a section of society, individuals enjoy a range of speech styles that vary according to context.

Talking and listening

This is the business of knowing when to speak, when to listen, and when you can just rest. We define it here as

- learning the rules of when to listen and when to speak
- learning how to make your contribution interesting and relevant, and not too long
- learning when to keep to the topic, and when you can change it.

We will now take our example of a conversation, this being the most typical case of listening and speaking in the home, following the analysis with a discussion of what we can learn from this example.

The conversation

The conversation is between a young boy, Mark, who is two-and-a-half years old, and his mother, his sister, and a family friend. It is about five o'clock in the evening, and Mark is simultaneously watching a video, talking about which drink he wants, talking about the video, and replying to questions about dinner. The extract was chosen precisely because it shows the kind of complex talking and listening tasks children in contemporary society undertake, giving their attention to a number of tasks and topics at the same time and trying to give a proper response each time.

The excerpt lasts about a minute.

Speakers:

Mother
Stella: family friend
Mark: younger child: age 2.5
Jane: elder child: 5.0

Key:

[= overlap: two people speak at once
Com: = a comment on or explanation of what is happening
[Line numbers relate to a larger transcript from which this is an excerpt.]

	Stella	Is this your video?
35	Mark	Yeh – and Jane brew . . . . won't work
	Stella	That one doesn't work?
	Mark	Her brew
	Stella	That's blue? Is he saying blue?
	Mark	Blue
40	Stella	Is that what he's saying, that's blue?
	Mother	What is, Mark?
	Com	[Eating cake]

	Mark	Brew
	Mother	Don't speak with your mouth full
45	Com	[Mark picks up his bottle]
	Mark	Bottle in here
		Bottle in here
	Mother	What do you want – milk?
	Mark	Bottle in here – tea
	Mother	No, that's coffee. Do you want tea or blackcurrant?
50	Mark	[No – I get it
	Jane	[I'll get blackcurrant
	Mother	No, you're not going to get it. What do you want, milk or blackcurrant?
	Mark	Want tea
55	Mother	Milk?
	Mark	Want tea . . . tea
	Com	[Mother fills bottle]
	Mother	What do you say?
	Mark	Thank you
60	Com	[Mother turns off video]
	Mark	Oh!
	Mother	What?
	Mark	I want teddy bear
	Com	[the Care Bears TV programme]
	Mother	Teddy bear?
65	Mark	Yeh

Analysis

In some ways this is a very standard conversation. Mark and his mother take turns, each replying appropriately; there are no breakdowns, no misunderstandings. The conversation progresses from one topic to a second: from drinks to teddy bears.

The mother's contributions

- Lines 40 and 41 are attempts to interpret Mark's language, by both talking about him (Stella) and to him (his mother).
- The mother repeatedly questions Mark about what he wants to drink. She has evidently decided in advance what the choices are, and her questions reflect this. The 'either/or' question at line 52, for example, is an (unsuccessful) attempt to limit his responses. This recurs in line 55 ('Milk?') – essentially an attempt to have Mark opt for a drink she approves of.
- She insists on politeness (lines 44 and 58).
- Her response 'Teddy bear?' (line 64) looks like a check: 'Did you say 'teddy bear', Mark?' – but is in fact a 'holding' remark while she works out her next move (which was in fact to insist on watching the video she had just turned off).

Mark's contributions

His language is easy to interpret, but it is not fully adult-like. He is using what are sometimes called 'reduced utterances': forms that look like simplified versions of the adult form. (The term 'utterance' is used in discussing speech; the term 'sentence' refers only to written language.)

Table 12.1

line	child's utterance	adult target
35	yeh – and Jane brew – wont't work	Jane broke it: it won't work
37	her brew	she broke it
39	blue	broke(n)
43	brew	broke(n)
46	bottle in here	I want a drink in my bottle
48	bottle in here – tea	I want a drink of tea in my bottle
50	I get it	I'll get it
54	want tea	I want some tea
64	I want teddy bear	I want the/my teddy bear

Table 12.1 shows us quite a lot about stages of language development (Crystal 1992) in children of this age. Roughly speaking, Mark's vocabulary seems to consist of one type of word but not the other.

Note that certain types of word are missing from the child version: we might agree that they are 'it', 'will', 'I' and 'the' or 'my'. If we compare these words to the ones Mark *does* use – words like 'broke' (though he produces both 'brew' and 'blue'); 'bottle', 'want', 'tea', and 'teddy bear', we see that this second type contains words that would have a lot of meaning even if they were uttered by themselves. If someone says to us 'teddy bear', we have an immediate image of a small (large?) furry thing that many of us take to bed at night. But if someone says 'it', or 'will', we have no such immediate response. Such words take their meaning from the context in which they occur. And there is a lot of evidence to suggest that these sorts of words – the ones with no 'picture' meaning, so to speak – are acquired later than the more concrete and visual ones (Lee 1986, p. 91–2).

Note however that Mark uses the word 'it' in line 50, but omits it in line 35, which might seem to weaken what we have just claimed. But that again tells us something about the study of child language: children are never precisely at one stage or another. They are continually in progression, and they sometimes even appear to slip back to an earlier stage of development. So when we focus on children's early language, it is vital to take a long view. The well-documented stages must be interpreted flexibly, and the child observed in the round and over time rather than by means of a one-off, snapshot assessment.

Discussion

It is easy to be critical of this very informal interaction. We have brought a microscope to bear on a minute segment of a family's private life, and one which we should in no way take as typical or representative. But it may still be *illustrative* of the talking and listening task that faces children in contemporary society. This is the reality of what we have to deal with as practitioners.

First, the multi-task nature of the conversation. Across the two excerpts, what Mark is expected to be able to do is to apply the 'rules for speaking and listening' suggested earlier. Specifically, in these particular excerpts, he can:

- give selective attention both to the TV and to people who speak to him
- follow changes of topic (the broken remote, drinks, the TV programme ('bear', line 63) – and changes of speaker
- understand everything that is said to him (note that he never *mis*understands what is said to him)
- apply the rules of the conversation game: when to speak, when to listen – he never slips up here either
- give suitable answers (they have to be relevant and polite)
- produce English at a level that communicates his message.

But a look at another side of the picture, that is the actual language produced by Mark, provides a different view. A striking feature of the extract is just how *little* he actually says, in terms of numbers of words contributed. Although he has as many turns (more or less) as his mother, and thus contributed successfully to the conversation, many of these utterances are responses to others rather than initiations. Stella and his mother mainly ask Mark questions, or give him orders. This raises this all-important question: in a dialogue like this, where are the opportunities for Mark to develop his abilities as a user of English? Mark 'passes' successfully in the conversation because he has learned the rules of that game. But we cannot tell from what we have seen that he is developing well in his *production* of language.

Beyond the home

The critical point for professionals in the field is to know what they can do to promote children's language development. To illustrate this, consider the differences that we can expect between the language of the home and that of early years settings. Imagine Mark as he comes to one such setting and see what he has to get used to.

In conversations in the home
- Topics are concrete things like drinks, the remote control, TV
- Each speaker knows the rules of the game
- People speak when they want to
- The speakers all know each other well and have similar status
- No specialised knowledge is needed to be able to join in.

There are some contrasts between these factors and what begins to happen in later settings.

A typical early years settings will have a number of activities available for children, with some whole-group activities also built into the session or day.

Thus children may select from play with water, for example, or sand, or sticking. They may operate in self-selecting groups or individually. Whole-group activities may take the form of all sitting on the floor while an adult tells a story, or conducts a more-or-less structured discussion on a recent event, or invites children to recount something from their own experience.

What changes are there for the activities of talking and listening compared with the home setting? There are at least two kinds. One is changes in how language is used in context – the pragmatics of language. The other is changes in discourse pattern: whereas a young child may be used to one-to-one conversations in the home, in new settings he or she will have to deal with larger settings, such as a group of children, with an adult providing structured interaction.

The pragmatics of talking and listening

Pragmatics is the study of how we use language to do things: to get people to do what we want, to make jokes, to hold conversations. In looking at Mark in his home, for example, we saw his mother appear to ask him questions, but the effect of those questions was to control or limit his behaviour in some way rather than to gain knowledge.

What is new about language use in the early years setting is only partly to do with new activities and experiences, as for many children these will already be familiar. But where that play involves unfamiliar children, language becomes important as a means of making one's meanings clear to somebody new. In the home, the people a child has grown up with can almost predict what that child will say in a given situation before it is said. (This works both ways, of course: children are skilled predictors of parents too.) But when children are unfamiliar with each other, they can take less for granted – *and* they have first to learn that this is the case. It is important to be explicit.

Such learning can be seen at a number of levels: the very words used, the patterns of play, how to interpret an adult's intentions, and so on. To take the example of words, some of the very familiar and intimate words of the home – words for parents and other family, for bodily functions, for routines like bedtime and bathing, are likely to be referred to differently by children from different backgrounds. Where children come from a minority cultural background, they may only have these words in another language, and in the early stages of the setting may need time but also actual tuition if they are to acquire them in English (as Rose Drury shows in chapter 10).

A structured interaction

Our second example illustrates some of these points. In the activity we now present, we see a familiar game – 'Spot the difference' – being played by three children and an adult in a nursery. While much in it could be typical of the home, there are some important differences.

First, there are four people co-operating in the game, and they are being controlled in a clear but friendly way by the adult. This control largely takes two forms: the allocation of turns and the demand for explicitness.

Second, the game itself provides a model of social and linguistic behaviour which is thereby held up to the children as a desirable way of behaving in conversation.

And finally, the adult introduces a small amount of semi-specialist vocabulary, and, while she does not expect this to be taken up in the children's contributions, she assumes it will be understood by them, and presumably that they will use it subsequently.

Speakers:

Jamie: age 3.6
Helen: age 4.0
Kelly: age 4.7
Pat: adult

Key:

Com: = a comment on or explanation of what is happening
[Line numbers relate to a larger transcript from which this is an excerpt.]

95	Pat:	Yes, OK, your turn now
	Helen:	I got a snowman.
	Pat:	A snowman, tell me what he is wearing.
	Kelly:	A scarf
	Pat:	A scarf. OK. A snowman wearing a scarf. Has he got any
100		buttons?
	Helen:	Yes
	Pat:	Is he wearing a hat?
	Helen:	No
	Pat:	No! I think it's mine. Is it mine?
105	Com:	[All say 'yes'.]
	Pat:	Now I've got a butterfly. Two circles on the top are green and purple. Who's got two circles on the top that are green and purple?
	Jamie:	Me
	Pat:	Yes, Jamie. Well done, what a good boy. It's your turn, Kelly.
110		What's that?
	Kelly:	A kite
	Pat:	What colour are the two top triangles?
	Kelly:	Red . . . pink and blue
	Pat:	Pink and blue. Who's got a kite that has pink and blue on the
115		top?

```
            Helen:  Me
            Pat:    Well done, Helen.
                    I've got a clown and he is juggling three balls.
            Com:    [Kelly puts his hand up.]
120         Pat:    Is it yours, Kelly?
            Kelly:  Yes
            Helen:  Three
            Pat:    Yes, one, two, three. Kelly, it's your turn. What's that? Tell
                    everyone what it is.
125         Kelly:  A mouse
            Pat:    What kind of balloon is he holding?
            Kelly:  A heart one.
            Pat:    Who's got the heart balloon?
            Jamie:  Thomas
130         Com:    [Thomas is not currently playing.]
```

This example can be seen as an activity providing a transition between the more intimate and less structured dialogues of the home and the public classroom events of the primary school. Consider in turn the notions of control, turn-taking and vocabulary.

Turns are allocated by Pat almost entirely by means of questions. These may be open questions – as at line 107: 'Who's got two circles on the top that are green and purple?' – to which any child can reply (though the distribution of cards is such as to prevent more than one child answering anyway). Or Pat may ask a directed, closed question, as at line 109: 'It's your turn, Kelly. What's that?' Even where there is no overt question, the children correctly understand that one is implied, and respond accordingly: 'I've got a clown and he is juggling three balls' (line 118), followed by Kelly's appropriate move.

The second type of control is the demand for explicitness. Pat is notably explicit in her own contributions: we have already seen her precise description of the butterfly card (lines 105–06). The children need to focus carefully on the cards they hold in order to play the game successfully. And Pat occasionally demands explicit language from them: 'What kind of balloon is he holding?' (line 126).

In terms of turn-taking, it is transparent that all contributions are structured by the game. As the game is built on turn-taking, so the language that emerges in it is structured in this way too. Pat allocates turns in the ways we have noted. Part of the effect of this is to create an ordered, perhaps rather idealistic model of conversation in which (unlike in the earlier excerpt) there are no overlaps and no shifts of attention. It is however a very focused and rather relentless type of interaction: no-one can escape their turn (the cards see to that), and in this we might see a forerunner of highly structured interactions in the classroom such as the public arena of story-time.

Finally, consider the level of vocabulary. The game depends on precision: players must be able to identify each card from its description. And the way the cards are designed is such as to promote the semi-specialist vocabulary ultimately demanded in the curriculum: the colour terms, but especially 'circle', 'triangle' and 'heart', and spatial referents such as 'top'.

Early learning goals

The expectation, as embodied in the Early Learning Goals (QCA 1999) is that at the end of the reception year, children will have acquired, among others, specific speaking and listening skills. Most of these are not controversial, though it is noticeable that they are a good deal less explicit than, for example those for reading and writing. It has always been more difficult for teachers and others to specify exactly what a good education in oracy actually meant. Speech is simply more difficult to measure than writing. In addition, especially where it is informal, it is so much more bound by its context that unless practitioners take the care to record and analyse what children actually say, they are in danger of missing the evidence. From the moment of a child's beginning to communicate, we expect so strongly that speech and language will develop naturally that, once they begin to develop, we almost forget to notice them.

The Early Learning Goals mentioned above include these:
that children will be able to

- sustain attentive listening, responding to what they have heard by relevant comments, questions or actions
- interact with others, negotiating plans and taking turns in conversations
- extend their vocabulary, exploring the meanings and sounds of new words
(QCA 1999, p. 27)

On the one hand, we can see that some of these skills are nurtured in the home, and that a child (such as Mark) needs to be able to develop selective listening skills in order to cope with the language demands of very informal situations. On the other hand, we have also seen continuity between home and school in the use of a (card) game which gave good opportunities for the greater order and precision that is demanded of children as they come to use language no longer primarily for social interaction, but as a tool for learning. Here, finally, we see the fusion between the language the child brings to the learning process and the guiding, scaffolding effects of structured interaction.

References

Cook, V. and Newson, M. (1996) *Chomsky's Universal Grammar: an Introduction*. 2nd edn. Oxford: Blackwell.

Crystal, D. (1986) *Listen to your child*. Harmondsworth: Penguin.

Crystal, D. (1992) *The Cambridge Encyclopedia of Language*. Cambridge: Cambridge University Press.

Gleason, J. *et al.* (1989) 'Social and affective determinants of language acquisition', in Rice, M. and Schieffelin, B. B. (eds) *The Teachability of Language*. Baltimore, MD: Paul Brookes.

Heath, S. B. (1983) *Ways with Words: Language, Life and Work in Communities and Classrooms*. Cambridge: Cambridge University Press.

Lee, D. (1986) *Language, Children and Society*. Brighton: The Harvester Press.

Ochs, E. (1982) 'Talking to children in Western Samoa', in *Language in Society* **11**, 77–104.

Qualifications and Curriculum Authority (1999) *Early Learning Goals.* London: Qualifications and Curriculum Authority.

Rice, M. and Schieffelin, B. B. (eds) (1989) *The Teachability of Language.* Baltimore, MD: Paul Brookes.

Snow, C. and Ferguson, C. (1977) *Talking to Children: Language Input and Acquisition.* Cambridge: Cambridge University Press.

Yule, G. (1985) *The Study of Language.* Cambridge: Cambridge University Press.

Chapter 13
Literacy learning at home and at school

Robin Campbell

We know that many young children learn about reading and writing at home, often before they move into an early years setting. By the time they are three years old many children are beginning to demonstrate reading and writing-like behaviour. They may not be reading and writing in the conventional sense as adults do. Nevertheless, they do read and write. How do young children acquire that knowledge without direct teaching? There are a number of activities and experiences, with support from adults, which help children as literacy learners.

Story reading

Children love to have stories read to them. Parents, grandparents and others with responsibilities for very young children will have experienced the joy of young children as books are read to them. That enjoyment of stories is extended when adults have taken the time to select worthwhile books to share with children.

In my study of Alice's development (Campbell 1999) we were able to see how a child develops as a reader in contact with story books. By the time she was one year old Alice looked at the pictures, listened to the stories, and pointed to characters. Later she asked questions – 'What's owl doing?' – repeated words from the text and learned the repeat lines from some books. Gradually, and by the time she was four, she was able to pick out some of the words which were important to her such as 'owl', 'zoo' and, strangely, 'and' in the books that were read to her.

It is evident that the story readings for Alice – and for other children at home – are not just a matter of the adult reading and the child listening. Instead the story readings are interactive, with both the adult and the child taking active roles. Inevitably the adult reads most of the text with the child making comments, asking questions and inserting words. But these contributions by the child, when the adult is willing to accept them, strongly support literacy learning.

The knowledge about books and recognition of some words that Alice acquired from interactive story readings meant that she was well placed to make rapid progress with reading, in the conventional sense, when she was five and six.

Of course, it is not just the study of individual children which tells us about the importance of story readings. A longitudinal study of many children growing up in Bristol indicated the positive influence of story readings on children's literacy development (Wells 1986). Quite simply children who had stories read to them on a regular and frequent basis were likely to make good progress as readers. They did so because the story readings had enabled them to know about books, know about stories, and to begin to recognise words in print.

Repeat readings

'Read it again' is a common request from young children as they listen to stories (Payton 1984), and being able to hear the same book read three, four, five or more times is important for them. First, it enables them to gain ownership of the story. Rather than having just a cursory awareness, the children 'capture' the story for themselves, getting to know its characters and events. When Lynley Dodd's Hairy Maclary stories (e.g. *Hairy Maclary from Donaldson's Dairy* 1983) are read aloud repeatedly, the children become excited about Hector Morse, Muffin McLay and other characters in the books. Indeed, if we listen to children's conversations at other times, we hear echoes of stories that have been read to them. The repeat story readings add to their subsequent talk as well as supporting their literacy learning.

The repeat readings also enable young children to join in. Some authors help young children to do this and to gain a sense of what it is to read. Authors may use rhythm, rhyme and repetition to facilitate children's participation. Of course, repetition of elements that serve a real purpose in the story, rather than the mechanistic repetition of any group of words, most benefits the child. For instance, young children love *The Very Hungry Caterpillar* by Eric Carle (1969). Because of the repetition in that story, they are quickly able to join in with the repeated 'but he was still hungry'.

Many young children go further and memorise complete stories that are read to them. That memorisation enables them to read the stories to themselves, to their toys or to other children. It also enables them gradually to make links to particular words in the print. For some children that leads to making a word-by-word link between the memorised story and the print on the page – they become readers.

Environmental print

Although story reading and the repeat reading of stories are important, print is seen in other contexts that can support children's literacy learning – see, for example, the extensive advertisements and notices that most children experience in industrialised societies. There is a very wide range of environmental print surrounding young children which can be enlisted in support of their literacy development. Elsewhere Linda Miller (1999) has detailed children's contact with that print and their response to it.

A simple example of environmental print is the large M logo for McDonald's. Many writers, including Lester Laminack (1991), have indicated how children as young as two are able to recognise the M and to link it clearly with food. There are the many different logos, colours, pictures and writing that are to be found on boxes, cans, bottles and wrappings of food generally. Young children learn very quickly to recognise particular products, using the information that is provided. That learning is aided dramatically when the adults who care for them take time to talk about the items being noticed.

Children see print regularly in other ways; for example, letters and junk mail coming through the letter box each day; writing on carrier bags provided by many shops; the newspapers and magazines in their households; and, later, the child's attempts to find out what is on the television. All of this creates contact with print for young children and it stimulates them to think about writing and reading.

Songs and nursery rhymes

Songs and nursery rhymes, jingles and finger plays, such as those in a collection provided by Matterson (1969), are activities that many children share with adults who care for them. Before they are one year old, many children are enjoying songs and actions such as 'Round and round the garden went the Teddy Bear, one step, two steps, tickle you under there'. Their understanding of the sequence of words is demonstrated as they indicate their anticipation of the tickle at the end of the rhyme.

Adults engage with children using songs and rhymes because the children enjoy them so much. The sheer enjoyment is reason enough to share these rhymes with young children (Meek 1990). However, children are gaining much more than just the pleasure of the activity and the sharing of a speck of their cultural heritage. As they become older and are able to join in with the singing and actions, they are learning new words and new meanings, incidentally widening their phonological awareness.

Traditional rhymes such as 'Humpty Dumpty' help children to hear and recite rhyming elements like 'wall' and 'fall'. Playing with and learning other such rhymes have been shown to help young children to develop as readers over a number of years (Goswami and Bryant 1990). Children become aware of the initial sound of the word, the onset 'w' and 'f' in these cases, and the rime elements, '-all' and that learning supports their subsequent reading and writing.

Opportunities to draw and write

Earlier, in chapter 2, Linda Miller demonstrated how play could provide many opportunities for children to explore writing in meaningful contexts. Writing shopping lists, taking orders in a restaurant, writing out prescriptions and the like can all be a part of the imaginative play of young children, providing opportunities for using and thinking about writing. Inevitably children are helped to develop such imaginative play and writing if, for instance, the adult caring for them takes a few moments to make a shopping list with the child before a shopping expedition. Providing models of functional literacy helps children to develop their own view of its place in life.

With younger children the writing they produce may initially look more like scribbles. However, as opportunities for writing are extended, children's efforts appear to be more letter-like as circles and lines appear in their work. After a time recognisable letters appear, although perhaps in no obvious sequence. Subsequently the letters begin to take on a meaning as they combine to represent recognisable words.

As well as writing during imaginative play, children benefit from opportunities to draw and write using a variety of paper and pencils, crayons and other implements. Children will draw and write, sometimes drawing only, while at other times they will add letter-like shapes or letters as explanations or descriptions of their drawings.

When children are given the chance to write on their own, they produce what are known as developmental, invented or phonic spellings. They produce their best attempt at getting down on paper the word that they hear in their head. That involvement with words is useful because the children are constructively developing their understanding of how literacy works. Alice's recipe for making a shepherd's pie when she was five years old (see Figure 13.1) demonstrated her knowledge of writing as well as the learning still to be achieved.

She was able to write 'to, a, of, and' in a conventional manner. Furthermore, her writing of hao (how), mack (make), sepas (shepherd's), piy (pie), uyn (onion), ptatos (potatoes), biass (beans), cess (cheese), and her attempts to write grams all demonstrated a good level of understanding of letters and sounds. With

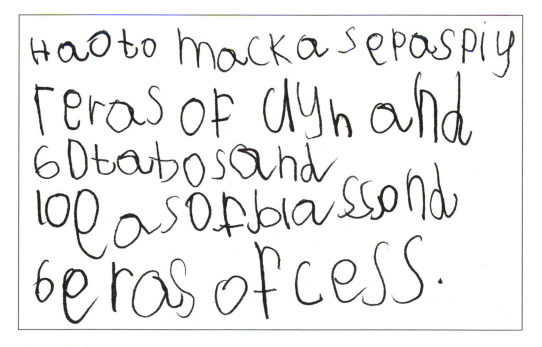

Figure 13.1

further numerous experiences of writing, and with adult support, those developmental spellings would become more conventional.

Writing one's own name

A very important word for young children is their own name and it should not surprise us that this is often the first word they write. Of course, it is not written perfectly from the start. Indeed many studies of young children developing as literacy users indicate that, to start with, the first letter of the child's name is written on its own to stand for the name. In a study by Judith Schickedanz (1990), we see how Adam first represented his name with just an A, and how the A became the most prominent letter produced in his writing for a few months. It was some months later, when he was three and a half years old, that he was able to produce a conventional written 'Adam'.

When children succeed in writing their own name in a conventional manner, they have created a foundation for their literacy learning. This achievement demonstrates a knowledge of some letters and the ability to memorise and reproduce those letters in a written format. Implicitly it also tells the children about the importance of creating the correct sequence of letters with spaces either side of each word. When one considers all the learning that has taken place in order to write their own name we can see what an important event it is for children. And for many children that learning takes place at home before starting at nursery or school.

Looking at the alphabet

Colourful alphabet posters are often found in the bedrooms of young children and alphabet books are commonplace. With those posters and books it is inevitable that young children will talk about, for instance, 'That's p for panda'. Sometimes saying the letter <p> and sometimes the sound /p/. They learn about letters and sounds during that talk with adults.

Children will also learn about letters as they ask questions about them. Part of that questioning will occur as they listen to story readings. For Adam and Alice it would not be uncommon to hear them say, 'That's an A like in my name,' as they share a story reading.

Support from adults focuses the attention that children give to letters and letter sounds and encourages them in their learning. Children also learn the alphabetic sequence as they join in with the singing of alphabet songs and this learning helps them to develop as readers and writers. The evidence suggests that children's knowledge of the alphabet at five is one of the best predictors of reading success (Riley 1996). The direct teaching of letters may not ensure that success so much as familiarity acquired through a wide range of experience with written language. Their knowledge is then broad-based rather than superficially learnt.

Television print

Torrey (1969) tells of a child who appeared to learn to read through listening to and looking at the print associated with numerous commercials on television. Learning to read in that way is probably unusual but some children do learn about print, letters and some words as they watch television. An early indication of their awareness of print on television is their reaction to the closing captions. Two-year-old children can demonstrate their awareness that the captions signal the end and they will move away from the television set as a favourite programme is completed.

Children will ask about the print they see on the television – 'What does that say?' – and they often comment on what they observe – 'There's an A'. Children who are fortunate to have an adult nearby to respond to their questions and comments have their literacy learning enhanced.

Literacy learning at home

In an article (Campbell 1998) I recorded the various literacy activities of a three-year-old during the course of a single day at home. Inevitably the day included many activities such as playing with constructional toys, imaginative play, as well as talk to self and others. It also showed how Caitlin moved in and out of literacy activities throughout the day.

Story books were read and reread by adults. There were conversations about television print and print on table mats. Songs and rhymes were sung spontaneously by Caitlin and she played 'I Spy' with her elder sister. She drew pictures and wrote her own name, made a birthday card and wrote the numbers from one to ten. At a supermarket she engaged with environmental print as she looked closely at items to choose the right product. An important feature of her day was the response of adults who answered questions that were important to her, so contributing to her literacy learning.

Weinberger (1996) has shown that children from different backgrounds experience a wide variety of literacy activities at home. Some activities are fleeting, as when a question is asked about television, or environmental print. Some last longer, as when the child listens to a story or draws and writes. All of such events and activities add to the child's knowledge about literacy.

Importance of adults

In this discussion of children's literacy development at home, the important role of the adult is evident. Parents, grandparents, and other carers have a crucial role to play. They provide resources and opportunities for children to experience literacy. They model literacy – as when reading stories or writing shopping lists – and sing songs and nursery rhymes with them.

Adults also answer the questions that children pose about literacy. Those adults are likely to be very busy, so responding to questions is not always easy, but it is important. Children who have their questions about literacy answered are likely to develop as readers and writers (Clark 1976).

From home to early years settings

As we have seen, some children will be reading and writing in a recognisable way before entering an early years setting. That is achieved by encouragement and the provision of literacy resources and activities at home, with the support of an adult or a sibling. Of course, there will be children who have not experienced numerous story readings and singing of rhymes (Weinberger 1996). And some children from a variety of cultural backgrounds will experience different literacy activities (Gregory 1996). What then does that suggest for early years settings?

As Eve Gregory (1996) suggested, the principle of building on the children's existing knowledge, working 'from the inside-out', needs to be one part of the approach. That implies that the adults in early years settings understand as much as possible about the family approaches to literacy and build upon that. (See chapters 10 and 11 for Rose Drury's exploration of the learning of bilingual children and Cindy Willey's reminders of the importance of working with parents. In addition to working from the inside-out, Gregory suggests introducing the unknown or working 'from the outside-in'. That view links to those expressed by Moustafa (1997) who advocated numerous story readings for children who had not been read to extensively. The literacy activities that were noted above provide part of the learning to be developed in early years settings (Campbell 1996). And those activities are consistent with the opportunities for learning and goals suggested by the QCA (1999).

Story readings support and extend children's literacy development and need a regular place in the early years classroom. The daily story readings will still be interactive: teachers become skilled at reading the story, responding to questions and comments, and then getting the story reading back on track. Repeat readings are important so that children can gain ownership of the stories and begin to recognise words and phrases in the text. For some of the story readings use will be made of big books so that children can see the print as it is read and learn from that experience.

The children will sing songs and recite nursery rhymes with the adult. From these events they will acquire knowledge, we noted earlier, about letters as well as onset and rime units such as 'w', 'f' and '-all' in 'wall' and 'fall'. That knowledge will help them to learn other words like 'tall' and 'call' by analogy. In the classroom the learning is made more systematic as word walls are developed to include key words from the books, songs and rhymes. As the word 'wall' is in alphabetic order, the children's knowledge of the alphabet is more firmly established.

Opportunities for drawing and writing will be extended, with the home corner becoming a shop, post office or travel agency to support the children's use of literacy during imaginative play. The provision of environmental print and writing materials in these settings and the modelling of literacy by the adult all add momentum to the children's move towards literacy. Additionally, the provision of a writing centre or writing table encourages the children to write.

As topics related to the environment are developed, other opportunities are provided for reading and writing. So the early years setting provides extensive opportunities, activities and support for literacy learning.

References

Campbell, R. (1996) *Literacy in Nursery Education.* Stoke-on-Trent: Trentham Books.

Campbell, R. (1998) 'A three year old learning literacy at home', *Early Years* **19** (1), 76–89.

Campbell, R. (1999) *Literacy from Home to School: Reading with Alice.* Stoke-on-Trent: Trentham Books.

Clark, M. M. (1976) *Young Fluent Readers.* London: Heinemann Educational.

Goswami, U. C. *et al.* (1990) *Phonological Skills and Learning to Read.* Hove: Lawrence Erlbaum Associates.

Gregory, E. (1996) *Making Sense of a New World: Learning to read in a second language.* London: Paul Chapman.

Laminack, L. (1991) *Learning with Zachary.* Richmond Hill, Ontario: Scholastic.

Matterson, E. (1969) *This Little Puffin . . . Finger Plays and Nursery Games.* London: Puffin Books.

Meek, M. (1990) 'What do we know about reading that helps us to teach?', in R. Carter (ed.) *Knowledge about Language and the Curriculum*, 145–53. London: Hodder & Stoughton.

Miller, L. (1999) *Moving towards literacy with environmental print.* Royston, Herts: United Kingdom Reading Association.

Moustafa, M. (1997) *Beyond Traditional Phonics: Research Discoveries and Reading Instruction.* Portsmouth, New Hampshire: Heinemann.

Payton, S. (1984) *Developing Awareness of Print: A young child's first steps towards literacy.* Birmingham: Educational Review, University of Birmingham.

Qualifications and Curriculum Authority (1999) *Early Learning Goals.* London: Qualifications and Curriculum Authority.

Riley, J. (1996) *The Teaching of Reading: The Development of Literacy in the Early Years.* London: Paul Chapman.

Schickedanz, J. A. (1990) *Adam's Righting Revolutions.* Portsmouth, New Hampshire: Heinemann Educational.

Torrey, J. (1969) 'Learning to read without a teacher: A case study', in *Elementary English* **46**, 550–56.

Weinberger, J. (1996) *Literacy goes to School.* London: Paul Chapman Publishing.

Wells, G. (1986) *The Meaning Makers: Children Learning Language and Using Language to Learn.* London: Hodder & Stoughton.

Children's books

Carle, E. (1969) *The Very Hungry Caterpillar.* London: Hamish Hamilton.

Dodd, L. (1983) *Hairy Maclary from Donaldson's Dairy.* Harmondsworth: Puffin Books.

Chapter 14
Literacy in reception classes

Pauline Minnis

Background information

This chapter explores how children's literacy is developed in reception classes. The role of adults in providing contexts and promoting literacy development is explored in relation to literacy goals. The material is based on observations of one child during his reception year at a Hertfordshire school.

In reception classes there has always been debate about the best provision to promote literacy development; what needs to be taught and how best to teach it. This has implications for the provision which early years practitioners working in reception classes make for their pupils in terms of their development as speakers and listeners, readers and writers.

Speaking and listening

In the past, speaking experiences may have been restricted to a child responding directly to teachers' questioning, with listening being perceived as all important. The status of child talk has now been acknowledged. Children are encouraged to talk in a variety of contexts, formally and informally, and to a range of adults and peers. A busy working atmosphere is preferred to a silent classroom. High quality interaction with pupils underpins the effectiveness of literacy development at this young age (Attainment target 1, DfEE 1989). The Early Learning Goals clearly emphasise the centrality of speaking and listening skills in pupils' development and to the specific development of language and literacy (QCA 1999). Likewise talk is an integral part of teaching promoted by the National Literacy Strategy (DfEE 1998).

Reading

Reading in the past may have meant being able to 'bark at the print' and reading aloud the words on the page. Today the emphasis is on reading for meaning; encouraging talk about the pictures and what is happening in the text, and an awareness of story structures (DfEE 1998 and QCA 1999). Children are also invited to relate fiction and non-fiction texts to their own experience and to express an opinion.

Writing

Writing in the past may have comprised handwriting and copying writing from the board. Today reception aged children are expected to be actively involved in composing for a range of purposes e.g. lists, signs, directions, labels, menus, greeting cards, stories and instructions (QCA 1999). The early years practitioner facilitates writing independently from an early age (DfEE 1998), and learning about writing by doing it. We encourage children to 'have a go' and work collaboratively, rather than individually and in silence. Talk is seen as vital to the writing process.

The strands of literacy are outlined briefly above, but early years practitioners in successful reception classes link experiences to make them meaningful. Although teachers need to ensure that pupils are developing in all areas of language, these are not typically taught separately and early years educators in the reception class need to consider the interrelationship between all of the modes and plan accordingly.

The current changes in literacy expectations for reception aged pupils are reflected in the English National Curriculum, the Early Learning Goals and The National Literacy Strategy objectives for the reception year. The developmental nature of literacy is emphasised in these documents.

How should we teach speaking and listening, reading and writing?

How children are taught is dependent on how early years practitioners think children best learn. In chapter 2 Linda Miller discussed the importance of play in the learning process and in chapter 13 Robin Campbell detailed early literacy experiences. In the reception class practitioners need to make decisions about appropriate approaches. This can be polarised through total free play at one extreme, to over-formalised direct teaching at the other. However, many early years practitioners would agree that:

> The distinction between play and learning is an outdated concept. Children learn through play and learning can and ought to be fun. Children don't distinguish between their learning and play and nor should we.
> (Margaret Hodge, the Education Minister, 1999 quoted in the *Daily Telegraph*, July 8th 1999 by Liz Lightfoot, Education Correspondent).

Most reception practitioners would agree that prior experiences should be built on, rather than dismissed and discarded. Nevertheless, to meet the reception child's growing needs literacy learning should incorporate a balance of approaches ranging from the informal to the more formal. Practitioners in the reception class will need to decide how appropriate objectives are, and how to sequence and best organise the learning of those objectives. Practitioners must also make the children and their development as literate beings the centre of their work, rather than solely meeting the objectives for teaching literacy. As Mary Jane Drummond reminds us:

It will not do to treat children as if they were nothing more than raw data for competitive league tables. The standards to which we aspire are in the quality of provision for the exercise of literacy and numeracy by all children, not in the levels of attainment reached. (Drummond 1998, p. 4–5)

The key to effective literacy teaching will be in quality interactions with children. A closer look at literacy experiences in a reception class today, and of one child – Kieran, will help to explore these interactions.

Kieran's experience in reception

Early years practitioners need to consider how to cater for pupils who spend differing time in the reception class according to their age; some may spend three terms in a reception class, some two and others one. As in pre-school settings, children in reception classes will be varied in their language experiences, literacy abilities and stages of development. Early years educators in reception classes need refined skills of observation and assessment in order to plan appropriately, differentiate and intervene constructively to support and extend literacy development. Kieran entered infant school last Autumn, just before his fifth birthday. The following is an account of his planned literacy experiences.

Organisation of reception aged children

First Kieran was placed in a small class of 17 children, all rising 5. After the first term, he joined Year 1 pupils and another teacher in a larger class, with the rest of his cohort. He remained there for the rest of the school year, being joined by the January entry cohort in the summer term.

Kieran started infant school in a small class which enabled the teacher to focus on individual needs. Kieran was quiet and shy at first, and the small and caring environment was conducive to settling into school. The need to establish a secure and stimulating environment and a trusting relationship with adults working in the classroom are important factors in literacy development, and indeed in all learning for young children.

The classroom context

Both of Kieran's classrooms were organised into areas for learning; art and construction areas, book corners and listening posts, role play areas, exploration/science areas and carpet spaces for larger group work. The book corner was small in the first class, but well stocked with a range of texts including fiction, non-fiction and poetry, big and small books. In the second class individuals, groups and the whole class could gather in the book corner.

In the first class, the role play area was a home corner, whereas the second began with a café and changed its focus throughout the two terms. Both classrooms displayed environmental print (Miller 1999) and adults' and children's writing. Both displayed alphabets, one which had been made by the children in the second class. Kieran had many stories read and told to him in both classes.

The value of creating such an environment to create an interest in print and to give a purpose and audience for the child's writing has been made elsewhere in this text (see Robin Campbell's chapter).

In both classrooms Kieran was able to work independently and self-initiate learning. He also worked on directed activities. Each room facilitated talk and gave opportunities for talk in differing contexts within the role play areas. He also had opportunities to see print recorded and to record in a variety of ways.

Self-initiated learning

At the start of each day children entered the first classroom and chose an activity for twenty minutes before the register was taken. This built on Kieran's earlier nursery experiences where children independently selected and initiated activities within the framework set up by the adults. Activities included listening to story tapes, playing in the role play area, working with large construction equipment, reading books, drawing and mark-making. During this time Kieran initiated his own work and would work in a variety of ways both collaboratively and independently. At times he would interact with the teacher, language support assistant or the student nursery nurse, but he selected what he would do. The adults observed and responded to Kieran if he approached them.

What was his literacy development? It was apparent that he was learning to use talk for a variety of purposes and was seen to:

- make a running commentary of his actions to himself, for example as he played with cars, or built with construction blocks;
- negotiate use of equipment and share construction materials with his peers;
- tell stories as he handled texts;
- verbalise his needs to others;
- communicate with a range of children and adults.

In the first class the emphasis was on oral development during self-initiated learning time, although Kieran did interact with print and handled texts. He was not seen mark-making during observations in the first class. In the next class Kieran was involved in similar activities, but related more to other children as he worked. By term three he was also observed confidently recording independently. The following is an example of his interactions with two other children.

Kieran, Edward and Davies were at a table. Edward and Davies were drawing swimming pools and Kieran a castle.

Edward:	Splash! The water's everywhere! Cor! He's wet! Wet! Wet!
Davies:	Mine's, (pool water), coming over the sides!
Edward:	What's that? Not a pool?
Kieran:	A castle. A giant castle.

They carried on drawing. Edward 'scribbled' all over his paper, got up and put it in the bin. Davies stopped drawing and watched. Kieran was engrossed in his drawing. Edward got a new piece of paper and began to draw turrets. Davies appeared to realise that Edward was drawing a castle and also got up, put his paper in the bin and got a new sheet. He also began to draw a castle.

Edward:	This is for the arrows. They're fired from here. (He pointed to the slots at the top of his picture.)
Kieran:	Who are they fighting?
Edward:	It's England v Wales.
Kieran:	Oh. Like the football.
Edward:	No! It's Wales v Scotland. This castle is silver. The other's gold. (Kieran drew a flag on one of the castle turrets).
Edward:	Oh! I forgot the flags!
Davies:	Why are they important?
Edward:	If someone goes out hunting they can find their way home. I've drawn an English flag but they're from Scotland and they're pretending to be from England! They're tricking the others! I could do a Man. U. Flag!
Davies:	That's not a country! That's a football club!

While Edward and Davies discussed Edward's picture, Kieran had taken another piece of paper and produced some writing. (Figure 14.1)

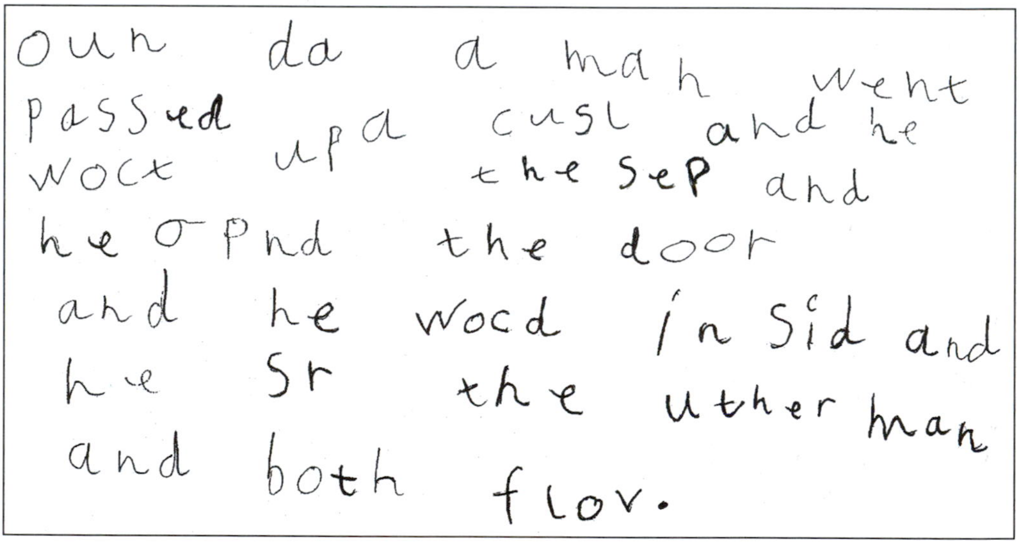
oun da a man went
passed up a cusl and he
woct the sep and
he opnd the door
and he wocd in sid and
he sr the uther man
and both flov.

Figure 14.1 Keiran's writing

One day a man went past a castle and he walked up the steps and he opened the door and he walked inside and he saw the other man and they both fell over.

So what are these children learning about literacy? All of the boys used talk to support their drawing and create narratives. Edward's picture and story were inspired by Kieran's castle drawing and his plot evolved as he drew the flag on his castle. We note that his plot is not simple and his oral narrative is a convoluted plot of deception. Davies clarified Edward's narrative by distinguishing between countries and football clubs. Meanwhile Kieran completed recording his own structured narrative with a beginning, 'one day', a middle 'went up the steps' and an ending, 'they both fell over.'

How children perceive the task of writing is immensely complex. Writing and drawing are symbolic activities. Children make marks on the page for a reason. As they become interested in the page the focus shifts to a connection with the page and an engagement with its form (Pahl 1999, p. 68).

So, without adult presence or direction, Kieran has engaged in story writing during an opportunity to self-select an activity. All of this has been completed, unaided, in twenty minutes or so. Apart from providing time for self-initiated tasks is the adult redundant in terms of literacy development? No, of course not. Firstly, the adult has given space and time for self exploration in literacy. The adults have read and told various traditional tales and books of traditional tales are on the bookshelves. The adults have also encouraged the children to experience traditional tales in a variety of forms and evidence of this can be seen in one of the classroom displays of paintings of 'Our favourite fairy tales' including Kieran's 'Jack and the Beanstalk' painting. (Figure 14.2)

We have painted pictures of our favourite Fairy Tales. Which is your favourite?

Jack and the Beanstalk.

Figure 14.2 Jack and the Beanstalk painting

Children had become involved with the content and structure of the stories and this is reflected in Kieran's writing. The Early Learning Goals state:

> By the end of the foundation stage, most children will be able to:

> show an understanding of the elements of stories, such as main character. sequence of events, and openings. (QCA 1999, p. 27)

They had been encouraged to make choices about their favourites. More importantly the early years practitioners in both reception classes have given Kieran the confidence, self-esteem and desire to write. He implicitly knows that the adults will value his contributions and that they will praise him for the capital letter at the start and the full stop at the end and make explicit to him the structure of his story in terms of his beginning, middle and ending. The adults will understand that this piece is at the appropriate developmental stage of writing and that his spelling will be phonetic in nature, and that 'and' will be overused as a connective. They will understand that his writing is good for his age and stage of development, take note of it and plan to move him forward. With the understanding that writing is a developmental process there is an expectation, and indeed acceptance, that errors will occur and that the writing will not be perfect the first time. These early attempts at writing are known as 'emergent writing' (Hall 1989).

As stated in the Early Learning Goals:

> By the end of the foundation stage, most children will be able to:
> use their phonic knowledge to write simple regular words and make phonetically plausible attempts at more complex ones;
> . . . begin to form simple sentences, sometimes using punctuation.
> (QCA 1999, p. 27)

Children are expected to write independently from an early age and to develop as writers by writing. Early years practitioners will understand the importance of valuing children's written contributions, praise these efforts and send them home to be seen by parents and carers. Of course they will have taken the trouble to explain the features of early writing to those parents/carers and involved them in encouraging and praising writing and mark-making too.

Both parents and carers are invited into the class to work alongside their own and other children during self-initiated time at the beginning of the day. They can read with their child and talk to them as they work. Some also stay to work alongside the educators during the morning session. The interactions observed in the two classrooms were positive and constructive for all children.

During self-initiated work times all children were engaged in a range of activities which involved speaking and listening for a range of purposes. Pupils were also observed reading independently, one to one with an adult, or with each other or in informal groups and mark-making for a range of purposes. In summary, it is difficult to specify for each child exactly what will be learned in terms of literacy, but that self-initiated learning time enables children to engage in:

- constructive dialogue between children for a range of purposes;
- reading and revisiting self chosen texts, (and in the above example with adult support);
- creating narratives through drawing and construction;
- opportunities for mark-making;
- revisiting areas worked on at other times;
- refining literacy skills by doing.

It is important that practitioners in the early years at the start of formal schooling, continue to monitor how the children in their care use self-initiated time, and to analyse and detail the value of work undertaken in times of non-direct teaching in relation to the role the adult should play in literacy development.

Planned learning opportunities: Direct teaching and shared text work

Alongside self-initiated pupil activities, early years practitioners working with reception aged children plan for direct teaching of literacy. In Kieran's reception classes direct teaching took place for the whole class group after the 20 to 30 minutes of self-selected work. In the first class the initial emphasis was on shared reading with big books, gradually moving to a balance of reading and writing.

In Kieran's first class shared text work took 10–15 minutes and was of a highly interactive nature. The children would discuss the front cover of the book and then collaboratively read simple texts following the model of the adult. The texts used had a repetitive or rhyme structure. The teacher engaged them in matching words one to one, and making and reading the sentences as a group. The emphasis was primarily on reading for meaning and enjoyment and only then decoding. (Figure 14.3)

Figure 14.3 'I Love Animals' shared reading

The shared approach to reading is 'valuable for less able readers who gain access to texts of greater richness and complexity than they would otherwise be able to read', (DfEE 1998, p. 11) and one can see the relevance of this to reception aged pupils. Through shared reading adults can also teach about grammar and punctuation in context. In reception classes shared reading can be lead by the teacher in one large group, or organised into two smaller groups with another adult. The National Literacy Strategy advocates that reading should be taught using the 4 searchlights model as detailed in Figure 14.4, (DfEE 1998, p. 4).

Readers use a variety of strategies, often simultaneously, to read. Practitioners in reception classes need to be aware of the strategies used and how children can be encouraged to employ them effectively. Kieran's first reception teacher drew on all of these strategies, and his teacher for terms two and three, made more explicit the use of varying strategies. The following interaction exemplifies this:

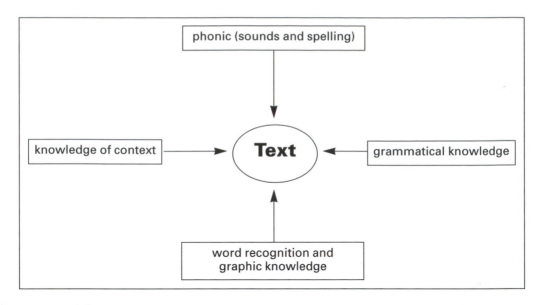

Figure 14.4

Teacher reads:	They are found dead under logs. (She substitutes logs for leaves)
She then asks:	Did I read that right? Can you spot the mistake I've made?
Children:	Leaves!
Teacher:	How do we all know that it's 'leaves' and not logs? Does logs make sense?
Children:	Yes.
Teacher:	So how do we know that it's not leaves?
Kieran:	It's got l and s but a different middle.
Teacher:	Yes. Look at the middle. It has eave. What would logs have?
Child:	O sound.
Teacher:	Yes. How would we write that?
Child:	O
Teacher:	Yes and this is an e sound . . .

This, of course, was done after the teacher had asked the children to recap what the information book was about and they had discussed the habitats of the various animals included in this information text. Comprehension is key and that is aided by re-reading a range of familiar texts frequently.

The teacher works with the class on shared writing. As with shared reading, the direct teaching and modelling aspects of writing takes place. Furthermore reception children are involved in composing for a range of purposes.

In Kieran's classes shared writing took place alongside the shared reading. This usually consisted of the teacher modelling writing and scribing the group's composition. In the first reception class the teacher developed the shared reading of 'I Love Animals' (McDonnell 1996) by asking the children to write a sentence about what they liked and first modelled on the whiteboard before asking them to have a go independently.

For Kieran, the shared text work was focused and enjoyable. A range of interesting texts at the level of the children were used and the adults used them in imaginative and interactive ways, using skilful questioning and physical interaction to involve all pupils. Kieran read aloud during shared reading sessions and joined in writing sessions. He appeared on task during independent tasks resulting from this work. Although a quiet member of the class(es), he was involved in the sessions observed and actively engaged during these daily sessions of 15–20 minutes.

Direct teaching time enables children to engage in:

- reading and writing texts which they would not be able to handle independently;
- talking about texts;
- considering the language features of texts;
- enjoyable whole text experiences.

It is important that early years practitioners consider how to mediate these literacy sessions to effectively engage children in activities which promote a love of reading and writing.

Planned literacy learning opportunities: guided and supported text work

Guided reading involves pupils working in small ability levelled groups to read texts supported by educators. Kieran worked with a small group plus the teacher, and demonstrated an ability to read independently and discuss the text within the group. He was also seen working alongside the teacher on his writing. The National Literacy Strategy has made explicit that there should be a variety of ways for writing to be developed. Opportunities for writers should include small group guidance which:

> allows the teacher to support and encourage pupils who are tackling a similar task and to monitor their use of the range of skills and processes in writing (Beard 1998).

More class teachers are planning for other adults to work with groups of children on the guided tasks. This is endorsed by the Additional Literacy Learning Support Materials (DfEE 1999) and has implications for practitioners in the early years with regard to understanding the processes involved in reading and writing and how to support children in a small group situation. Adults need to see their role as one of working alongside children to model writing and to discuss or conference with children the features of their writing. In the discussion the adult will respond to the content and technical features, praise what is correct as well as attempts at unknown words and structure. The adult will edit the work with the child. Whilst it is considered legitimate for adults to write for children, this now takes the form of scribing or underwriting. The value of copy writing has been questioned. Scribing is writing down what children want to write in order to support the composition. Underwriting is writing the conventional form of the child's writing either underneath or alongside the child's writing after the child is given time and space to 'have a go.'

Planned literacy opportunities: independent learning

Alongside direct teaching of literacy, there also needs to be opportunities for independent work where children can explore their literary interests and compose, practice and consolidate taught experiences. Early years practitioners need to consider how to organise independent literacy activities which are both self-initiated by pupils and adult directed. Kieran's reception classes both gave opportunities for self-initiated work at the start of the day. In the first class more opportunities were given after the shared text work, as pupils were able to plan their work for the bulk of the independent session, although withdrawn to work with the teacher on directed literacy work for a few minutes. During this directed time the adult guided the pupils to work independently, often observing if pupils could complete the task unaided, or intervening through questioning and demonstrating to give successful literacy experiences. During the second class, the teacher worked with a group of pupils while the learning assistant took on the same role as the first reception teacher to support pupils in the literacy tasks. Both classrooms encouraged independence and gave focused support and quality interactions. The value of play was apparent and adults were aware of their crucial role in:

- planning and resourcing a challenging environment;
- supporting children's learning through planned play activity;
- extending and supporting children's spontaneous play;
- extending and developing children's language and communication in their play.

The practitioners were also aware that through play children can:

- think creatively and imaginatively;
- communicate with others as they investigate or solve problems.
  (QCA 1999, p. 12)

Planned literacy opportunities: language development across the curriculum

In the early years, literacy learning takes place across the curriculum and practitioners maximise literacy opportunities as all other areas are developed. Young children are given the opportunity to talk, read and write about numerous topics, and to develop their understandings in different, but complementary ways.

Implications for practitioners of reception aged children

The task of supporting children through the crucial stage where they realise they cannot actually read 'word for word' but are retelling stories and 'play reading', and that their writing cannot actually be read by a wider audience, usually falls to practitioners in reception classes. Therefore early years practitioners need to be skilled at maintaining pupils' confidence and self-esteem as talkers, readers and writers. They need to organise a variety of literacy experiences, which not only meet teaching the objectives and goals for literacy, but effectively develop all pupils, and give reception children the confidence and the desire to want to talk, read and write. How to, and when to, intervene in order that pupils develop effectively is always an issue for practitioners in the reception class. The environment in the reception class should be organised to support a range of literacy opportunities (QCA 1999).

Reception educators need to nurture literacy development and have high expectations for pupils' literacy achievements but need to:

Strike a balance between promoting early progress and avoiding an inappropriate emphasis on academic provision for children so young (Beard 1998).

Acknowledgements

Thanks to practitioners, pupils and parents of St Andrew's J. M. I. School, Hitchin for their patience and collaboration during this case study work. Special thanks to Kieran's parents and to the reception class teachers Alison Brooks and Helen Peto for allowing their practices to be recorded and the head teacher, Sue Sanderson, for enabling the research to take place.

References

Beard, R. (1998) *Review of the National Literacy Strategy and Research Related Evidence*. Sudbury: DfEE Publications.

DfEE (1989) *English In The National Curriculum*. London: HMSO.

DfEE (1998) *The National Literacy Strategy: Framework for teaching*. Sudbury: DfEE Publications.

DfEE (1999) *Additional Learning Support Materials*. London: HMSO.

Drummond, M. (1998) 'Warning: Words Can Bite'. *Co-ordinate*. Issue No 66.

Hall, N. (1989) *Writing With Reason. The Emergence of Authorship in Young Children*. Sevenoaks: Hodder & Stoughton.

Hodge, M. (1999) 'Four year olds are not too young to be taught the three Rs'. London: *The Daily Telegraph*, reported by Liz Lightfoot, Education Correspondent, July.

Miller, L. (1999) *Moving Towards Literacy with Environmental Print*. Royston, Herts: United Kingdom Reading Association.

Pahl, K. (1999) *Transformations: Children's Meaning Making In A Nursery*. Stoke-on-Trent: Trentham Books.

Qualifications and Curriculum Authority (1999) *Early Learning Goals*. London: Qualifications and Curriculum Authority.

Children's book

McDonnell, F. (1996) *I Love Animals*. London: Walker Books.

Chapter 15

Children growing and changing: the interpersonal world of the growing child

Patti Owens

What is so important about interpersonal development?

As an early years practitioner for over twenty years, I have had the opportunity to observe a lot of young children and adults interacting as they spend time together. Nowadays I also work as a psychotherapist with adult clients. Time and again I hear stories of love and care offered to these people as children by nursery nurses, nannies, teachers and playgroup workers, as well as parents. And, of course, I hear the bleaker tales of rejection, humiliation and sometimes abuse at the same hands. Our responsibility as early years practitioners is a serious and important one in human terms; we play a key role in both the *intra*personal and *inter*personal development of human beings. Our work with the youngest children has a profound effect on the way they come to feel intrapersonally, or 'inside themselves', and on the manner of being they adopt as adults, in interpersonal relationships with others.

Interpersonal development is, perhaps, an area of human development that we could be more aware of. As a result largely of political factors, 'child development', as it has traditionally been called, has come under some suspicion in current educational thinking. In teacher education, with its emphasis on 'academic subjects', child development has been widely relegated to a special 'option'. Even amongst early childhood educators there has been a tendency simply to keep teaching the major theorists from the past (Davenport 1991, Owens 1997).

These trends seem doubly unfortunate. First, poorly informed professionals can not adequately support a child's interpersonal development, and we pay the cost in society as children grow up into adults who do not relate effectively to others, or even feel good about themselves. Secondly, despite the great contribution made by past theorists, it is easy to criticise some of their ideas from a modern perspective. Without an understanding of important research conducted more recently, early years practitioners can be left feeling that it is better to trust one's intuition in these matters, rather than a faulty or mistaken developmental theory.

A new approach to developmental theory

In this chapter I want to argue that some of the more recent research on children's development is worth knowing about because it can help enrich our observation and understanding of the inner world of children. Though you might want to return to the earlier theorists indicated in the References of this chapter to see the historical context, you do not need to know their work in detail in order to make use of the newer research.

I have identified three themes which together inform current developmental theory and create a background for my discussion, later on in this chapter, of Daniel Stern's model of interpersonal development in very young children (Stern 1985).

1. There is now an emphasis on 'whole' child development. In effect this means that we are no longer easy with the notion of separating out areas of development. When I focus here on interpersonal development I keep in mind that this is only one, though a very important, aspect of every child's experience and perception. The notion of 'whole-ness' also transcends old-fashioned terms like 'phase' or 'stage' of development, favoured by earlier theorists. We concentrate on young children, but of course interpersonal development continues throughout human life, and it is often experience rather than ages, phases or stages, that triggers off new learning at a particular point.
2. The old debate about 'Nature versus Nurture' does not in fact get us very far, much as this has preoccupied past theorists (Bee 1992). We now give due recognition to the fact that human development takes place in a social context. The process whereby a child grows in human character and understanding is more like a 'transaction' than a battle where one side is dominant. We are learning much more about the complexity of neonate and infant experience (Kagan 1984, Berry Brazelton and Cramer 1991). Recent researchers, furthermore, have identified the critical influence that even young children bring to bear on their carers and their environment, so changing the course of their own development (Woodhead *et al.* 1991).
3. Unlike major theorists such as Freud, who seems never to have actually observed an infant whilst constructing his theories about human developmental psychology, recent researchers base their theoretical models on close, detailed infant and child observation. Whilst accepting that observations provide the evidence for ideas about how children develop, most researchers also see the practical impossibility of a totally objective 'scientific' stance. The observer will be influenced by, amongst other things, their own early experiences, often seeing events through the filter of their own childhood memories (Houston 1995). Modern researchers try to take account of this unavoidable subjectivity. Daniel Stern (1985), for example, uses the notion of the 'participant observer' where he checks out his own observations and intuitions against those of any other adults, usually parents or carers, who are participating in the observation.

Without a theory, such observations and intuitions can be very interesting and rewarding to follow up, but they remain un-grounded. Current researchers, therefore, construct models of development that offer a kind of map, or template against which we can orient our observations. Unlike past developmental theorists whose work has often been presented as scientifically true, or even proven, modern researchers tend to take a more humble attitude, but one that enables them to continually check their theory against what they actually observe, revising the model in the light of further research. In this way, a theory can only ever be more or less 'useful', not more or less true.

These three characteristics of modern developmental theory are evident in the work of Daniel Stern, and it is to that research I now turn.

Daniel Stern's model of infant interpersonal development

Daniel Stern draws on two perspectives in constructing his model of infant development: psychoanalysis and developmental psychology, notably attachment theory (Bowlby 1965, Barnes 1995). As a developmental psychologist he is a committed infant observer; as a psychotherapist he makes some inferences about the infant's 'inner' psychological world, based on his experience of taking adults through the process of psychoanalysis. Stern gives a detailed account of the first two years of life, during which period he argues that the infant goes through the process of developing four distinct 'senses of self'. Each sense of self begins its development only when the infant has particular experiences and gains particular human capacities, during the process of wider growth and change. Stern refers to these sets of experiences as 'domains of experience' — not stages or phases of development.

In the first eight weeks or so of life the infant's sense of self is 'emergent' and the primary need seems to be for 'relatedness' with the primary care giver, usually the parent(s). Stern sees as crucial the infant's capacity at this point to perceive events and experiences with their 'whole' self. Think for a moment of a baby feeding: he or she touches, smells, sighs, desires to be fed, experiences satisfaction. These experiences do not distinguish between the physical and the emotional, for the infant's perception of the world takes place using their whole being. Correspondingly, Stern notices the importance of a key 'parental assumption', namely that this infant is a person with developing human characteristics. Consider how we might say to a very young infant things like, 'You want your nappy changed don't you?', or 'I bet you wish your sister was here.' Stern thinks, rightly in my view, that past developmental theorists have been wrong to see this neonate behaviour as purely based on physical survival needs. In doing so they have 'looked right past' what was happening in front of their eyes, as infant and parent/carer make those significant initial contacts; the beginnings of human relatedness. Hence Stern's labelling of this first domain of experience, the 'domain of emergent relatedness'.

Then between about two and six months of age, the infant develops what Stern calls a 'core sense of self', based on experiences and perceptions in the domain of 'core relatedness' to another human being, usually the parent or carer with whom the infant spends most interactive time. If we imagine for a moment that the infant could speak, he or she might say, 'I am a being with a physical presence. I can feel physical sensations, which for me are not separate from my emotional feelings. If I am happy I feel good in my body; if I am distressed I feel pain. I am aware that other beings (parents/carers) can influence how I feel.'

What is more, Stern's observations lead him to hypothesise that the infant begins at this time to remember the most often repeated events, and then make generalisations based on these rememberings. Stern calls this process the establishment of RIGs, or 'Repeated Interactions that are Generalised'. The experience of, say, having a bib put on comes to be associated in the infant with nourishment, which is a physical need. But the experience is also strongly associated with closeness to the parent/carer, and with that more of a sense of himself or herself as both distinct from, and related to, that other person. If the physical nourishment goes along with welcome, appropriate interaction from a parent/carer who tunes in to the infant on more than just a physical level, these experiences can be generalised to form special RIGs that will persist very strongly throughout their coming life. Good experiences of this kind, which include the special interaction with another person who gives emotional, as well as physical, nourishment, can help the infant to experience what Stern calls an 'evoked companion', or the experience of being 'not alone' psychologically, even when this is materially the case. Work with insecure children and adults suggests that where this process has not happened for some reason, the individual can not 'evoke a companion'; they can not believe that they will be protected and nurtured, however safe they are in fact (Gillie 1999).

The third sense of self, the 'subjective' sense, begins to be experienced, according to Stern's observations, around seven to nine months. This is the domain of 'inter-subjective relatedness' where, all being well, the infant comes to trust that his or her own feeling states are both unique to himself or herself, and capable of being understood by significant other people, mainly parents or carers. The infant realises for the first time, perhaps, that 'I have a mind, and so does this other person'. Intimacy can be more or less deep and fulfilling for the infant, depending on how he or she experiences the other person in relation to himself or herself. Crucial to this new development is the 'care-giver's empathy', or indeed lack of it. This is the first time, says Stern, that the care-giver's 'socialisation of the infant's subjective experience' becomes an issue. The parent or carer has responsibility for affirming or denying the infant's inner, subjective experience. A child can learn that some of their feelings – the need to weep, the urge to reach out and love another, for example – are, or are not, acceptable. These attitudes, as Stern notes, tend to move forward with us into adulthood, as strong and persistent RIGs.

All three domains of experience and perception continue through infancy and beyond, and we need to bear in mind that these are not stages or phases of development like those traditionally outlined, but ways of experiencing ourselves and other human beings that have their beginnings in our infant histories. These early experiences become part of our adult ways of being; part of how we experience ourselves in relation to others, helping to form our habitual attitudes and predispositions to the ever changing circumstances of ordinary human life.

The fourth domain of 'verbal relatedness' depends on language acquisition and comes to the fore, according to Stern, at around fifteen to eighteen months. The infant becomes capable of making clear to others that they know things, using symbols and words. This gives them another way of thinking about themselves, others and the wider world; they begin to develop a 'verbal self'. Central to this process is the forging of 'we meanings'. Think of the kind of example where a toddler tries to make himself or herself understood; fails at first, then succeeds. Such verbal agreement, though necessarily symbolic (words are in themselves abstract entities) adds a kind of concrete-ness to the child's reality. Before words, a lot depends on the child's ability to respond to, then initiate, interactions with their parents and carers, in conjunction with the parent/carer's empathetic and welcoming response to the child's efforts. Now, says Stern, words can be used to solidify the sense that 'we' understand things together. The child can gain enormously in confidence and ability to relate and communicate with others, in generalising from these verbally supported RIGs. As with the other domains of infant experience, however, there is also the possibility to distort or fracture the child's experience. Words add another even more powerful dimension in such cases. An all too common example is the child who experiences violence or abuse from a 'carer' who at the same time speaks kind words like 'I love you, I don't want to hurt you, but . . .'. Or there is the example of the child whose attempts to reach out in affection to another person are met with words that should express reciprocation, but do not; the child instead hears harshness of tone, or experiences emotional coolness, not the warmth the words alone might suggest. As psychotherapists know, there are many ways in which the experience of 'words not matching my reality' can become part of the adult's way of being in the world, and their habitual expectations in relation to others.

Some implications of Stern's research for early years practitioners

So what are we to make of Stern's model of infant interpersonal development, as early years practitioners? Many of us will have dealings with infants and very young children so the relevance may be immediately apparent. Others will be working mainly with older children in the 0–6 years age range. It might be interesting then to notice how Stern's notions of 'domains' of experience, and development of different 'senses of self', for instance, can inform your observation and understanding of older children's interpersonal development.

With these issues in mind, I want to finish this chapter with an infant observation I recently undertook and analysed in the light of Stern's model of infant interpersonal development.

Observation of Thomas

Contextual note

I observe Thomas in June 1999 when he is ten months old (43 weeks). He is with his father, who shares childcare with Thomas' mother; both parents do paid part-time work. They are at a toy library group close to their home, which Thomas has visited twice before with his mother. Thomas and his father are playing on a large mat where four other children, all under a year, are using the selection of colourful and soft toys set out by the toy library leader and her assistants.

Observation method

As the observer, I have known Thomas' parents for several years. Thomas is their first child, and I have observed Thomas in the home setting on a number of occasions since his birth. I try to keep myself in the background, though if Thomas approaches me I will interact with him as normally as possible. Thomas' father has agreed to be a participant observer, and discuss the observation with me after it has been completed. The observation lasts about 5 minutes.

Record of observation

Thomas has been sitting near an eleven month-old girl, picking up and dropping squares of coloured felt fabric. He rolls from a sitting position into a crawl, moving across the mat for a couple of metres. He sits up, head turned to the right, and points, making excited 'Ee-ee-ee-ee!' sounds. Thomas' father, who has been watching him, looks in the direction of Thomas' pointing finger. Thomas first looks at his father's face, then back in the pointing direction. Thomas' father says, 'What do you want, Tom? Yes, cubes . . . they look exciting, don't they?', and pointing at them himself, says, 'Ye-e-e-e-eh – cubes!'. Thomas looks at his father's face again and chuckles, then points, looking at his own hand, then at his father's face again, then his father's hand. Thomas suddenly lurches into a crawl, going over to the soft, coloured cubes. He sits up again, and bangs his hand down a few times on one of the cubes, making the 'Ee-ee-ee!' sound again. Thomas' father comes over. 'Bang, bang, bang!' he says, tapping his fingers on the cube. Thomas watches him do this then looks away, this time pointing in front of himself towards another cube. He makes as if to crawl towards it then stops and looks up at his father's face. Seeing his father look away (he has noticed another child throwing toys in a rather dangerous looking manner) Thomas whimpers then starts to cry, banging his arms and kicking his legs. 'Oh, what's the matter?' whispers Thomas' father, 'Wasn't I looking at the cube with you?' He strokes Thomas' face and Thomas stops crying and points again to the cube in front of him. 'OK Thomas', says his father, 'This cube is a yellow one – Ye-e-e-llow!' Thomas laughs and looks up, touching his father's smiling mouth.

My response to this observation, in the light of Stern's research

This observation reflects very clearly some of the key points in Stern's model of the development of a 'subjective sense of self'. Thomas is apparently seeking what Stern calls a 'shared subjective experience' with his father. He is not content merely to enjoy his own knowledge (That's a cube over there!) and mastery (I can sit, crawl, grasp, be excited, feel happy, be worried, point my finger and make daddy look . . .). He wants to do what Stern calls 'sharing the focus of attention' with his father. Being 'preverbal', Thomas needs experiences of the kind that do not require language, though his 'Ee-ee-ee-eeh!' sounds communicate excitement effectively enough. He uses pointing himself, to make his father look in a particular direction, as well as looking in the direction that his father points, rather than simply looking at his hand as a younger infant might have done. All this indicates a shared experience where Thomas is both aware of his own physical and feeling state, and trusting that his father will understand that too, because somehow the father seems to have similar feelings.

These early interpersonal experiences rely on a special kind of empathy that Stern labels 'affect attunement'. I noticed that Thomas' father responded to his son's excited 'Ee-ee-ee-eeh!' sounds with words spoken at a similar vocal pitch: 'Ye-e-e-eh, cubes!', accompanied by a sort of wriggle in his upper body. When I asked Thomas' father why he might have done this, he said that although he had not thought about it at the time, on reflection this 'wriggle' was another way of letting Thomas know that his excitement was 'contagious' – a shareable human experience. Stern thinks that these experiences of affect attunement 'recast the event, and shift the focus of attention to what is behind the behaviour, to the quality of feeling that is being shared'. So here Thomas learns that he can have feelings of excitement, enthusiasm, concern, fear, all of which are capable of being understood by this important other person, his father. And further, Thomas can know more about his own inner feelings now, as well as responding to more overt parental behaviour.

Of course, Stern's model leaves some things unanswered and may generate some objections. Stern himself wonders if 'different societies could minimise or maximise this need for intersubjectivity'. He is aware that in a society like many in the West, where individualisation of human experience is highly valued, we run the risk of losing out in interpersonal terms. Certainly the many signs of personal and social breakdown seem to point to this trend, so it is not surprising that Stern, like myself and others in the field of psychotherapy and counselling, should see a need to attend to the interpersonal, as well as the individual development of the infant (PCSR 1997, AHPP 1999). Stern's model, however, may not be generalisable across the spectrum of different human societies.

In conclusion

Writing as an early childhood educator, I can see that Stern's ideas lend more weight to some of the principles we already hold dear, such as the guidelines on appropriate adult to infant childcare ratios enshrined in the Children Act (1989), or the principle that 'children need relationships with significant responsive adults' at the foundation of the 0–3 *Educare* curriculum (Rouse and Griffin 1992). If we are to have infants and very young children in institutionalised childcare situations at all, these must be centres not just of excellent educational practice, with trained professionals to care for the children in a well resourced environment, but also places where these 'unseen' interpersonal processes can be nourished in the growing child. Whether an infant or young child is cared for in their own home, by a trained childminder, or in some other early years setting, 'what is at stake here is nothing less that the shape and extent of the sharable inner universe of the child' (Stern 1985).

Writing as a psychotherapist, I see daily the effects of neglecting the interpersonal world of the growing child, in favour of other kinds of 'success'. The majority of people who attend my practice are outwardly successful and have achieved a great deal 'out there' in the world. Their lameness is internal; their pain is often silent and hidden from others. Long ago, they lost the trust that others will be capable of understanding how they feel; as adults their apparent self confidence is not supported by the internal strength that can only grow, it seems, in the company of another person who affirms and encourages interpersonal efforts.

I make use of Stern's idea that the 'domains of experience' go on developing throughout a human life. It is never too late, I suspect, to experience another's empathy and attunement to one's inner world; this experience can bring healing, even to adults quite advanced in years. How much better then, to show our children that feelings matter as much as mental arithmetic; that caring for each other is no less important than learning to read (QCA 1999). Our support for the interpersonal development of young children is no 'optional extra'; it provides the solid ground on which to build a healthy and happy human life.

References

AHPP publications (1999) *Association of Humanistic Psychotherapy Practitioners.* London.

Barnes, P. (1995) *Personal, Social and Emotional Development of Children.* Milton Keynes and Oxford: Open University and Blackwell.

Bee, H. (1992) *The Developing Child.* New York: Harper Collins.

Berry Brazelton, T. and Cramer, B. G. (1991) *The Earliest Relationship.* London: Karnak House.

Bowlby, J. (1965) *Child Care and the Growth of Love.* Harmondsworth: Penguin.

Davenport, G. C. (1991) *An Introduction to Child Development.* London: Collins.

Gillie, M. (1999) 'Daniel Stern: A Developmental Theory for Gestalt?', *British Gestalt Journal* forthcoming, December 1999.

Houston, G. (1995) *The Now Red Book of Gestalt.* London: Gaie Houston.

Kagan, J. (1984) *The Nature of the Child.* New York: Basic Books.

Owens, P. (ed.) (1997) *Early Childhood Education and Care.* Stoke on Trent: Trentham.

PCSR Publications (1997) *Psychotherapists and Counsellors for Social Responsibility.* London.

Qualifications and Curriculum Authority (1999) *Investing in our Future: Early Learning Goals.* London: Qualifications and Curriculum Authority.

Rouse, D. and Griffin, S. (1992) 'Quality for the under threes', in Pugh, G. (ed.) *Contemporary Issues in the Early Years.* London: NCB/Paul Chapman.

Stern, D. N. (1985) *The Interpersonal World of the Infant: A view from psychoanalysis and developmental psychology.* New York: Basic Books.

Woodhead, M. *et al.* (1991) *Becoming a Person.* London and New York: Routledge.

Chapter 16
Number in play and everyday life

Val Warren and Susan Westmoreland

We only need to reflect on the past twenty-four hours to see how maths and especially number are part of everyday life: reading bus or train timetables, following recipes or selecting the correct coins to pay for the newspaper. However, research (Munn and Shaffer 1993) suggests that young children do not naturally focus on number unless they are encouraged to do so by adults around them. Adults need to actively engage children in opportunities to count and use number in everyday events, play, rhymes, songs, books and games. Similarly, in chapter 13 Robin Campbell emphasised the importance of adult support in children's acquisition of knowledge about reading and writing at home.

This chapter uses a case study of Amber (aged four) to illustrate how her numeracy in the areas of counting, addition and subtraction, number recognition and representation has developed as a pre-school child. It also offers some indication of her anticipated experience as she starts school at five years of age in the Reception class. There is a distinction between a child's experience of numeracy in the home, in an early years setting and later in school, illustrated in Figure 16.1. There is also a change in the nature of adult interaction during these three phases.

At home early numeracy experiences occur in play and during everyday activities, although the extent to which this takes place is dependent on culture

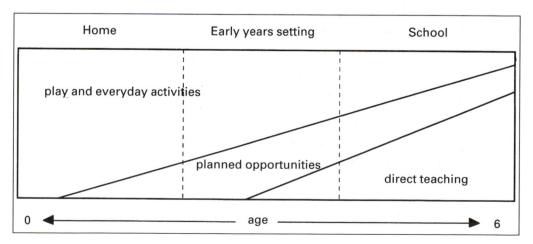

Figure 16.1 Early numeracy experiences

and social context (Rogoff *et al.* 1998). These experiences continue in early years settings with the addition of planned opportunities for numeracy and there may also be some direct teaching. At school this balance changes so that direct teaching (whole class or groups) provides the main numeracy experiences. This change denotes a move from informal learning at home to more formal learning at school (Tizard and Hughes 1984).

Teaching and learning early numeracy

By the time they start school research has shown that children are already competent mathematicians (Aubrey 1997). For example, before the age of two young children show an understanding of quantity. This contrasts with the deficit or empty vessel model which focuses on what children do not know rather than what they do know.

How do children learn about number? Clarke and Atkinson (1996) describe learning mathematics as being like a jigsaw made up of interlocking pieces. They emphasise the complexity of the process, pointing out that children often learn things which we have not taught them and fail to learn the things that we have taught them. This can be explained by the idea that from the earliest age children attempt to make sense of their world and therefore construct their own knowledge by assimilating new ideas and experiences into existing ones. It follows that this process is different for every child.

Play can be regarded as children's active involvement with their environment (Neaum and Tallack 1997). At home and in early years settings it is the most appropriate way of learning. It provides practical, first-hand experiences in meaningful contexts with opportunities for the use of language about number. Adult support in this language development is essential. They need to be aware of the potential of activities, know when to intervene and when not, consolidate existing learning and extend to new learning. Although free play has benefits, children's learning is maximised by high level of adult–child interaction during play (Meadows and Cashdan 1988). For example, one evening Amber decided she would like some cheese and crackers for her supper.

'How many would you like?'

'Three please'.

(One cracker was taken out and buttered).

'I said I would like three crackers, Mummy'.

'How many more crackers do I need to butter for you?'

'Two more', she replied.

(Another cracker was taken out of the packet and buttered).

'Just one more now, Mummy.'

Amber's mother could have simply opened the packet, taken the three crackers out and given them to her. However, the opportunity to develop her understanding of calculation and use the appropriate mathematical vocabulary would have been lost.

Counting

'Say and use the number names in order in familiar contexts' 'Count reliably up to 10 everyday objects.'

These statements are included in the National Numeracy Strategy Key Objectives for children in Reception classes. They are the same as the Early Learning Goals for mathematical development for three to five year olds.

To an adult, counting seems a simple, straight forward task. However, a closer look at what is involved in the process of counting reveals the complexity of the task. Furthermore, we use number words in three different ways: cardinal, ordinal and nominal. Cardinal refers to the quantity in a given set or group, e.g. Ten green bottles or Five little speckled frogs. Ordinal refers to the order or position in a sequence, e.g. the first little pig or the second Billy Goat Gruff. Nominal refers to a name or a label, e.g. telephone numbers and house numbers.

Counting involves several skills which have been classified as counting principles (Gelman and Gallistel 1978). First, the counting words need to be repeated in the correct order (the stable-order principle). These words have no logical pattern until sixteen (e.g. 'thirteen', not 'threeteen') and the lower decades are irregular (e.g. 'twenty', not 'two-ty'). Reciting the words, however, is not enough to count correctly. Many young children are able to recite the numbers in order like singing the words of a song but cannot count accurately. As a toddler Amber could sing, '1, 2, 3, 4, 5, once I caught a fish alive!' yet had no understanding of the significance of the words as indicators to aid counting the number of fingers on her hand. Second, everything must be counted only once (the one-to-one principle). This means that the child must assign one number name to each object and in the early stages this can give rise to a number of errors (Montague-Smith 1997). The third skill is knowing that the last number in the count is the size of the set (the cardinal principle). This represents a later stage of development as it is dependent upon the first two principles. Amber (aged 3 years ten months) drew her family 'Mummy', 'Ruby', 'Daddy', 'That's me'. and unprompted counted, 'There are one, two, three, four people in my family' (Figure 16.2).

Once these skills have been mastered the child also needs to learn that they can be applied in any situation (the abstraction principle) and that objects can be counted in any order (the order-irrelevance principle).

In addition to these specific counting skills young children also use subitizing. This is a perception-based strategy in which the child automatically recognises the number of objects (up to five or six) by their arrangement without counting them. When eating her breakfast cereal, Amber noticed a group of five Sugar Puffs clustered together and called, 'Hey look Mummy, there's five altogether!' When asked how she knew, she said it looked like a dice. At three years old she could recognise instantly one, two and three. Her ability to subitize was developed by opportunities to count and see patterns in the arrangement of numbers, particularly board games and dominoes.

In order to be successful at counting children need a broader experience than simply counting objects which can be touched. Montague-Smith (1997, p. 10) suggests that they need opportunities to count:

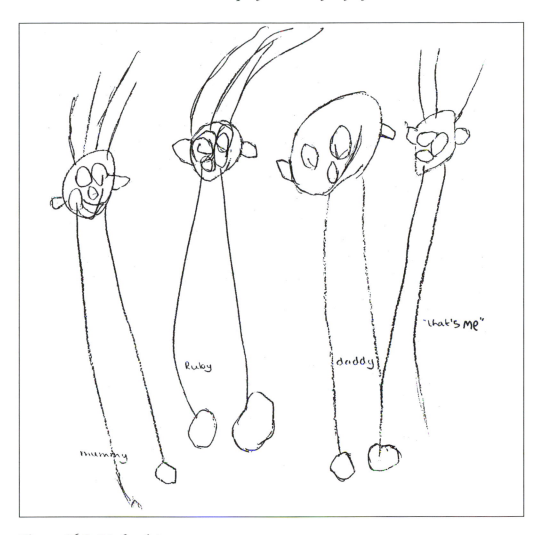

Figure 16.2 'My family'

- items in a set which can be counted again with the items in a different order
- items which can be touched but not moved (e.g. in a book)
- items which can be seen but not touched (e.g. trees)
- sounds
- physical movements
- given quantities of items (e.g. Amber counted out five sweets for each party bag before her birthday party).

The importance of counting for number development has been increasingly emphasised as a result of research since the 1970s. Thompson (1997, p. 157) stated that 'counting should constitute the basis of the early years number curriculum and not the 'sorting sets, matching and ordering' approach'. That approach involving pre-number activities owed much to the thinking of Piaget who believed that children could not understand number until they could think logically. He also maintained that until children reached the age of six or seven, they could not conserve number (i.e. the number of objects in a set remain unchanged regardless of how they are arranged) and therefore they could not develop the concept of number. Counting brings together the cardinal and ordinal aspects of number when the child recites the number names in the correct order and gives the final number as the size of the set.

Early addition and subtraction

'Find one more or one less than a number from 1 to 10'
'In practical activities and discussion begin to use the vocabulary involved in adding and subtracting'
'Begin to relate addition to combining two groups of objects, and subtraction to "taking away"'
(*National Numeracy Strategy*, DfEE 1999)

Very young children are able to compare two small groups of sweets and know that one group has more! This comparing of quantities is the beginning of addition and subtraction which will become more formalised with the use of the appropriate language 'more', 'the same' and 'fewer' or 'less'. However, until recently formal work on the number operations of addition and subtraction has not been considered appropriate until the age of five or six. The work of Hughes (1986) challenged thinking about the capabilities of pre-school children and their ability to calculate. He found that children could add and subtract providing situations were meaningful and the numbers involved were very small. This change in expectation was reflected in *Desirable Outcomes for Children's Learning* (SCAA 1996) and now the Early Learning Goals (QCA 1999).

Early addition and subtraction arise from the counting process. Initially in addition children will 'count all', i.e. they will count out each set, put them together into a new set, and then count all the objects in the new set. Even at four years of age, although Amber knew that she had five fingers on one hand she still counted them all to work out one more. The next stage is to 'count on' starting from the number which indicates the size of the first set, e.g. 6, 7, 8, 9. This is further developed by 'counting on' starting with the largest number. Finally young children may progress to calculating using known number facts e.g. number bonds to ten, and then using derived number facts, e.g. doubles (Carpenter and Moser 1984).

Subtraction requires the ability to count backwards as well as forwards. Songs like 'Five currant buns' and 'Ten green bottles' both require the ability to count back. As a toddler, Amber would sing the song but wait for the adult to say the next number in the sequence. At almost five years old, although Amber is able to count back from ten, she is just beginning to calculate one less and predict each time the next number in the sequence.

In early subtraction there are four main strategies (Thompson 1997). These are:

- 'counting-out' in which children count out the initial quantity, remove the specified number of objects and then count what is left;
- 'counting-down-from' in which children count backwards from the initial quantity the amount to be taken away;

- 'counting-up-from' which is better known as the 'shopkeeper's method';
- 'bridging-down-through-ten' e.g., 13 - 6 is seen as 13 take away 3 is 10, take away another 3 is 7.

In the past, addition was taught separately from subtraction and it often received considerably more attention within the number curriculum. There is now an emphasis at Key Stage 1 on children understanding that subtraction is the inverse of addition (it 'undoes') and they are often taught alongside each other. For example, when playing shops, Amber started with five sweets and sold two of them leaving her with three. She put the two back with the three and said, 'Look, I've still got five sweets.'

Number recognition

'Recognise numerals 1 to 9'
(*National Numeracy Strategy*, DfEE 1999)

Numbers, like words and letters, are part of the environment, e.g. price labels, house numbers, speed limits. Young children will also encounter them at home and in early years settings in books, board games, the clock, their birthday cards etc. Number recognition can be further supported by the use of numbers in displays (e.g. '4 children' by the water tray); the availability of wooden/plastic/magnetic numerals and number matching puzzles, and a calculator, a telephone and a till in the role play area.

Number lines are particularly valuable as they can help children understand number order and the relative position of numerals, and a washing line with pegs and moveable numerals allows children to order them. A number line can be particularly successful when the children are involved in its construction, starting with numerals which are meaningful to them, such as their age and the ages of brothers and sisters (Carruthers 1997).

Although the Key Objectives for Reception and the Early Learning Goals only refer to the recognition of numerals up to nine, young children are fascinated by big numbers. They will encounter them in the environment long before they start school in telephone numbers, their birthday on the calendar, 500g on a cereal packet etc. At three years old Amber was observed in the role play area of her Nursery answering the telephone and accurately reciting her number. It is not unusual to see a 100 square in an early years setting as a reference point for identifying numbers which have arisen in play or discussion. The calculator also provides a valuable opportunity to discover and play with big numbers. Amber enjoyed entering numbers into the calculator and asking, 'Which one is that?' She liked the names of big numbers such as 321.

Representation

Although the Early Learning Goals and the Key Objectives make no reference to representation or recording, the National Numeracy Strategy teaching programme for Reception classes states that children will 'begin to record numbers, initially by making marks, progressing to simple tallying and writing numerals'. (DfEE 1999) This reflects the increased emphasis on mental calculation and the consequent delay in the introduction of written methods of calculation.

At home and in early years settings young children will imitate adults and make their own representations, especially in role play situations, e.g. telephone numbers, price lists. All of these situations are meaningful contexts for the child. At Nursery Amber's teacher had written 'Who is hiding behind the door?' Amber wrote her house number (95) on the front and teddy behind the door (Figure 16.3). At the age of four years two months Amber attended a barn dance and was disappointed not to win a raffle prize. She created her own raffle at home selling tickets to members of the family. She wrote two sets of numerals one to ten, one set for the prizes and one set for the participants. She was also able to match the numbers and read them (Figure 16.4).

Hughes (1986) work with three year olds showed that they were able to represent small quantities and understand those representations in the context of leaving a message for someone about the number of bricks in a tin. Meaningful contexts provide the opportunity for young children to begin to make the connection between the concrete objects and the abstract symbol.

He identified four stages in early numerical representations:

- idiosyncratic   ('scribbles' or mark making)
- pictographic   (pictures of the objects showing 1:1 correspondence)
- iconic   (tallies showing 1:1 correspondence)
- symbolic   (conventional symbols)

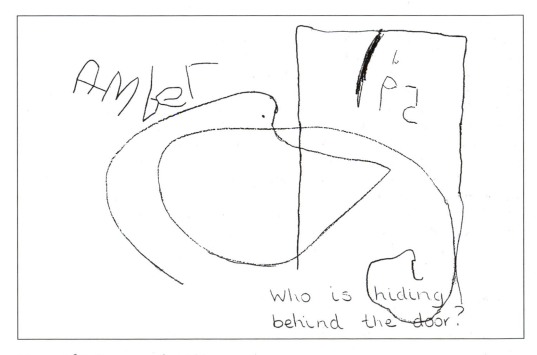

Figure 16.3 House number 95

School

Within the first few weeks of starting school, Amber completed the statutory baseline assessment to identify her strengths and weaknesses in mathematics and other curriculum areas. Baseline Assessment enables appropriate targets to be identified and provides the basis against which her progress can be measured.

Amber's start at school also coincided with the introduction of two key initiatives. The first was the establishment of a foundation stage from the age of three to the end of Reception and the replacement of the Desirable Outcomes by the Early Learning Goals. The second was the introduction in England of the National Numeracy Strategy for Reception to Year 6, based on the National Curriculum for Key Stages 1 and 2. These initiatives are linked in that the Early Learning Goals are the same as the Key Objectives for the end of Reception. The guidance in the Introduction of the National Numeracy Framework about numeracy in Reception reflects good early years practice and is intended to provide similarities and continuity for early years settings.

The National Numeracy Strategy will also mean that Amber's experience in Reception will differ from that of an older brother or sister. The emphasis on mental strategies and the delay in the introduction of written calculation is a key element of the Strategy. This should have two main consequences. The first is that she should receive more direct, interactive teaching in which she will be encouraged to explain her answers. The second is that although she may record some of her mental work she will not spend a large part of her numeracy lessons completing workbooks.

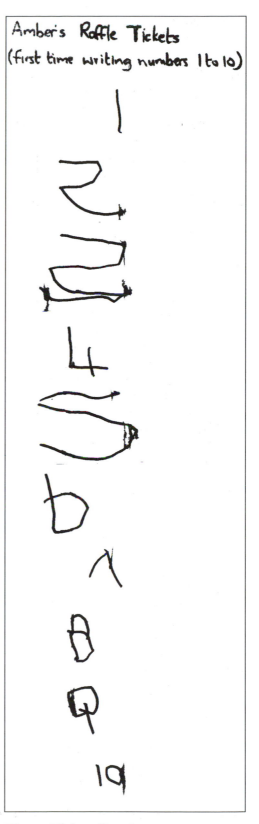

Figure 16.4 Raffle tickets

Conclusion

Amber, like many four year olds, already had considerable competence in numeracy when she started school. This presents a challenge to parents/carers and adults working with young children in the early years to be aware of opportunities which have potential for developing numeracy and to engage in high-level interaction with the children in their care to support their learning. In early years settings and in school adults need to build upon children's previous experiences so that they can make links between informal home experience and knowledge and formal school knowledge.

Finally, if you have the opportunity, spend part of a day with a young child at home or in an early years setting noting and then *maximising* opportunities for numeracy development.

References

Aubrey, C. (1997) *Mathematics Teaching in the Early Years: An Investigation of Teachers' Subject Knowledge*. London: Falmer Press.

Carpenter, T. P. and Moser, J. M (1984) 'The acquisition of addition and subtraction concepts in grade one through three', in *Journal for Research in Mathematics Education* **15**(3), 179–202.

Carruthers, E. (1997) 'A number line in the nursery classroom: A vehicle for understanding children's number knowledge', in *Early Years* **18**(1), 9–14.

Clarke, S. and Atkinson, S. (1996) *Tracking Significant Achievement in Primary Mathematics*. London: Hodder & Stoughton.

Department for Education and Employment (1999) *The National Numeracy Strategy: Framework for teaching mathematics from Reception to Year 6*. London: DfEE.

Gelman, R. and Gallistel, C. R. (1978) *The Child's Understanding of Number*. Cambridge, MA: Harvard University Press.

Hughes, M. (1986) *Children and Number. Difficulties in Learning Mathematics*. Oxford: Basil Blackwell.

Meadows, S. and Cashdan, A. (1988) *Helping Children Learn*. London: David Fulton Publishers.

Montague-Smith, A. (1997) *Mathematics in Nursery Education*. London: David Fulton Publishers.

Munn, P. and Schaffer, H. R. (1993) 'Literacy and numeracy events in social inter-active contexts', *International Journal of Early Years Education* **1**(3), 61–80.

Neaum, S. and Tallack, J. (1997) *Good Practice in Implementing the Pre-school Curriculum*. Cheltenham: Stanley Thornes Publishers.

Qualifications and Curriculum Authority (1999) *Early Learning Goals*. London: Qualifications and Curriculum Authority.

Rogoff, B. *et al.* (1998) 'Toddlers' guided participation with their caregivers in cultural activity', in Woodhead, M., *et al.* (eds) *Cultural Worlds of Early Childhood*. London: Routledge/Open University.

School Curriculum and Assessment Authority (1996) *Nursery Education. Desirable Outcomes for Children's Learning on Entering Compulsory Education*. London: DfEE and SCAA.

Thompson, I. (ed.) (1997) *Teaching and Learning Early Number*. Buckingham: Open University Press.

Tizard, B. and Hughes, M. (1984) *Young Children Learning*. London: Fontana.

Chapter 17

Exploring our world

Peter Bloomfield, Max de Boo and Bernice Rawlings

We are explorers from the cradle to the grave. We seem to be born with curiosity, 'a need to know', although in unfavourable circumstances this can be stifled (Tizard and Hughes 1984). The young child reaches out from the cot or crawls towards to the flower bed or presses the buttons on the TV remote control, all with unspoken questions such as, 'What is it?' What will happen if . . . ?' 'What will it feel like if I . . .?' As children acquire vocabulary their enquiries spiral upwards, with new words fuelling subsequent questions and actions, such as Cindy (4 years) 'What's that?' (A stapler), then 'What's a stapler for?' . . . 'Can I have a go?'

The linguistic format of the question is used appropriately from very early on. Indeed, the development of structured speech patterns may be an innate characteristic (Chomsky 1976). There is a universality to the kind of questions we ask from an early age that are common to all languages, cultures and curricula. For example, questions such as, 'Where did you get it?', 'Can I have it?', 'Can I eat it?' are recognisable children's questions from China to Chester-le-Street (de Boo 1999). As children grow, their questions become more sophisticated. There is a search for identity – 'Who am I?', 'Where do I live?' and an awareness of the future 'What will I be when I grow up?' and 'What will happen to me when I die?'

Not all questions are articulated, either by children or adults. Some questions are implicit in body language and actions, for example, looking at the back of a packet to see a date stamp or peering into a hand lens to see a beetle under magnification. Not all questions have answers or easy solutions. Some questions can be answered by research (books, experts), some questions can be explored and investigated in early years settings. Questions open doors to ideas, thinking and actions (Elstgeest 1985). Questions, and the search for answers, can change our lives. Whatever the outcome, learning to ask questions is crucial – an enquiring mind makes for an independent learner (de Boo 1999). Independent learners cope better with the changing nature of a hi-tech world or a fast-changing community.

However, learning to ask questions does not happen in isolation (Vygotsky 1986). 'Social contexts, like attitudes and emotions, are not simply background factors but have major effects on individuals' learning' (Merry 1998, p. 95). It is vital that adults encourage play experiences that include exploration and investigation (Johnston 1996). Children need stimulating environments and opportunities to communicate with adults and other children. In these contexts, our own questions provide a role model for children's enquiries. The following questions encourage skills, positive attitudes and a sense of awe and wonder:

Observation: What do you notice? What can you see? What's underneath? What's inside? How is it changing? (a sense of time)

Classification: What does it remind you of? Which ones are the same as each other? Why do you think that? What do you call it/them?

Predictions: What do you think will happen? What will happen if . . .? When do you think . .?

Testing: How can we find out? Shall we do it again? Shall we change anything this time?

Reasoning and explanation: What happened? Why do you think it did that?

Neutral questions: Or? Anything else? (open questions develop and expand on ideas).

Our questions can encourage the acquisition of knowledge and self-esteem:

Ownership: What's special about it? When do you like it best? (temporal)

Locality and connections: Where is the place where you live? What is it like there? Who else lives there? What other things can you find here . . . living things? . . . . not-living things?

Journeys: Where are we going? How are we going to get there? What will we find there?

Materials: What is my world made of? What do we use these materials for? What can I make with them?

We can support children's effective exploration of their world by posing questions in a wide variety of contexts and encouraging children's own questions (Qualter 1996).

Who am I?

One of the most important questions we will ever address is that of our identity. Exploring 'ourselves' in early years settings gives opportunities for learning in science and mathematics, social skills and self-esteem, learning in language and motor skills. Questions can be investigated, children measured or surveyed, and the results recorded in words or pictures, by hand or on the computer.

Questions about ourselves can help to develop children's sensitivity to each other and reduce prejudice (Siraj-Blatchford and McLeod-Brudenell 1999), and involve parents and other significant adults. When Sarah (4 years) was asked about her family, she said, 'I live with my Mummy and Joe (little brother) but my Daddy lives in a different house.' The adult replied, 'Yes, my 'Daddy' lives in a different place too.' Two or three other children chimed in with, 'Mine too.' Sarah's face showed relief – her family was fine, she was accepted and valued.

We need to be sensitive when children investigate themselves. Self-esteem is precious and can be lost if we appear to have biases or values that our children do not share. Some children will be genetically shorter or taller than others – they need to understand that 'big' does not equate with 'better'. Research shows that young children are sensitive to adult perceptions and can gain or lose self-esteem very quickly (Fisher 1990).

In reality, the human body is beautifully designed and adapted to our earthly environment. Children need to learn that we are all the same in terms of features, limbs and cycles of growth. There are a million times more similarities between people from different cultures and ethnic groups than there are differences. We need to emphasise and take delight in our shared characteristics as well as the differences. Story books can help, for example, *Tall Inside* (Richardson *et al.* 1989) and *Hue Boy* (Mitchell 1992) and the activities below will support this.

Sorting and classifying

Sorting and classifying activities help to simplify a complex world (Bruner 1996) and encourage mathematical and scientific skills and knowledge. For example, the questions, 'How many boys are there in our class? How many girls?' can lead to making pictograms and using ICT skills. The questions 'What is your favourite toy? TV programme? book?' encourage language skills and decision making. The question 'Do you think the clothes in the Home Area will fit you?' could lead to measurement with handspans or tape measures.

Exploring the senses

Questions which explore and investigate the senses require other stimulating resources. Such questions encourage the use and development of descriptive language and labelling (de Boo 1999), for example, 'What can you see out of the window? Through the magnifying glass? Underneath the fallen tree?' Children can be given ownership of the questions with the starter phrase 'Can you see . . . ?' They and the other children have to look closely before they ask or reply. For example:
Aisha: Can you see the little bird?
Noam (excitedly): I can. I can. It's on the tree . . . no, it's flying away.
Going out and asking what sounds can be heard in the playground, the park or the supermarket encourages careful listening. Asking about the feel of leaves and bark, water and ice, sand and dough encourages sensory perception.

Guess who!

Looking in mirrors and recording images encourages thinking and motor skills, observation and the development of symbolic representation. Ask: What do we look like? Draw self-portraits using mirrors, or portraits of a partner (See Figure 17.1). Use paper plates for making faces. We need not be afraid to ask about skin colours but we must supply a range of colours and accept children's perceptions of themselves. Ling (Chinese family) mixed brown and yellow for her face colour whilst Brian chose pale green. 'I like green', he said. Displaying the portraits sends the implicit message that the children are valued.

Figure 17.1

Our hands are one of the most important tools we have for exploring our world. We can encourage awareness of this, as well as motor skills and habits of hygiene whilst investigating hands (Figure 17.2). For example, we can explore the use of two hands, and one hand only and compare this with the size of our hands. Playing hand games and rhymes (de Boo 1992) and showing posters of dancers using their hands expressively makes constructive links with language, movement and dance. Investigating feet and legs and the different things we do with these can be followed by turning the Imaginative Area into a shoe shop and reinforcing mathematical and social skills.

Young children are curious about their origins as babies. A parent visiting with a small baby could be asked how the baby differs from, and is the same as, the children. Children can be encouraged to ask their questions, such as 'What does the baby eat? What can she do on her own? Why does she wear a nappy?' It is easy to follow this up by investigating a pack of new nappies to see how much water a nappy can absorb.

What do we eat?

There is a Chinese saying that 'you are what you eat'. Identity is tied up in our diet, individually and culturally, although with global mobility, this last is changing. What we eat determines our state of health and well-being. There are major issues to discuss with young children (e.g. care of our teeth, cultural taboos, family celebrations and personal hygiene) which make it vital that children are introduced to exploring foods and cooking from a very early age (de Boo 1999). They need as much experience and self-confidence as possible to

My hands can punch
my hands can stretch
my hands can pull.   Dean

Figure 17.2

make informed decisions about their choice of a healthy and enjoyable diet. As discussed in chapter 9 (Health Issues) children need to know of the importance of cereals and fruit and vegetables in our diet. Whenever possible, food explorations should include growing foods also. Adults will need to be sensitive to different expectations and potential health hazards (e.g. peanut allergies, diabetes), with different likes and dislikes, cultural and religious taboos. Cultural awareness can be encouraged by exploring different kinds of bread, rice and pasta and asking children to speculate on what is inside the bread.

Exploring different fruits and vegetables, including unfamiliar ones, and asking the children 'What might the fruits look like inside and taste like?' develops skills of prediction. Children can be asked to make block graphs of favourite foods and develop motor and social skills by making fruit salad and vegetable soup. Literacy skills are developed by reading 'Nail Soup' and 'The Tiger Who Came to Tea'. Making sandwiches and allowing children to choose from a limited choice of ingredients develops decision making skills. Cooking rice and pasta provides experience of change and children can draw familiar and unfamiliar foods (Figure 17.3).

Figure 17.3

Preparing and cooking foods

Children will have had different experiences of cooking. It is important to discuss different approaches, such as: shared cooking at home, eating out (burgers, etc.), buying take-aways and special family celebrations. Some children will have had experience of fasting. As role models, we need to show children that we value all the varied approaches, for example by inviting parents to come and cook chosen foods with the children, such as burfi, potato latkes, halva and oat cakes. In an atmosphere of enquiry, children learn about tastes and textures, changes, rituals and hygiene and have a lot of fun too.

Where does food come from? How does food grow?

Very young children may assume that all food comes from the shop and before that from a bigger shop. We need to discuss how and where the food might have grown and the parts of food we eat: roots and tubers (carrots, potatoes), stalks (celery, rhubarb), leaves (cabbage, lettuce), fruits and seeds (wheat, corn, rice). There are opportunities here for safety awareness, that is, which parts of food *not* to eat.

Seeds are fascinating but where are they? Some fruits are seedless – these cannot reproduce. Exploring strawberries, apples (cut horizontally), bananas, mangoes can help children to find and look at the size and number of seeds. Children can be asked to imagine and draw how bananas or mangoes grow. Growing cress or lettuce and measuring the growth reinforces knowledge of the world. Making and decorating paper packets for some dried seeds, and writing growing instructions uses literacy skills, and can help turn the Imaginative Area into a garden nursery, embellished with seeds and paper flowers on sticks.

Nearby shops or supermarkets can be visited to look at the range of foods, feel the 'cold' in the freezer section and look at the different packaging. Children can be invited to suggest reasons for this. Small packets of different breakfast cereals can be explored on your return.

With experience and encouragement, children will become thoughtful 'scientists' and apply their knowledge in new situations, as did the 5–6 year old children when visiting the fishmonger. They were awestruck at the sight of a fish with no eyes.

Alistair:	It's got no eyes!
Brenda:	They've been cut out by the fishmonger.
Kristal:	You don't need eyes in the sea.
Alistair:	Why not?
Brenda:	'Cos it's too dark in there.
Alistair:	How does it find its way then?
Kristal:	Maybe it finds its way by smelling.
Siva:	(scornfully) You can't smell nothing in the sea!
Brenda:	Yeah, 'cos you sniff up all the water.
Alistair:	Maybe it finds its way by listening . . .?
Siva:	Where's its ears then?

The children stand thinking. Then the fishmonger turns the fish over.

Alistair:	It's got both eyes on one side!

The chorus of 'Ooohs' and 'Aahs' reflected the children's wonder, delight and surprise in their fascinating world. The children used their prior experience to think, come to conclusions and speculate to make sense of the peculiarities of their world. They applied their language skills: because, maybe, where and how, in a new and unfamiliar context. They gained confidence by being allowed to discuss without interruption. It simply wasn't necessary for the adult to intervene.

Where do we live?

Young children's exploration of where they live, their developing skills knowledge and understanding that helps them 'to make sense of the world' in the Early Learning Goals (QCA 1996b), will progress to 'locality studies', the key focus of geography in at Key Stages 1 and 2 of the National Curriculum. Working from the 'known to the unknown', areas of the children's locality can be explored using items brought in or explored from the early years setting. Children develop a sense of spatial awareness from birth. As babies, they quickly learn where their toys are kept and where their food comes from. In effect, they are developing mental maps of the organisation of their home space. It is important that we recognise that children come to us with this bank of spatial awareness and build on it rather than assume no knowledge or skills. This is well documented with respect to young children in work which uses the school grounds (Palmer 1994). It is very important that children should identify with their local area and be able to talk about their roads and position of their homes and apply this to a map. A really large map enthuses and motivates children (Bloomfield 1992). Productive questions and activities about local features will prompt thought and action:

Homes and gardens

Exploring the children's close environment can develop language skills (adjectives and prepositions) and knowledge of time in daily and seasonal changes (Bloomfield 1999). Enquiry through questions such as: 'Where do the children sleep?' 'Where do they keep their toys?' 'Which is the quickest way from bedroom to breakfast?' all develop spatial and environmental awareness. Children should be encouraged to draw maps of commonly used routes. Figure 17.4 is the response Sara gave when asked to 'draw her journey to the nursery'. Through questioning she articulated that the journey had a beginning, her home, went around some roundabouts, along some roads, stopped to collect friends and ended at the nursery. She has some idea of elements of a journey but little spatial awareness in the sense of direction, scale, or perspective. These concepts remain to be learned.

Good practice in the early teaching of spatial awareness should be related to questions about children's experiences in the early years setting and reinforced with positive, simple mapwork, for example asking where the children play games like catching and where they push toy cars and buggies. This could be followed up by putting a symbol of a ball and a car or buggy on a large wall-map of the nursery. In exploring a garden, allotment or park children should look carefully (and safely) at the soil to investigate its colour, texture and smell. They should be encouraged to say what is growing in the soil and whether they are flowers, vegetables, weeds or grass, and asked to describe the colours and shapes and whether these change through the year. This might lead to discussion about whether this is somebody's home and can they see any birds, tadpoles, frogs, slugs or snails or anything else.

Roads and streets

Fieldtrips in the neighbourhood encourage knowledge of the diversity and individuality of the local environment. Children will begin to learn that there are different kinds of buildings and that they can be classified into groups, for example, flats, semi-detached and bungalows. They will learn about the

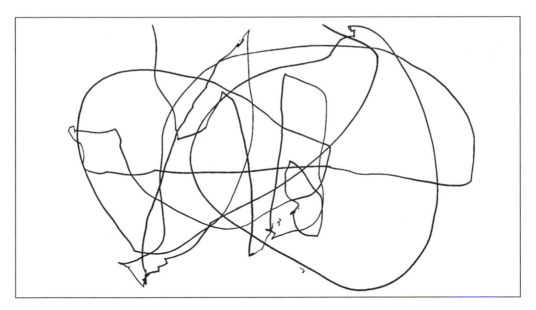

Figure 17.4 The way to nursery

infrastructure of pavements, post-boxes, telephones, road signs and trees. Making models of these and arranging them to represent relative positions on a large three-dimensional playmat consolidates learning through play.

Local shops

An awareness of local people and their needs encourages a sense of community and citizenship (QCA 1999b). Discussion of where children shop, why they think they shop there, the range of goods sold and the alternatives will highlight the difference between local and city centre or out of town shops. It can also encourage thinking about what shops people need, or would like, in the local area.

Special places

We can all have a 'special place' even if only in imagination. This concept encourages a sense of self-worth and creativity. Asking the children whether they have places where they play, hide or just sit quietly and whether these places are at home or near the early years setting or in-between again consolidates their known spatial environment. 'My special place is wild with long grass and lots of leaves and near the trees' or 'I like thinking I'm under the ground with the moles' can be consolidated through creative art or map work, or models and may be related to a children's story.

Exploring journeys (with links to locality)

Children make journeys every day when they go to playgroup, nursery or school, shopping, to the park and to friends and family for tea. Children read, or are read to, about the journeys of postmen, animals and space travel, all of which explore our world and beyond.

Adults take children on visits or 'fieldwork' where they develop observation skills, and valuable emergent geographical language (Lewis 1998, Walters 1998) and skills (orientation, mapping and route following). Journeys and locality work can be recorded and processed using computers. Children can be encouraged to talk about personal journeys, such as visiting family or friends. Discussing holidays needs sensitivity as these can be divisive and discriminatory – the holiday of a familiar adult or imaginary journeys are good alternatives (Norris Nicholson 1996). All such activities will encourage directional language and knowledge of keys and symbols. An exploration of journeys to the early years setting can be facilitated with the use of colour codes for routes on large prepared maps, encouraging the children to describe their journey, making a word bank and symbols of key places or features, would be a natural progression from Sara's route to the nursery (see Figure. 17.4).

There are many visitors to nurseries; post-people, waste collectors, health visitors and parents. Children could be encouraged to ask them questions about their journeys and with help, record and display the journey as mentioned above. This begins to take the learning from the known to the unknown.

Other journeys take place in the context of visits from the classroom, for examples fieldtrips to local parks, the seaside, woods, shops and even an airport (SCAA 1997). The best of these write the key place names on cards (car park, bus stop, railway station, sea, beach, aquarium) and link the cards to a wall picture/map with string. These can be discussed before, during and after the trip with additional information from the children added to give more detail.

Journeys do not have to be 'real-life' journeys but can be journeys in books. '*Rosie's Walk*' (Hutchins 1968) and *Spot's Walk in the Woods* (Hill (1995)) are excellent examples of children's books which illustrate a journey and it is possible to convert the stories into actions and textured maps, such as 'We're going on a bear hunt' (de Boo 1992).

Young children adapt well to using computers (Donart 1998) and often do not have the phobias and concerns common in adults. Asking them to send letters and e-mails to other children, nurseries and schools in the area then looking up the locations on local maps; discussing telephone and Internet 'journeys'; contacting 'Voices of Youth', which is a website where children can talk to each other across the world: (www.unicef.org/voy), are all examples of how exploration of places and journeys can lead to an appreciation of the local environment and form the fundamentals of care and responsibility, duties and rights and thereby, citizenship.

Exploring other places

Exploring places beyond the immediate environment expands a child's world in a safe way, developing her or his self-esteem, knowledge of different climates, seasonal changes and open-minded attitudes to people in other places. For young children 'other places' are places that are 'not home'. These can be near or far, real places (a garden centre or a friend's home) or imaginary places (in their heads or in a story). Children learn about other places from first hand experience and from images in books and television (Milner 1997).

For a number of years learning about and exploring other places has been dominated by the questions first proposed by Michael Storm (1989) and subsequently adapted by others, and which can be used in an early years setting. These questions can be used to express ideas about positional location in familiar terms. For example, children from a nursery class visited the local allotments. Albie (5 years) asked, 'Where are the allotments?' The adult responded 'On Walkern Road'. Asha said, 'Oh, that's where my Grandma lives!' The best way to find out about other places (garden centres, the seaside, the fire station) is to visit them and explore them as you have explored your own environment.

Where is this place?

Making or collecting pictures of a journey nearby and trying to sequence them; drawing maps and asking questions such as 'How long will it take to get there?' will all help children to develop an understanding of how places are related to each other. If the place is far away, children can be introduced to a large inflatable globe. They can be asked to find the place and a discussion can follow about how long it might take to get there.

Bringing other places to life

Children are fascinated by the lives of other people, especially other children. They ask questions such as 'Do children in other places do the same things as us?', 'Do they wear the same clothes?', 'Do they eat the same kinds of food?', 'Do they play with the same kind of toys?' Photographs of other places are a wonderful resource especially if they are large and have children in them. The adult can ask the children to describe the clothes that the children in the photograph are wearing, leading to a discussion about whether the place in the picture is a hot place or a cold place, a rainy or a dry place, and how we can tell. Questions about what the children in the photograph are doing and what their favourite games might be encourages children to consider the similarities as well as the differences between their lives and other peoples. Children can be encouraged to think of questions they would like to ask of the children in the photograph. A speaker from another place could be invited to come and talk to the children and the children could be encouraged to ask questions of this person too. A role play area, related to the other place, such as a garden centre, a fishmonger or an airport (Milner 1997) could be developed and the children could be involved in its design and construction.

Using simple props and artefacts can help to bring the other place alive to children. When talking about the weather in other places clothing can help to bring the idea alive to children. An example is to bring a bag or case packed with clothes to wear in another place, taking out and discussing the clothes one by one, asking questions such as, 'Why have I packed my swimming costume?' 'Do you think the weather will be hot or cold?' 'Can anybody think of anything else that I might need to take?' 'I wonder why I haven't packed my boots?' Role playing a weather forecast for the other place and their own place, after watching a video clip of a weather forecast can help to reinforce the idea of the different weather.

Comparing our place and other places

If it is possible to visit another place you could carry out a footprint activity. To do this children cut out a paper footprint that they place on the ground. The adult can encourage them to look carefully at what is inside their footprint (Figure 17.5). The children can be encouraged to look in each other's footprints to see whether they are the same or not. Skills of prediction can be developed by considering what will happen if the footprints are moved to another place. Footprints such as these can be used in rural or urban environments and can be completed in the local area before visiting the other place to focus the children's observation.

Collecting materials, such as grass, leaves, small stones and paper, can be used to show what a place is like. By assembling these onto a sticky card they can be taken back and referred to in the early years setting.

Conclusion

Positive exploration of ourselves and our environment leads to children who are confident of their own identity and background and are more likely to value other people and customs which differ from theirs. Curiosity can be stifled if not encouraged in the early years (Tizard and Hughes 1984). By adopting an enquiry approach themselves, adults will offer good role models and encourage children to become independent learners (Elstgeest 1985). The young children of today are the citizens of tomorrow. The more they know about their world, the more likely they are to make decisions to enjoy and protect their environment for themselves and others.

Figure 17.5

References

Bloomfield, P. (1992) 'The Map', in *Education 3-13* **20**(2), 24–29. Harlow: Longman.

Bloomfield, P. (1999) 'Where's Teddy; Part 2: A walk to find Teddy and some simple mapwork', in *Primary Geographer* **36**, 28–9. Sheffield: Geographical Association.

Bruner, J. S. (1996) *The Culture of Education*. Cambridge, MA: Harvard University Press.

Chomsky, N. (1976) *Reflections on Language*. London: Temple-Smith.

de Boo, M. (1992) *Action Rhymes and Games*. Leamington Spa: Scholastic.

de Boo, M. (1999) *Enquiring Children, Challenging Teaching*. Buckingham: Open University Press.

de Boo, M. (ed.) (2000) *Science 3–6: Laying the Foundations in the Early Years*. Hatfield: ASE.

Donart, K. (1998) 'Developing Progression through IT', *Primary Geographer* **33**, 22–5, Sheffield: Geographical Association.

Dowling, M. (1992) *Education 3–5*. London: Paul Chapman.

Elstgeest, J. (1985) 'The right question at the right time', in Harlen, W. (ed.) *Primary Science – Taking the Plunge*. London: Heinemann.

Fisher, R. (1990) *Teaching Children to Think*. Hemel Hempstead: Simon & Schuster.

Johnston, J. (1996) *Early Explorations in Science*. Buckingham: Open University Press.

Lewis, L. (1998) 'Geography and Language Development', in Carter, R. (ed.) *Handbook of Primary Geography*, 163–181. Sheffield: Geographical Association.

Merry, R. (1998) *Successful Children, Successful Teaching*. Buckingham: Open University Press.

Milner, A. M. (1997) *Geography through Play. Structured Play at Key Stage 1*. Sheffield: Geographical Association.

Norris Nicholson, H. (1996) *Place in Story Time: Geography through stories at Key Stages 1 and 2*. Sheffield: Geographical Association.

Palmer, J. (1994) *Geography in the Early Years*. London: Routledge.

Qualifications and Curriculum Authority (1999a) T*he Secretary of State's Proposals: Curriculum Review* . London: DfEE.

Qualifications and Curriculum Authority (1999b) *Early Learning Goals*. London: Qualifications and Curriculum Authority.

Qualter, A. (1996) *Differentiated Primary Science*. Buckingham: Open University Press.

SCAA (1997) *Looking at Children's Learning; Desirable Outcomes*. London: SCAA.

Siraj-Blatchford, J. MacLoed-Brudnell, I. (1999) *Supporting Science, Design and Technology in the Early Years*. Buckingham: Open University Press.

Storm, M. (1989) 'Key questions of place', *Primary Geographer* **2 (**4). Sheffield: Geographical Association.

Tizard, B. and Hughes, M. (1984) *Young Children Learning: Talking and Thinking at Home and at School*. London: Fontana.

Vygotsky, L. (1986) *Thought and Language*. Cambridge, MA: MIT Press.

Walters, A. (1998) 'Progression and Differentiation', in Carter, R. (ed.) *Handbook of Primary. Geography*, 43–54. Sheffield: Geographical Association.

Watling, R. (1995) 'Our village: Freire, Freinet, and practical work in the early years', *Early Years* **14** (2), 6–12.

Children's books

Hill, E. (1995) *Spot's Walk in the Woods*. Harmondsworth: Puffin.

Hutchins, P. (1968) *Rosie's Walk*. New York: Macmillan.

Mitchell, R. (1992) *Hue Boy*. Gollancz.

Richardson, J. *et al.* (1988) *Tall Inside*. London: Methuen Children's.

Chapter 18

Creative expression

Rosemary Allen, Tricia Lilley and Gill Smith

The importance of creative experience and self-expression in boosting children's self esteem and confidence has recently been acknowledged by David Blunkett (1999). In his foreword to the report entitled 'All Our Futures: Creativity, Culture and Education' (NACCCE 1999) he pledged Government support for young people both at school and in the community, enabling them to explore and develop their creativity. It is essential that early year's practitioners in all settings have a thorough understanding of the ways in which young children's creativity develops and can be supported by the adult.

This chapter places particular emphasis on children's musical and artistic creativity and expression from birth while acknowledging that creativity is equally important in the sciences and all aspects of our lives. We have identified key stages in young children's creative development and raise some issues for early year's practitioners to consider in providing quality support for this aspect of development.

Creative expression through the visual and tactile senses

Supporting young children in their creative development requires sensitivity, skill, knowledge and judgement. Understanding how and why children develop from infancy into early childhood and beyond, enables the early years practitioner to provide an appropriate physical, intellectual and emotional environment for learning to take place (QCA 1999). Creative intelligence can be expressed, for example, in the way someone approaches a problem, or interprets music through a series of movements or coloured marks, or the ease with which an engine may be taken apart and then reconstructed. All of us can recognise these attributes in ourselves and in others. Valuing strengths and interests and helping to develop skills is a key part of the role of the early year's practitioner (Ofsted 1995).

The curriculum for three to five year olds is structured to take account of the way humans organise and begin to make sense of themselves and their world. This supports the argument that intelligence is complex and multi-faceted and not restricted to a narrow range of skills, knowledge and understandings (Gardner 1985).

Whilst many early years practitioners recognise, nurture and value these qualities, some are unsure of the value of fostering creativity especially with current concerns regarding literacy and numeracy. The scaffolding necessary for effective learning has, as part of its structure, the range of concepts and skills associated with creativity and imagination. These include the skills of painting, constructing, drawing, dancing, gymnastics, music, role-play, speaking and imagining. Important concepts include space, shape, form, pattern, tone, direction and time. These transcend subject areas and can be seen as central to children's learning (HMI 1989). Creativity is usually seen as a critical feature of arts subjects and it is through these activities that creative expression can often be fostered most easily (NACCCE 1999). However, creativity and imagination can be developed through a broad range of activities within a framework that supports open-ended, imaginative thought and action (QCA 1999).

Milestones in creative development can be seen and recorded through the way a child draws, moves, thinks and speaks (Einon 1998). Researchers in the field of child art development such as Lowenfeld and Brittain (1970), Kellogg (1969), Goodnow (1977), Gardner (1985), Matthews (1994) and Cox (1997) have documented clearly the stages of development in children's drawing. These stages can provide insights into the child's world and give us markers for our own actions (Chisholm 1999). The key characteristics of drawing structures are common to all known cultures and early years practitioners throughout the world are familiar with the scribbled marks on such surfaces as foodtrays, walls and faces as well as on paper. Selleck (1997) calls this stage 'baby art' and describes the ways in which young children can create meandering patterns, shapes and textures with their food, dribbling or splattering yoghurt or gravy across the plate and the table. Selleck reminds us that babies are themselves sculptural forms curling, twisting, nestling and she signals the dangers of crushing babies' creativity by ignoring these early creative, sensual and artistic experiences perhaps by focusing on later developmental stages more commonly associated with the toddler. She challenges 'parents, nannies and childminders in homes, and . . . day care staff in nursery centres' to consider the ways in which 'baby art' should be observed and nurtured (p. 18). It is certainly food for thought.

Paintings follow similar patterns to drawings with movement and direction being more important than colour. Short brushes or fingers in creamy paint make satisfying marks. Young children also love to manipulate soft, pliable materials such as playdough, food or clay. Sensation is more important than appearance, so adults must be prepared to offer encouragement related to what is happening rather than expecting a particular outcome. Working in three dimensions helps children to develop an awareness of shape, space and form, concepts that relate to both art and mathematics. Our concerns regarding numeracy should not ignore the importance of this early years scaffolding of underlying concepts.

First drawings are made with balanced side to side movements and follow the natural arm movements made by babies. At first it is the movements themselves that are important – the marks are incidental. Before long however, usually with adult help, the child gradually makes connections between the movement and the mark and attempts to repeat and reinforce what they have learnt (Michotte

1963). At this stage, early year's practitioners can provide a range of suitable surfaces and materials for mark-making. In addition they can show their appreciation of the results by talking and encouraging and, as in sound and movement development, by providing an audience. Most children will accompany drawing with vocal sounds that relate to the pace and character of the movement, thus establishing the interdependence of aural, kinaesthetic, visual and tactile senses (the Arts in Schools Project Team 1990).

By the age of about two, although drawings and paintings are still focused on movement, the child's repertoire of marks has increased dramatically. As more tools are used in addition to hands and other body parts, modification takes place and the interaction between body, tool and surface becomes more structured. As a child moves more, their relationship with space and objects changes and a greater awareness of self develops. Marks are now made with both hands moving simultaneously making large sweeping shapes that meet in the middle. The child may stand to draw or paint and, in doing so, may drip paint at first accidentally and then deliberately. They may 'stab at the result thus making dots and blobs and showing evidence of intention' (Matthews 1994, p. 43). It is common for a child to deliberately paint over marks they have made, obliterating the original, emphasising that it is the process that takes priority at this stage. Wolf (1989) makes links between speech, movement and mark making and Matthews reminds us that the apparent random nature of these forms of communication actually conceal 'sub-structures of highly organised sequences and patterns' (p. 44). These sequences enable children to develop the structures and formalities needed for drawing, painting and marking and, in turn, contribute to emergent literacy and numeracy.

As mark making and pattern making becomes more intentional and controlled, children begin to order what they see, touch and know. Sorting and matching skills enable them to group marks, colours, shapes and textures together showing an early awareness of composition. By about two to three years children are engaged in sophisticated ways of representing their feelings, observations, memories and ideas. Colour, surface and pattern become increasingly important and provide the child with a visual means of storytelling and by the age of three many children are drawing and painting representations of aspects of their world. Fysh (1998) has collected drawings over an eleven year period showing how they provide a commentary on the development of the whole child, demonstrating that 'an order exists' and should be built upon and responded to by all those involved in early childhood education (Jameson 1968).

Drawings and paintings from observation begin to emerge at around the ages of three to four and should be encouraged as a sign of the child's growing interest in representing what they see. Imagination continues to develop through sight, touch, movement, sound and speech. Pattern making of all kinds echoes a greater range of expression leading to emergent writing and reading, a process described in more detail by Hall (1989) and Miller (1996).

By the ages of five to six years, control in making paintings and drawing is much more advanced. Smith (1979) argued that young children are aware of differences between letters, numbers and pictures and begin to understand new functions by incorporating them into their early play worlds. Thomas and Silk

(1990) emphasise that in order to understand how children read we should look closely at how they draw. Early years practitioners must take this seriously if they wish to ensure that children's development is seen in a holistic way.

By the ages of six to eight years children are able to include fine detail in their drawings and paintings and show an impressive degree of control and sophistication in their imagery. Elaborate storytelling through words and pictures is of central interest to the child and covers a vast range of subject matter associated with memory, imagination, observation and experience (Clement and Page 1992) A combination of styles emerge displaying a distinctive combination of symbolic features, together with increasing realism. As the child moves towards a greater understanding of the world and their relationship to it, his or her creative work reflects a growing maturity and sophistication. This is apparent not only in visual and tactile form but also in the way children express themselves through sound and music. These areas will now be considered in greater detail.

Creative expression through sound and music

Hearing is one of the earliest senses to develop and it has been shown that a baby responds to sounds before birth through physical movements and an increased heart rate (Evans and Parncutt 1998). Familiar sounds – notably the mother's voice and repeated passages of music – as well as sudden loud sounds provoke physical responses, which continue after birth. Babies may even show a preference for familiar sounds. They quickly learn to perceive and interpret the qualities of sound-movements as meaningful within a familiar context and can identify the different voices of those caring for them, modifying their behaviour accordingly. Awareness of fixed sound sources, sounds getting closer and sounds moving further away, gradually combine with visual perception and recognition to provide infants with additional clues as to what is happening in their world. These early experiences help to form the experiential basis for the continuously expanding world of the child. As perceptual awareness increases, the child's physical and sense development help to establish a growing repertoire of creative, expressive responses and interactions. Orsmond and Miller (1999) have discussed in further detail the nature and importance of the symbiotic relationship between aural, visual, tactile and kinaesthetic development in the young child.

All children create sounds. They bang, shake and scrape objects to explore sound qualities. A baby reaches out and touches a brightly coloured object and is often rewarded by a sound response. Later, deliberate dropping of particular objects becomes a game which helps in the development of spatial awareness and generates a response from others. The toddler who delights in the sound produced from dropping a spoon from a high-chair soon realises that dropping a sock does not have the same effect. The pre-school child becomes absorbed in trying out sounds, thus building a knowledge base about creating sounds. Later these sounds will be used to express mood and emotion, perhaps to accompany an imaginative story or a song (song-speak). Repeating sounds and actions helps fix in the memory the sensations, qualities and effects that are being experienced.

These stored memories can later be recalled to be used in a variety of contexts. As basic skills are learnt children can express ideas through movement and sound more effectively. Young (1995) urges early years practitioners to support creative expression by understanding how music making develops in young children and the contribution that this makes to their overall development, including early literacy and numeracy skills and concepts. Campbell (1999) reminds us that singing and chanting nursery rhymes helps to prepare children for the patterns and rhythms of reading and writing. The early years practitioner plays an important part in laying the foundations of numeracy and literacy through their interactions with the child at such a receptive stage in their learning.

The pattern of a child's creative development is shaped through the interactions of involved and informed adults. First words, songs, sound and movement games help to establish a growing maturity and provide markers for healthy development. Sophisticated elements of music such as rhythm, pitch and articulation provide a foundation for creative expression through sound and are a starting point for instrument learning at a later stage. In stressing the importance of adult and child interactions, the power of the media to influence music and sound should not be underestimated. Television in particular has enormous impact on children's exposure to music and early years practitioners can help children to enjoy and learn from this rich medium.

Craft (1999) stresses the importance of structuring a child's learning in music as they grow, in order to ensure progression and continuity and to allow the development of sufficient skills to enable imaginative thinking and response. Whitebread (1996), Beetlestone (1998), Duffy (1998) and others have demonstrated that the attitudes and understanding of the adult in fostering creativity are crucial to a young child's physical, emotional and intellectual development and require a wholehearted commitment to early years education in the full range of settings. The guidance for early years practitioners in the Early Learning Goals regards the support given to children at this early stage as 'fundamental to succesful learning' (QCA 1999, p. 40).

The role of the adult in supporting children's creativity

If young children are to develop their creativity to its full potential, they need to gain a wide range of experiences in an atmosphere in which their ideas, explorations and achievements are identified, fostered and valued. Early years practitioners need to recognise and become knowledgeable about the processes of creativity, and understand how to support a young child's early attempts at activities such as mark making or interacting with sounds, to encourage playfulness and experimentation with a variety of media (NACCCE 1999).

Earlier in this chapter the important stages in the development of children's imagery and musical awareness were outlined, raising key issues about the processes of creativity. It is well established that all children pass through discrete stages of learning and development and actively explore their world seeking to make sense of their surroundings, assimilating and accommodating new knowledge into existing schema. Research by Athey (1990) and Nutbrown

(1994) into the development of children's schema or 'repeatable patterns of behaviour, speech, representation and thought' (Nutbrown, p. 13), indicates that early schemas can form the foundations for later learning. One of the roles of early years practitioners is to recognise and identify particular schema and then provide a range of experiences to nourish and extend children's learning. The circular marks and movements that children make in the sand, with the paints, in their drawings and in making sounds with certain musical instruments – perhaps cymbals or a tambourine – can provide valuable insights into current schematic interests. The early years practitioner is then able to make provision for individual needs by encouraging children to explore circular patterns in a wide range of contexts, perhaps providing printing objects that are cylindrical or oval, or looking at paintings and photographs of snails, flowers or spirals in the natural and made environment. The key role at this stage for the early years practitioner is one of careful observation, noticing what interests children in their settings and how learning can be taken forward.

Recent research on the development of children's self-esteem (Roberts 1995) suggests that a child's overall sense of self-worth is strongly influenced by the ways in which significant others – parents, carers, siblings, key workers and peers in early years settings – regard the child and his or her activities. Despite these findings, many adults do not always recognise children's creative talents or their efforts to represent their world in their art work or through sounds or movements (Moyles 1989). Some early years practitioners are themselves anxious about visual representations and feel particularly threatened or under pressure to display children's art work that has a 'likeness' to an original, many feel compelled to adapt, cut out, or even take over the painting of a picture for a child without realising the potential damage that such actions may cause to the child's self-esteem. Many adults have a personal memory of thoughtless negative comments made by a relative or teacher about their talent in drawing or singing as a child that is still recalled in adulthood.

The relationship between our interactions and informal comments made to children and the potential effect on their future development cannot be over-estimated. We should make an explicit commitment to value what children produce through their own creative expression, free from adult interference, and show respect for their work whatever their level of ability. In addition, early years practitioners need confidence to communicate these principles to parents, carers and colleagues and identify opportunities for a child's creative expression to be encouraged and fostered in all settings. The guidance for early years practitioners in the Early Learning Goals regards the support given to children at this early stage as 'fundamental to succesful learning' (QCA 1999, p. 40).

Art is a 'visual language', which enables the young child to develop his or her ideas and concepts of visual elements such as shape, space, colour, tone, pattern and texture. Music also has certain basic elements such as sound qualities, rhythm and melody, which the child explores from her earliest experiences of sound making. There is a close relationship between art, music and movement and the development of children's language, ability to solve problems, their imaginative play and the growth of positive self-esteem (Moyles 1989). The provision of an environment which stimulates curiosity and a sense of excitement can also promote enquiry, self-expression and the children's use of all their senses to develop awareness of their world. Encouragement to experiment freely with a range of media, can help children to develop an understanding of the elements of art and music and express ideas and feelings in a variety of ways (Moyles 1989, Early Childhood Education Forum 1998).

Adults can play a vital role in helping young children to develop their skills and express their ideas by talking to children about their work, encouraging them to look and listen carefully, to experiment with different materials to produce sounds and art work, and by helping them to make connections between favourite stories, music making and dramatic, imaginative play. Given the opportunity, children will use early experimentation with the elements of art or music or movement to express ideas and feelings. Early years practitioners need to recognise the importance of these early creative experiences for the development of the whole child in terms of imagination, self-discipline, sensitivity, ability to make decisions and solve problems (Herne 1995). It is not sufficient simply to provide art or musical resources for the child, such provision must be underpinned by a thorough understanding of the ways in which children learn and develop, the role of the adult in scaffolding learning for the child and the range of experiences in the arts that will foster creativity and well-being.

References

The Arts in Schools Project Team (1990) *The Arts 5–16: A Curriculum Framework.* Harlow: Oliver & Boyd for The National Curriculum Council.

Athey, C. (1990) *Extending Thought in Young Children.* London: Paul Chapman Publishing.

Beetlestone, F. (1998) *Creative Children, Imaginative Teaching.* Buckingham: Open University Press.

Campbell, R. (1999) *Literacy from Home to School: Reading with Alice.* Stoke-on-Trent: Trentham Books.

Chisholm, A. (1999) *Teaching Art.* Unpublished paper.

Clement, R. and Page (1992) *Principles and Practice in Art.* Harlow: Oliver & Boyd.

Craft, A. (1999) 'Creative Development in the Early Years: some implications of policy practice', in *The Curriculum Journal* **10** (1) Spring.

Cox, M. (1997) *Drawings of People by the Under 5's.* Lewes: Falmer Press.

Duffy, B. (1998) *Supporting Creativity and Imagination in the Early Years.* Buckingham: Open University Press.

Early Childhood Education Forum (1998) *Quality in diversity in early learning. A framework for early childhood practitioners.* London: National Children's Bureau.

Einon, D. (1998) *Learning Early.* London: Marshall Publishing.

Evans, S. and Parncutt, R. (1998) 'Foetus has an ear for music at 20 weeks'. *The Times,* March 30th.

Fysh, A. (1998) *Discovering Development with the 3–5s.* Unpublished thesis.

Gardner, H. (1985) *Frames of Mind.* New York: Basic Books.

Goodnow, J. (1977) *Children's Drawing.* London: Fontana/Open Books.

Hall, N. (1989) *The Emergence of Literacy.* Sevenoaks: Hodder & Stoughton.

Her Majesty's Inspectorate (1989) *Aspects of Primary Education: The Education of Children Under Five.* London: HMSO.

Herne, S. (ed.) (1995) *Art in the Primary School.* London: London Borough of Tower Hamlets Inspection and Advisory Services.

Jameson, K. (1968) *Pre School and Infant Art.* London: Studio Vista.

Kellogg, R. (1969) *Analysing Children's Art.* California: National Press Book.

Lowenfeld, V. (1970) *Creative and Mental Growth.* New York: Macmillan.

Matthews, J. (1994) *Helping Children to Draw and Paint in Early Childhood – Children and Visual Education.* London: Hodder & Stoughton.

Michotte, A. (1963) *The Perception of Causality.* Methuen Manual of Modern Psychology. London: Methuen.

Miller, L. (1996) *Towards Reading: Literacy Development in the Pre-School Years.* Buckingham: Open University Press.

Moyles, J. R. (1989) *Just Playing? The Role and Status of Play in Early Childhood Education.* Buckingham: Open University Press.

National Advisory Committee on Creative and Cultural Education (1999) *All Our Futures: Creativity, Culture and Education.* Sudbury: Department for Education and Employment.

Nutbrown, C. (1994) *Threads of Thinking: Young children learning and the role of early education.* London: Paul Chapman Publishing.

Ofsted (1995) *Guidance in the Inspection of Nursery and Primary Schools.* London: HMSO.

Orsmond, G. and Miller, L. (1999) 'Cognitive, Musical and Environmental Correlates of Early Music Instruction', *The Psychology of Music* **27** (1) p. 18–37.

Qualifications and Curriculum Authority (1999) *Early Learning Goals.* London: Qualifications and Curriculum Authority.

Roberts, R. (1995) *Self-Esteem and Successful Early Learning.* London: Hodder & Stoughton.

Selleck, D. (1997) 'Baby Art: art is me', in Gura, P. (ed.) *Reflections on Early Education and Care.* London: British Association for Early Childhood Education.

Smith, N. (1979) 'Developmental origins of structural variations in symbol form', in Smith, N. R. and Franklin, M. B. (eds) *Symbolic Functioning in Childhood,* 11–26. Hillsdale, NJ: Erlbaum.

Thomas, G. and Silk, A. M. J. (1990) *An Introduction to the Psychology of Children's Drawings.* New York: Harvester Wheatsheaf.

Verney, J. (1999) 'Language and Music in the Early Years', *Primary Music Today,* Summer.

Whitebread, D. (ed.) (1996) *Teaching and Learning in the Early Years.* London: Routledge.

Wolf, D. (1989) 'Artistic learning as a conversation', in Hargreaves, D. (ed.) *Children and the Arts* (23–29). Milton Keynes: Open University Press.

Young, S. (1995) 'Listening to the Music of Early Childhood', *British Journal of Music Education* **12**, 51–8.

Chapter 19

Meaningful history with young children

Rosie Turner-Bisset

What is history?

On her way into school one day, five year old Harriet asked her mother: 'Why are there three gates into school and we only use this one? Her mother explained that there had been a girls' entrance, a boys' entrance and an infants' entrance. She showed Harriet the words over each gate and the date, 1870, set in the brickwork. Harriet was intrigued that in the olden days, boys, girls and infants would have used different gates. She began to understand that the school had been there a long time, that other children had used that gate many years ago just as she did now, and that some things in the past were different. Thus Harriet was engaging in some of the processes and skills of history: asking questions about visual evidence of the past in the world about her. She was also beginning to develop an understanding that the school had existed before she did, showing embryonic notions of time and change.

History is included in the early years curriculum as part of knowledge and understanding of the world. Children talk about where they live, their environment, their families, and past and present events in their own lives. In addition, they explore objects and events and look closely at similarities, differences, patterns and change (QCA 1999). This is a relatively new perception of what it means to do history with young children. There have been several long-standing arguments against teaching history to young children. Some educationalists argue that it is more sensible to concentrate on literacy and numeracy in the early years. Since the Plowden Report (DES 1967), there has been a widespread view that teaching subjects to young children is not appropriate because it imposes artificial divisions on their learning; it is argued that they do not learn in this way naturally. In addition, our understanding that children learn best through their own experiences seems at odds with common perceptions of the nature of history as a subject concerned with abstract ideas such as cause and effect or change over time, evidence and interpretations of evidence. There are misconceptions about the nature of history: that it is about learning facts and dates. Adults remember the kind of history they were taught at school and rightly perceive this as being unsuitable for young children. An understanding of the true nature of history is essential for doing history with young children.

History is the imaginative reconstruction of the past using what evidence we can find. We can state what we definitely know from the evidence. We can hypothesise about the things we are unsure of, and we can use other knowledge and experience to inform our interpretations. These are the processes of history. In addition, doing history involves many skills, some of which are cross-curricular: for example, observation and use of the senses, sequencing, hypothesising, reasoning and deducting, evaluating, reflecting and remembering, predicting, comparing and contrasting, sorting and classifying. Finally there are key concepts: time, change, continuity, cause and effect, interpretations, evidence, and historical situations. Young children can be introduced to the concepts, processes and skills of history providing that the evidence selected for use is appropriate for this age-range, and that suitable teaching methods are employed.

If history involves the investigation of evidence, we need to decide what are the best sources of evidence for use with young children. Evidence of the past takes many forms. It is not merely written evidence, and in any case much of this would be unsuitable for use with young children. Evidence includes artefacts, pictures and photographs, adults talking about their own past, written sources, music and dance, stories of the past, buildings and sites, as well as documentary sources. Some of these forms of evidence, in particular, artefacts and stories, are very appropriate for children in early years settings.

Using artefacts

Artefacts are ideal to use with children in early years settings. They involve first-hand experience and enquiry-based learning (Wood and Holden 1995). They are not just an interesting addition to other forms of evidence: they are an important primary source of evidence in themselves. All societies, including those who do not have written forms of evidence, such as the Australian Aborigines, use or have used artefacts in their daily lives. Study of these artefacts can tell us a great deal about people's lives in the past.

Before embarking on a play/learning session with artefacts, early years practitioners need to be aware of several points, which can influence the success or otherwise of working with artefacts. These points are: the importance of working from familiar experiences; the need to establish a framework of questions, so that the activity does not just become a guessing-game (Andreetti 1993); and the way in which young children will often flit between fantasy and reality (Wood and Holden 1995). In addition, young children will need much support and demonstration from early years practitioners in observing closely and in using descriptive language. Finally, children need time to play with the objects and relate to them actively and imaginatively. Through play, children can begin to understand what an artefact is for, and what it might have been like to be the person who used it.

Some of these points are illustrated in the following example of work with a group of 3- and 4-year-olds in a nursery setting. They were given a number of objects to examine and play with, including a bright yellow enamelled candle-holder of the type which has a circular tray to catch the wax and a handle to carry the holder.

Sita:	It's yellow!
Teacher:	Yes, it's very yellow! Do you know what it is?
Oliver:	It's a wine-holder.
Teacher:	Is it? How do you know?
Oliver:	People have these on holiday . . . they put the wine in there, see (points to central part which holds the candle) . . . and hold it up like this, (mimes tipping it back, holding it by the handle) and drink the wine.
Teacher:	I suppose it does look a bit like that.

The artefact in question was very unfamiliar to the children. They had no knowledge of lighting before electric lighting, to inform their interpretation of the candle-holder.. Oliver shows us in his confident explanation that it was a wine-holder, that he is trying to relate the object to his previous experience, perhaps of seeing people use things of a similar shape used for drinking wine on holiday. A better preparation for investigation of the candle-holder would be to use a torch with the children first: a modern object with the same purpose as the old artefact, and one which they are more likely to have seen on camping trips or around the house. After the modern object has been handled, played with and questions asked about it, the early years practitioner can introduce the old artefact and say it was used for the same purpose.

A framework of questions should be used to guide discussion and enquiry. The reasons for using such a framework are to avoid the tendency towards a guessing-game, noted above, to encourage the use of the senses and of descriptive language and to help the children to make some beginnings in interpreting historical evidence. I have used the framework in Figure 19.1 with children between the ages of 3 and 6. It is best to keep the number of questions small with very young ones, as their concentration span is shorter than that of older children.

> What does this look like?
> What does this feel like?
> What do you think this is made of?
> Have you seen anything like this?
> How is/was it used?
> Who uses it/who used to use it?
> What would it be like to use it?

Figure 19.1 A framework of questions

Such a framework encourages children to describe what they perceive through their senses. Note there is no direct question: 'What do you think this is?' Instead the children are able to explore and use language to describe what they perceive. They may well ask this question themselves, but the 'guessing-game' type of activity is avoided. An additional problem is that once children have thought of what an object might be, their ideas are often difficult to shift, even though the physical evidence might suggest a different purpose. This was the case with Oliver, who clung to his initial idea that the candle-holder was a wine holder. There is no question in the framework about the age of the object. Young children, who may still be learning to count and sequence numbers, are not usually able to estimate how old an object might be.

The most valuable parts of this activity with the three and four year olds were their playing with the artefacts and the talk which accompanied their play. Over and over again they poured pretend hot water from the kettle into the hot-water bottle and pretended to drink the 'wine' from the 'wine-holder'. As they did so they described what they were doing: 'I'm going to fill the bottle, look!' Through active engagement with the objects in play, they were able to use their imaginations as to how people in the past used these objects. Wood and Holden (1995) give an example of how artefacts such as washboards, dolly pegs, tin baths, soap and grater can be used in a role-play area, enriching children's understanding of how people washed clothes in the past.

With slightly older children in Reception and Year 1 classes, play is still important. The experience of handling artefacts, and role-play with them is an essential part of promoting their understanding of people's lives in the past. It can also begin to develop some understanding of change and continuity. A group of five- and six-year-olds were given the same set of artefacts as the nursery-age children. They investigated some of the artefacts using the framework of questions shown in Figure 19.1. As the teacher and children talked, the objects were passed around the group and children handled them. They played with them extensively, miming their use and feeling such qualities as hardness, softness, smoothness, roughness, heaviness, lightness, and size and shape. The skills of observation were being developed in this activity, and the children were encouraged to use a range of adjectives to describe what they perceived. They spontaneously used terms such as 'in the olden days'.

Teacher:	Now this is a very heavy object, a very heavy thing. I want you to look at it and tell me what you think it's made of.
Abigail:	China
Teacher:	China, yes. How does it feel?
Abigail:	Cold. Hard.
Teacher:	Yes, it does feel cold, doesn't it? Is it heavy?
Abigail:	Yes, it's heavy!
Teacher:	Do you want to pass it over here so that Heidi and Jane can see how hard and cold it is . . . and heavy?
(Children pass the hot-water bottle around)	
Teacher	. . . and what do you think it's used for?
Neil:	Money! Money!
Heidi:	Water?
Teacher:	Why do you think it's used for water?
Heidi:	Because if you turn that the water can come out (points to protruding end)
Teacher:	Is there a hole so that water can come out?

Heidi: (points to screw cap) It could come out of there.
Teacher: It could come out of there . . . Or you could put water in there . . .
             Sam, does that come off?
(Sam unscrews the cap)
Neil: It's dark in there.
Teacher: So . . . you think you put water in there?
Heidi: Is it a hot-water bottle?
Teacher: Well done! How did you know it was a hot-water bottle?
Heidi: It looks like one.
Teacher: It looks like one. Is that what a hot-water bottle looks like?
Children: No.
Teacher: What does a hot-water bottle look like that we have now?
Neil: It's a bag, and it's got water in it and it's like, squashy.
Heidi: Was this a hot water-bottle in the olden days?
Teacher: Yes, that's excellent . . . well done!
Neil: This was a hot-water bottle in the olden days.
Neil: It's rolly (pushes the bottle from side to side).
Heidi: I thought I knew what it is.
Teacher: So you knew what it was all the time? But you kept very quiet? That
             was really good!
Heidi: It's just we've got one of those at home.

In this example, the children investigate the object through the use of their
senses and with the support of the teacher, through a series of open-ended
questions. They are asked to observe first, and only later to say what the object
might be. In this example, one of the children had seen an old hot-water bottle
before: she was able to use her previous knowledge to inform her interpretation
of it. Some young children may well have seen some old artefacts before in
museums or at home. Their parents may collect such things, or they may have at
home, for example, a copper kettle standing by the fire, or granny's old flat-iron.
Five and six year olds can record their understanding by drawing objects and
either labelling the important parts, or writing a couple of sentences about their
qualities and use. If necessary early years practitioners can scribe for them. The
group of children above were asked to choose their favourite object to draw and
write about. Abigail, just turned six, chose a milk-jug cover, a circular piece of
lace work with beads hanging down from it, as her special object. Rather than
tell the children its purpose directly, the teacher asked a child to fetch a jug and
she placed the cover over the rim. The children were able to say it was to keep
dirt or flies out of the milk. Abigail was enchanted by the noise the beads made
as we slipped it over an empty mug, and thought that the sound of the beads
would help to keep the flies away. She recorded her understanding in the work
shown in Figure 19.2.

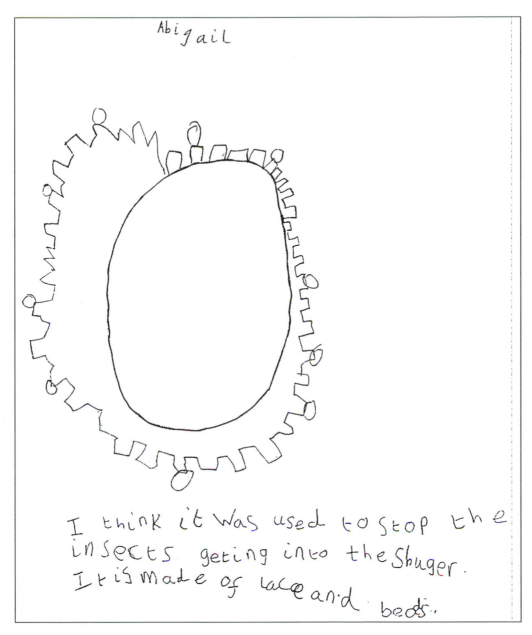

Abigail

I think it was used to stop the insects geting into the Shuger. It is made of lace and beds.

Figure 19.2

Using stories

Stories are an ideal way to develop an understanding of the past, of historical situations and of why people behaved how they did. Wood and Holden (1995) state that stories are central to the development of historical thinking and understanding in young children. They provide, as well as a shared experience for children and adults, a meaningful vehicle for understanding the past, and for 'introducing children to "different worlds" beyond their own experience' (Cox and Hughes 1990, p. 4). Wells (1986) argued that stories are one of the fundamental ways of ordering experience. We sequence events, real or imagined, into narratives which show our understanding of those events and the people to whom they happened. Story is of crucial importance as a foundation for all sense-making (Egan 1991). Cooper (1995) also argued for the centrality of stories to everyday life: she added that stories affect children's intellectual growth, through listening actively and using their imaginations to create new worlds.

Children can learn a great deal through listening to stories of the past, of other cultures in place and time. Firstly, stories are an excellent means of communicating information. The narrative structure allows the teller to convey facts, concepts, ideas and technical language in a way which holds children's attention. Recently I told a story about King Henry VIII and Thomas, a boy who wanted to be a falconer, to a group of five and six year olds (story adapted from 'The King's Feather' in Fines and Nichol (1997)). They were rapt from beginning to end, in spite of the fact that some of the ideas and vocabulary were new to them. They did not know 'falcon', or 'falconry', yet by the end of the story, they had some idea of what falconers do. Neil asked, to confirm his knowledge of the new word: 'What did you call that bird thing again?' I asked them what else they had learned, and they said: people travelled on foot or by horse in the olden days.

Stories create a context for abstract ideas such as kingship, loyalty, authority, community and duty, as well as for the overarching historical concepts such as change and continuity. They create a sense of wonder: for example in the story used above, the moments spent describing the richly dressed King Henry VIII, not only showed how wealthy people dressed in Tudor times, but also allowed the children to exercise their imaginations in picturing the gorgeousness of his clothing. Stories also help in relating the past to the present. In the story of Thomas, the children were able to relate his longing to be a falconer to aims and ambitions of their own, though admittedly these can change very frequently in such young children.

It is important to tell stories as well as to read them. There is something very special about telling stories. It is almost as if human beings are programmed to listen to stories. In the telling of a story one can make eye-contact with the children. Eyes convey meaning very powerfully: emotions can be understood in this way. Storytelling also allows one to use gesture and movement. In this way, one can act out part of a story. Stories can help children understand how and why people behaved as they did. In this particular story of 'The King's Feather' I stopped the telling just before the end, and asked the children what they thought Thomas would do next. They were able to predict that he asked to be a falconer, having understood the story within the context.

Many different kinds of story can be used to develop historical understanding, say of life in the past, or simply to develop skills of sequencing, or understanding cause and effect. Early years practitioners can use well-known stories such as 'Little Red Riding Hood', 'Three Little Pigs' or 'Goldilocks' as a means of teaching sequencing of events, cause and effect, and as a way of approaching moral issues about behaviour, right and wrong. In a story one action leads to another: 'Goldilocks lay down *because* she was tired.' This is an illustration of cause and effect. Through a story such as 'Three Little Pigs' children can begin to understand the processes of reasoning which led the third pig to build his house of bricks.

Such stories are not necessarily historical stories, but can be used for the development of some historical skills and concepts, for understanding of human behaviour, and for personal and social development. All kinds of stories: fairytales, myths and legends, folk tales from other cultures and from our own culture, as well as stories based on evidence of real people and events in the past, can be used in this way. One example of an historical process which can be developed through story is that of interpretations of history.

The process of interpretation of evidence would seem to be too sophisticated to develop with very young children, but stories can be used to begin some interpretation. Children can begin to understand that there are versions of stories and of past events. Cooper (1995) describes how through telling different versions of well-known stories from the point of view of other characters, for example the wolf in the 'Three Little Pigs', four and five year olds can begin to see that different people would report the same events in different ways. This does not happen spontaneously: such young children need discussion and adult intervention to move from thinking that two versions are two unlinked stories, to thinking that there are two versions.

Play

Play can be linked to both stories and artefacts. It is an excellent way of developing historical understanding in young children. They can re-enact stories they have been told, or parts of stories. Such play helps to reinforce understanding of people's actions and behaviour: children can internalise the kinds of feelings the people in the stories experienced. Cooper (1995) suggests that stories from the past have a structure which children can reinvent through play, recreating and internalising their meanings. In play the boundaries between imagination and reality are blurred: children can hypothesise about what might happen if events took a different turn. They can be in control, shutting out of the play any events or characters which may be too threatening or beyond their understanding.

However this kind of play needs input and inspiration from the teacher. A story or artefact such as an old doll or teddy can be the initial starting point, but the early years practitioner has an essential role in ensuring maximum value in play (Sylva *et al.*, 1980; Bateson 1985). In examining an old teddy with a group of five year olds, the teacher asked where Teddy might have been before she had him. The price tag still attached gave the clue that he had been in a shop or on a stall. This led to speculation about who might have owned and played with the teddy before he was in the shop. Thus the children and teacher collectively made a story about the artefact.

A nursery teacher working with three and four year olds provided a setting and toy animals for the children to 'play' the story of the 'Three Billy Goats Gruff'. In evaluating the activity afterwards, she stated that the props were essential to get the children started. Simple costumes, such as long skirts, cloaks and hats can help to fire imaginations, and the home corner can be turned into a variety of settings: a castle, a ship's cabin, or a Victorian kitchen, for example.

It is important that adult intervention is sensitive: early years practitioners should observe the children and supply information or ideas based on observation. Sometimes this can be in the form of questions, to advance the children's ideas, for example: 'What will you do when the Romans attack your village', or 'What do you think Robin Hood would do next?' Talk of this kind with slightly older children could be used as the basis for creative writing. All the time the children are making narrative structures through enactment of stories, and coming to understand how such structures work.

Meaningful history

There are many different sources of evidence and approaches to teaching and learning from which one could choose in planning for young children's learning in and through history. In this chapter, I have selected just three: artefacts, stories and play, because they are the most suitable for children in early years settings. Pictures and storybooks, photos, buildings and adults talking about their lives can all be used, but the three approaches presented here are of great value in promoting historical understanding in young children; and in developing the beginnings of key historical concepts, skills and processes.

References

Andreetti, K. (1993) *Teaching History from Primary Evidence.* London: David Fulton Publishers.

Bateson, G. (1985) 'A Theory of Play and Fantasy', in Bruner, J. S. *et al.* (eds) *Play, its Role, Development and Evolution.* London: Penguin.

Cooper, H. (1995) *History in the Early Years.* London and New York: Routledge.

Cox, K. *et al.* (1990) *Early Years History: An Approach Through Story.* Liverpool: Liverpool Institute of Higher Education.

Department of Education and Science (DES) (1967) *Children and their Primary Schools: A Report of the Central Advisory Council for Education* (The Plowden Report). London: HMSO.

Egan, K. (1991) *Primary Understanding: Education in Early Childhood.* London: Routledge.

Fines, J. (1997) *Teaching Primary History.* Oxford: Heinemann.

Qualifications and Curriculum Authority (1999) *Early Learning Goals.* London: Qualifications and Curriculum Authority.

Sylva, K. *et al.* (1980) *Childwatching in Playgroup and Nursery School.* London: Grant McIntyre.

Wells, G. (1986) *The Meaning Makers: Children and Using Language to Learn.* London: Hodder & Stoughton.

Wood, L. and Holden, C. (1995) *Teaching Early Years History.* Cambridge: Chris Kington Publishing.

Index